Workshop
Theory

Workshop Theory

for Metalwork and Engineering

Vincent Austin BSc (Econ) ND Agr E

Third (Metric) Edition

MACMILLAN

© Vincent Austin 1963, 1969, 1975

All rights reserved. No reproduction, copy or transmission of this publication may be made without written permission.

No paragraph of this publication may be reproduced, copied or transmitted save with written permission or in accordance with the provisions of the Copyright Act 1956 (as amended).

Any person who does any unauthorised act in relation to this publication may be liable to criminal prosecution and civil claims for damages.

First edition 1963
Reprinted 1964, 1966
Second edition 1969
Reprinted 1971, 1972
Third (Metric) edition 1975
Reprinted 1977, 1979 (twice), 1981, 1982 (twice), 1983, 1985, 1986

Published by
MACMILLAN EDUCATION LTD
Houndmills, Basingstoke, Hampshire RG21 2XS
and London
Companies and representatives
throughout the world

Printed in Hong Kong

ISBN 0-333-15773-7

Preface to Third (Metric) Edition

The new edition has enabled the author to re-examine the requirements of examination candidates taking *Metalwork Theory* to Ordinary and Advanced level and *Engineering Workshop Theory* to Ordinary level of the General Certificate of Education for the following Boards:

Associated Examining Board for the General Certificate of Education (AEB)
Northern Universities Joint Matriculation Board (NU)
Oxford and Cambridge Schools Examination Board (O & C)
Oxford Delegacy of Local Examinations (OLE)
Southern Universities Joint Board for School Examinations (SU)
University of Cambridge Local Examinations Syndicate (CU)
University of Durham School Examination Board (DU)
University of London School Examination Council (LU)
Welsh Joint Education Committee (WJEC)

The appendix now includes a sample of past questions for the Certificate of Secondary Education, for the following Boards:

Southern Regional Examinations Board (S)
South Eastern Regional Examining Board (SE)
Welsh Joint Education Committee (WJEC)
East Midland Regional Examinations Board (EM)
West Midlands Examinations Board (WM)
East Anglian Regional Examinations Board (EA)
Metropolitan Regional Examinations Board (M)
North Western Secondary School Examinations Board (NW)
Associated Lancashire Schools Examining Board (L)

The abbreviations in brackets after each name have been used to identify each of the past GCE and CSE questions printed in Appendix B of this book. The author wishes to acknowledge the copyright of the Boards for their own questions and to thank the Boards for their permission to include questions in his book. In order to give the greatest possible range of metric questions, some past questions in imperial units have been converted to metric units. These questions are indicated by an asterisk.

Other boards which have a policy of not permitting the reproduction of their examination questions, but have had their syllabuses taken into consideration are:

South Western Examinations Board
West Yorkshire and Lindsey Regional Examining Board
Yorkshire Regional Examinations Board
North Regional Examinations Board.

In order to reduce the problems faced by students in this transitionary period of change from imperial to metric units, the author has omitted all reference to imperial units. Those who may still require conversion tables, Model Engineer's Thread tables, etc. should keep a copy of the Second Edition for reference purposes.

The basic layout of this book has not been changed and, as in previous editions, it should be pointed out that it is not intended that the chapters should necessarily be read in order. Indeed, the complete beginner would be well advised to start by reading the first half of Chapter 8, which deals with fundamental benchwork.

Since writing the First Edition the author has travelled widely in his work, to Africa, Asia and Latin America, utilising his knowledge of both Engineering and Economics. This experience has confirmed his belief that if the student wishes to achieve his highest attainment in Metalwork and Engineering he must work equally hard at the more academic subjects such as Maths, Science, English, and Geography, and include a foreign language if possible.

The author has been pleased to receive correspondence from students overseas and if it is felt that the text or past questions could be expanded to cover additional syllabuses, this will be considered for the next edition.

V. A.

1974

Acknowledgements

I would like to offer my sincere thanks to Mr C. H. Walker, BSc, AMIEE, to Mr J. H. Perkins, AMIProdE, AMBIM, and to my wife for her constant encouragement.

The author also wishes to express his thanks to the firms and organisations mentioned below, who have supplied information, drawings, photographs and blocks.

Abingdon King Dick Limited
William Allday and Company Limited
The Aluminium Development Association
J. E. Baty and Company Limited
Boxford Machine Tools Limited
The British Cast Iron Research Association
The British Oxygen Company Limited
British Steel Corporation
W. Canning and Company Limited
The Carborundum Company Limited
Rabone Chesterman Limited
Charles Cooper (Hatton Garden) Limited
Clarkson (Engineers) Limited
Copper Development Association
Coventry Gauge and Tool Company Limited
Foundry Services Limited
Fry's Metal Foundries Limited, Research Department
The Glacier Metal Company Limited
G.K.N. Screws and Fasteners Limited
C. and J. Hampton Limited
T. S. Harrison and Sons Limited

Edward G. Herbert Limited
The Horstmann Gear Company Limited
Imperial Chemical Industries Limited, Paints Division
The Jacobs Manufacturing Company Limited
Johnson, Matthey and Company Limited
Kasenit Limited
Lead Development Association
Lehmann, Archer and Lane Limited
W. J. Meddings Limited
Moore and Wright (Sheffield) Limited
James Neill and Company (Sheffield) Limited
John Oakey and Sons Limited
Tom Senior (Liversedge) Limited
The Sheffield Twist Drill and Steel Company Limited
Shell-Mex and B.P. Limited
Peter Stubs Limited
Suffolk Iron Foundry (1920) Limited
Wilkinsons Tools Limited
Wolf Electric Tools Limited
Zinc Development Association

Drawings from BS 122: Part 1: 1953, Milling Cutters, and BS 328: Part 1: 1959, Twist Drills, are reproduced by permission of the British Standards Institution, 2 Park Street, London W1A 2BS from whom complete copies of the Standards may be purchased.

Contents

1 **Metals**   1
1 Introduction. 2 Properties. 3 Pig iron. 4 Steel. 5 Cast iron.
6 Wrought iron. 7 Aluminium. 8 Light alloys. 9 Copper. 10 Brass.
11 Bronze. 12 Lead. 13 Tin. 14 White metal. 15 Zinc. 16 Heat
treatment. 17 Case hardening. 18 Workshop tests and methods of
identification.

2 **Preliminary Considerations**   28
1 Safety. 2 Design. 3 Working drawings.

3 **Foundrywork**   33
1 Patterns. 2 Cores. 3 Castings. 4 Die casting. 5 Shell moulding.

4 **Joining Processes**   41
1 Introduction. 2 Sources of heat. 3 Fluxes. 4 Soft solders. 5 Hard
solders. 6 Brazing. 7 Welding. 8 Rivets. 9 Screws, bolts, studs and
nuts.

5 **Sheetmetalwork**   57
1 Developments. 2 Marking out. 3 Wire and sheet gauges. 4 Snips.
5 Bench shearing machines. 6 Punches. 7 Stakes. 8 Mallets.
9 Bending. 10 Edges. 11 Joints.

6 **Silversmithing**   71
1 Introduction. 2 Cleaning. 3 Sinking. 4 Hollowing. 5 Raising.
6 Stakes. 7 Planishing. 8 Built-up work. 9 Rolling and wire drawing.
10 Application of wires. 11 Piercing. 12 Chasing. 13 Further
decorative techniques. 14 Finishing.

7	Forgework	93

1 Smith's hearth. 2 Anvil. 3 Leg vice. 4 Upsetting. 5 Drawing down. 6 Fullering. 7 Swaging. 8 Cutting tools. 9 Flaring and scrolls. 10 Drop forging.

8	Benchwork	105

1 Marking out. 2 Holding devices. 3 Cutting. 4 Filing. 5 Scraping. 6 Measurement. 7 Riveting. 8 Threading. 9 Bolting.

9	Drilling	153

1 Drilling machines. 2 Methods of holding work. 3 Drills. 4 Reaming. 5 Countersinking, spot facing and counterboring.

10	Lathework	166

1 Lathes. 2 Self-centring chuck. 3 Independent jaw chuck. 4 Centres. 5 Face plate. 6 Mandrels. 7 Steadies. 8 Lathe tools. 9 Surfacing. 10 Sliding (parallel turning). 11 Taper turning. 12 Boring. 13 Screwcutting.

11	Machinework	215

1 Shaping and planing machines. 2 Milling. 3 Grinding. 4 Abrasives. 5 Cutting fluids. 6 Lubrication. 7 Surface finishes. 8 Surface protection.

12	Economic Considerations	230

Appendices	234

A *Tables.*
B *Past GCE and CSE theory questions.*

Index	267

1

Metals

1.1 Introduction

The craft of *Metalwork* covers all the basic processes of working in metal. Practice may develop a vocational interest, or suggest an occupation for leisure such as model engineering or silversmithing. *Engineering* is a vocational subject and offers a wide range of careers.

The student should realise that the working of metal is an exciting and expanding occupation. The industrial countries of the world are continually making fresh discoveries and advances; and many of the underdeveloped countries have now built their own metal industries. To keep abreast of the latest developments, the student can receive help from special features in newspapers, periodicals and more particularly, technical journals.

The natural *sources* of metals are distributed throughout the world, and may be mined from under the ground, on the surface, or even dredged from under water. The *production* of the metal may continue in the country of its origin or it may be transported in the raw or semi-raw state to an industrial region, perhaps on the other side of the world. The final *forms* that metals can take are varied, some may be only cast, whilst others are available in many forms, such as castings, plate, sheet, foil, bar, tube, wire, extrusions, rollings, forgings, stampings and powder.

The *properties* of a metal are the various qualities it possesses such as strength, ductility, malleability, toughness, hardness, heat and electrical conductivity, fusibility and resistance to corrosion. The possibilities of *working* in either the hot or cold state, and the after-effects produced, vary from one metal to another.

The *uses* of metals are almost limitless. Metals are required pure or commercially pure, as alloys (containing one or more metals and perhaps non-metallic elements such as carbon), or as chemical compounds.

All metals are divided into one of two groups:

(1) Those which come from iron, called *ferrous* metals, which include all irons and steels. (2) Those which do not come from iron, called *non-ferrous* metals, which include aluminium, copper, lead, tin, zinc, their alloys, and many other less common metals.

1.2 Properties

The **strength** of a metal is the maximum force the metal will withstand in *tension, compression* or *shear*. The *ultimate tensile strength* of a metal is usually expressed in meganewtons per square metre (MN/m^2) of cross-sectional area.

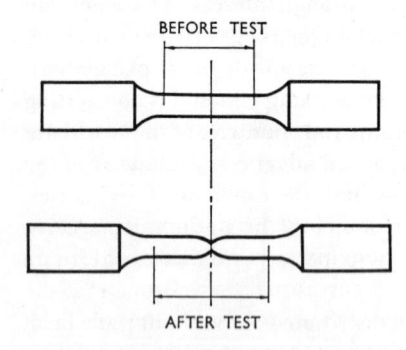

Fig. 1. Tensile test piece

Ductility The percentage increase in length of a tensile test piece before breaking is called the *elongation* and is a measure of the *ductility* of a metal. A ductile metal may be drawn out in tension without rupture, as in wire drawing.

Malleability is the property of permanent deformation without rupture. Lead is a very malleable metal but has low ductility.

Toughness is the amount of energy a metal can absorb before fracturing, and is expressed in joules (J). A test piece is broken at a notch by a heavy pendulum, and the loss in height of swing after impact is a measure of the energy consumed.

Hardness is the resistance of a metal to cutting and surface indentation. Under a given load a hardened steel ball (Brinell) or diamond pyramid (e.g. Vickers) is forced into the surface, and the width or depth of indentation is measured. Standard tables are then used to assess the hardness number.

Fig. 2. Hardness testing

Heat conductivity is a measure of the rate of flow of heat per unit area and per unit temperature gradient.

Fusibility. The melting point of metals varies considerably and it is interesting to note that lead (melting point 327°C) and tin (melting point 232°C) when alloyed together in equal proportions produce an alloy which melts at a lower temperature (very approximately 200°C).

1.3 Pig Iron

The main *sources* of the rich black magnetite ores (up to 65% iron) are in Sweden, Austria, USSR, and Brazil, whilst reddish-brown haematite ores (50% to 60%) are widely distributed throughout the world. In Great Britain the main deposits are in an impure form (20% to 30%). The iron ore is mined either underground or by the open-cast method.

The iron ore may require 'crushing' to reduce the lump size or 'sintering' to partially fuse loose particles into a hard porous mass. Magnetite ores can be concentrated by magnetic means.

The production of pig iron requires a high quality coke, hard, porous and low in sulphur content; also limestone is needed to act as a flux.

The blast furnace is a vertical steel cylinder, 25–30 m high, 5–9 m in diameter, and lined with fire bricks.

The charge to produce 1 tonne of pig iron will vary, but a British ore containing 30% iron would require over 3 t of ore, 1 t coke and 0·3 t limestone.

During charging, the double bell arrangement prevents gases escaping, which are later cleaned and used. One use is to heat the air entering the bustle pipe, to about 800°C, which practically halves the amount of coke required. The oxygen in the air causes the coke to burn fiercely, generating heat and reducing gas, which with limestone extracts the iron.

Iron, which is the heaviest product, drips to the bottom of the hearth and the lighter slag floats on top of the iron. The slag is tapped out at the slag notch and can be treated for road-making materials, cement manufacture, concrete aggregate and lightweight building material.

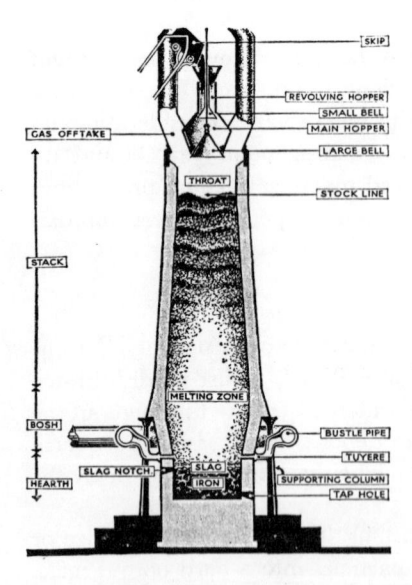

Fig. 3. Diagram of blast furnace

The iron is tapped out at the tap hole, which is simply a hole about 300 mm square, plugged by forcing in clay under pressure and tapped by drilling and then burning the remainder away with an oxygen lance.

The process of feeding in raw materials and tapping out iron and slag continues day and night until the fire-brick lining wears out, averaging over 1 000 000 tonnes for each lining.

The molten iron may be cast into small metal moulds on an endless chain, sprayed with water and the resulting pig iron tipped out of the moulds into railway wagons. If the blast furnace is situated close to a steel works, the blast furnace metal or hot metal, as it is termed, can be carried in the molten state, in steel, brick-lined ladles.

The iron produced varies in chemical composition, and may be divided into two groups, depending upon high or low phosphorus content.

1.4 Steel

The production of steel requires the carbon content of the pig iron to be reduced from over 3% to less than $1\frac{1}{2}$%, and usually to less than $\frac{1}{4}$%.

Iron with a low phosphorus content is treated in a furnace with an 'acid' lining (silica bricks), removing carbon, silicon and manganese.

A furnace in which phosphoric iron is refined requires a 'basic' lining (crushed dolomite rammed with tar), to remove carbon, silicon, manganese, sulphur and phosphorus.

In recent years there has been a marked change in the production of steel, as shown in the table below:

UK Steel Output 1960–1970

Process	1960 %	1970 %
Open Hearth	84·5	47·2
Basic Oxygen	2·4	28·1
Electric Arc	6·9	18·9
Bessemer Converter	5·7	*

* Only one plant remained in 1970 and this was phased out in 1973.

Courtesy of the Iron and Steel Statistics Bureau, British Steel Corporation

The Open Hearth Process has changed in recent years from a process depending on gas or oil to provide heat, and oxidation by flame and iron oxide, to an oxygen-assisted process. In the Ajax method, oxygen is injected into the furnace by means of long, retractable, water-cooled lances. This intensifies the chemical reaction and speeds up production.

The furnace consists of a shallow bath holding from 60 to 400 tonnes. Some are fixed and others have a tilting device which enables slag to be removed easily. At each end of the bath there are open chequered brickwork chambers to pre-heat air (and gas if used). The very hot spent gases heat one side and then the flow is reversed.

The basic open hearth process has by far the biggest output in Great Britain. In the basic process, in addition to the metal charge of pig iron and steel scrap, a specified quantity of lime is added to absorb impurities. The flame and oxygen oxidise some of the silicon and carbon, and the further refining is carried out by oxidisers such as iron ore and mill scale (the broken-off oxide skin of a steel ingot); more lime is then added.

Samples are taken regularly and the final additions, alloying elements, deoxidisers and a carbon adjustment, are made to the furnace and then to the ladle whilst tapping.

Fig. 4. The open hearth process

The Basic Oxygen Process is a development from the Bessemer Converter process where air was blown through the molten iron from holes in the bottom of the converter in the vertical position.

The LD–AC converter process (Fig. 5) is the most widespread and the converter is charged with molten iron in the conventional manner (Fig. 5a) together with steel scrap and lime, after which the vessel is brought to a vertical position ready for the blow. The lance is lowered and the jet applied, using oxygen alone for the first few

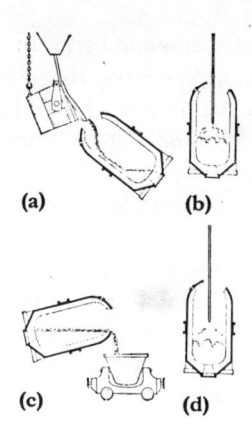

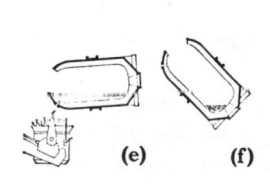

(a) *CHARGING*
The ladle pours molten iron into the mouth of the converter which tilts forward to receive the charge.

(b) *THE FIRST BLOW*
The lance descends into the mouth of the converter directing a jet of oxygen and powdered lime on to the surface of the molten iron.

(c) *SLAGGING*
Tilting backwards the converter pours the primary slag, which contains most of the impurities, from the surface of the metal into a ladle.

(d) *THE SECOND BLOW*
The converter returns to its position in **(b)** and a second oxygen/lime injection further purifies the metal.

(e) *POURING*
Tilting forward completely the converter pours the steel into the waiting ladle.

(f) *PREPARATION*
The residual slag remains in the converter which returns to its position in **(a)** for the next charge.

Fig. 5. The LD–AC converter process

minutes, after which lime is injected through the lance in the gas stream (Fig. 5b). After most of the phosphorus and carbon have been removed the vessel is tilted for slag removal (Fig. 5c), and checks are made on the metal and slag. The converter is returned to the upright position and the oxygen/lime blow continued (Fig. 5d) until the desired composition is attained when the steel is tapped (Fig. 5e). The provision of a tap hole enables the metal to be run off underneath the second slag, which is retained in the vessel for use in the next heat (Fig. 5f), the iron content of this slag increasing the yield of steel from the raw materials charged. The first slag removed is rich in phosphorus and, when cold, is finely crushed, forming a valuable agricultural fertiliser (Basic slag).

The electric process can melt steel under neutral conditions and alloys can be added without loss in the slag.

The bulk of electrically melted steel is produced in the *arc furnace*. This consists of a circular shallow bath with acid or basic lining, with a capacity of up to 80 tonnes of steel. Three carbon electrodes are suspended above the bath. The raw material is selected scrap of known composition. Lime, ore or mill scale are then added and the 'arcs struck'. After about 1½ hours or more, most of the silicon, manganese and phosphorus can be removed in the slag. Further treatment is sometimes made by adding a reducing slag of lime, fluorspar carbon and ferro-silicon; this deoxidises and desulphurises the steel. Alloy additions are made and samples checked before tapping.

The second electrical method is the *high frequency induction furnace* with a capacity of up to 5 tonnes. Round the furnace runs an insulated copper coil. When a high frequency electrical current is passed through the coil, a current is induced in the metal charge. This causes the metal to melt, and eddy currents ensure thorough mixing. The furnace is used not for refining, but for making the highest-quality alloy steels.

When the steel has been made in the open hearth, converter or electric furnace, it is first tapped into a steel ladle which has one or two 'nozzles' in the bottom, closed by vertical 'stopper rods'. Pouring or 'teeming' from the bottom prevents the inclusion of slag, and may be either into a mould as a steel casting, such as locomotive wheel centres, or into an ingot mould for subsequent rolling or forging.

The ingots, which are usually between 4 and 20 tonnes, are held in a 'soaking pit' to allow them to attain a uniform temperature

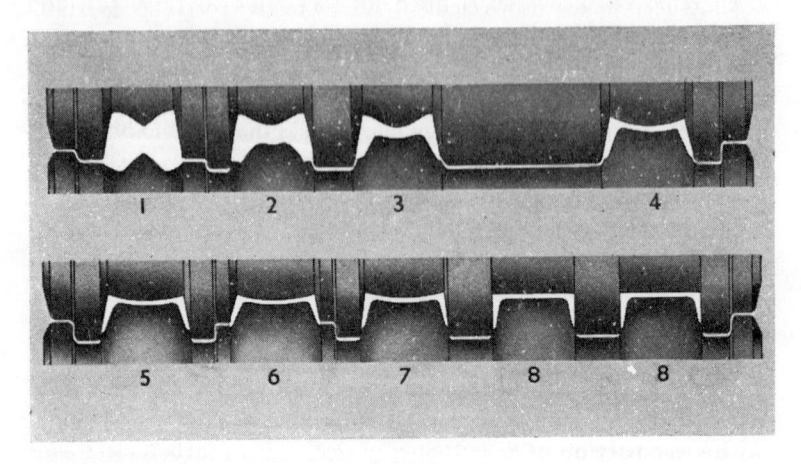

Fig. 6. The sequence of passes used to roll a channel

suitable for rolling. The initial rolling of the ingot is known as 'cogging' to produce 'blooms' or 'slabs'. The steel is again reheated and passed through the finishing rolling mills, which are graduated down to the *forms* required. Some blooms (about 200 mm square) are rolled to smaller square-section lengths known as billets (about 60 mm square) for the smaller sections flats, bars, strip, tubes, rods, wire, and sections (angles, tees, channels, etc.).

In continuous casting, the molten metal is teemed direct into a casting machine to produce billets, blooms, slabs and similar products.

Slabs are rolled to plate and sheet, for tinplate, see 1.13. The forging of steel is discussed later in Chapter 7.

Not only is there a wide range of shapes available but also of types of steel, which can be divided into plain carbon steels and alloy steels. The *properties, working* and *uses* of steel can vary considerably.

(1) Low Carbon Steels less than 0·15% carbon: wire, rivets, etc.
(2) Mild Steels 0·15%–0·25% carbon: general purposes
(3) Medium Carbon Steels 0·25%–0·5% carbon: garden hoes, spades, shafts and gears
(4) High Carbon Steels 0·5%–1·4% carbon: hammers, springs, chisels, drills.

Alloy steels have various elements added to give special properties, such as retention of strength at high temperatures (e.g. gas turbines for jet aircraft) and corrosion resistance (e.g. stainless steel sink units). Important alloys in the workshop are high-speed steel for cutting tools, the main additions being 14–18% tungsten, 3–5% chromium and 0·6% carbon, and Ledloy steels for improved machinability with the addition of 0·18% lead.

Tool steel is any steel suitable for making into a cutting tool, and may be either a carbon or an alloy steel.

1.5 Cast Iron

The grade of pig iron used in the foundry is called 'Foundry Iron' and generally contains approximately 3·2–3·6% carbon, 2–3·5% silicon, 0·5–0·8% manganese, 0·1% sulphur and 1–1·4% phosphorus.

The production of cast iron is in effect, re-melted pig iron cast into sand moulds. Very little iron is cast into die castings, see 3.4.

The furnace most generally in use is the cupola furnace into which is charged pig iron, scrap, coke and limestone. Although similar to a blast furnace which operates for years without being shut down, the cupola may be shut down after 8 hours' work. The limestone acts as a flux and the coke as a melting agent, taking little chemical part in the process. Except in such modern developments as hot-blast cupolas, the waste gases from the cupola merely pass to the atmosphere.

The actual foundrywork is described in Chapter 3.

The properties of cast irons are wide and varied, according to specification. Cast iron is not just a single alloy: the name covers a wide range of alloys with widely varying properties and *uses*.

White cast irons can be recognised by the characteristic white fracture and are extremely hard and brittle and virtually un-machinable. They are therefore used for crushing machinery, etc.

Grey cast iron has a characteristic grey appearance of the fracture and most of the castings made today are grey iron castings. Grey iron is fairly soft and readily machinable but its properties can be varied over a wide range by suitable adjustments to the chemical composition, particularly to the carbon, silicon, manganese and phosphorus contents. Low grade irons are comparatively weak. Within this range low phosphorus irons are used for large castings such as ingot moulds for steelworks, and bed-plates for machinery; whilst high phosphorus irons are used for light and intricate castings such as domestic gas, electric and solid fuel cookers, grates, pipes, rain water goods and many other applications.

The higher grades of grey iron are used for the so-called engineering castings, which cover large fields such as cylinder blocks for automobile engines, brake drums and various machine parts.

Malleable cast iron is a soft, machinable product with some measure of ductility. It is produced by oxidising at red heat to remove some of the carbon of white cast iron and is used in special pipe fittings and in the automobile industry.

Nodular (or Spheroidal) cast iron is produced by alloying ordinary grey iron with small quantities of magnesium. It has very high strength and considerable ductility, particularly in the heat-treated form.

For special properties grey cast irons can be alloyed with such elements as nickel, chromium, copper and molybdenum. It is unusual for cast iron to be given any form of hot or cold *working*.

1.6 Wrought Iron
The production of wrought iron by puddling has been almost completely replaced by steel.

Pig iron is melted on the hearth of the puddling furnace by the roof reflecting down the heat of the flames from a coal fire. Silicon, phosphorus, manganese and carbon are oxidised by the air passing through and by the addition of iron oxide. Finally when the iron is at the pasty stage and the slag liquid, the puddler gathers the iron

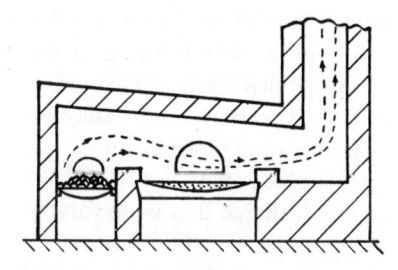

Fig. 7. The principle of the puddling furnace

into balls or 'blooms', as free from slag as possible and drags them out. The balls are then hammered to squeeze out as much slag as possible and finally rolled.

The wrought iron always contains fibres of slag, and to reduce them in size for better quality iron, one bar is placed on another, reheated and re-rolled. The *forms* of supply are usually bars and rods.

The properties are extremely valuable: extreme ductility, toughness, resistance to atmospheric corrosion, and weldability and forgeability at moderate temperatures.

Uses include chains and railway drawgear, where a possible failure of the metal would be disastrous. Wrought iron gives some warning by stretching before breaking. Less common today is ornamental wrought ironwork, for gates and railings, grilles, candelabra, etc. Modern 'Wrought Ironwork' is often mild steel.

1.7 Aluminium
Aluminium is the most abundant metal in the earth's crust, but the only commercial *source* of the metal is bauxite, a hydrated form of alumina. Deposits of the requisite high purity are found in Surinam, Guyana, Jamaica, USA, France and Ghana.

Production For the economic production of aluminium a cheap and plentiful supply of electricity should be available (usually hydro-electric power).

The crushed and dried ore is first 'digested' with hot caustic soda solution, dissolving the aluminium hydroxide and forming sodium aluminate. Filter presses remove the impurities and the filtrate passes to tall precipitation tanks, where the dissolved aluminium hydroxide collects at the bottom.

Filtered hydroxide is washed and heated to 1100°C giving alumina of 99·4% purity.

Reduction of alumina to aluminium is carried out in rectangular mild steel tanks up to 8 m in length, with a carbon lining as the negative electrode; the anodes are suspended carbon electrodes. Molten cryolite is maintained at 950–1000°C and up to 5% alumina is added. The alumina is decomposed, liberating molten aluminium which sinks to the bottom, while oxygen is given off.

Aluminium and aluminium alloys are available in a wide variety of *forms*:

(1) wrought forms: rolled plate, sheet, strip and foil; extruded bars, rods and sections; drawn tubes and wire; forgings and stampings;
(2) castings made in sand or metal moulds;
(3) aluminium powder for paint.

The production by rolling and wire drawing is fundamentally the same as described for silver, see 6.9; for forging see 7.10 and casting see Chapter 3.

Extrusion consists in forcing a heated billet of metal through an orifice cut in a hardened steel die, the orifice having the profile of the section desired.

Properties Pure aluminium (melting point 660°C) is white, light, soft, malleable, ductile, highly conductive to heat and electricity, and corrosion-resistant.

As normally produced, the surface of pure aluminium is covered with a thin inert film of oxide which renders the metal practically immune to attack by the atmosphere and by many chemical substances.

When *working* aluminium in the cold state, the metal will sooner or later become work-hardened and will require annealing; either rub a soap mark on the surface and heat gently until the mark turns to a chocolate brown colour, or heat until a matchstick rubbed on the surface leaves a brown mark.

The uses of aluminium and its alloys include aircraft, lifeboats, crankcases and pistons for internal combustion engines, body and chassis work of railway coaches and road transport, window and curtain walling frames, gutters, down-pipes, steel-cored aluminium overhead conductors of the Grid network, refrigerators and cold storage rooms, domestic holloware, aluminium foil for food wrappers and bottle caps.

1.8 Light Alloys

Light alloys are distinctive for lightness, of which the major proportion are aluminium alloys.

By alloying with other metals, aluminium increases in tensile strength and hardness and the machinability is also improved.

There is a broad division between alloys used in the form of castings and alloys in various wrought forms; in each group some are susceptible to heat-treatment (alloys of highest strength).

Both wrought and cast aluminium alloys are produced to British Standard specifications which govern their composition and mechanical properties.

Wrought alloys not strengthened by heat-treatment, but by cold work, are of outstandingly good resistance to corrosion, and contain 1·25% manganese, or 2·25 to 7% magnesium.

The principal alloying elements of heat-treatable alloys are copper, magnesium, silicon, zinc and manganese. Heat treatment of aluminium alloys normally takes two stages. First the alloying elements are taken into solid solution, and secondly they are precipitated in extremely fine form throughout the structure of the metal, with a consequent increase in strength. For example, one particular alloy, when heated to 490–505°C and quenched in water, proceeds to age at room temperature resulting in an increase in strength which reaches a stable maximum after four days; this is known as age-hardening.

The strongest alloys are often coated on both sides with pure aluminium (cladding), thus combining high corrosion resistance with high strength.

Cast alloys differ considerably in their properties and in their casting characteristics; for example in their ability to fill the mould completely (fluidity) and their proneness to show surface depressions or cracks due to contraction. The casting alloys most favoured are those containing 5% or more of silicon, of which LM 4 and LM 6, BS 1490: 1970 account for about 40% of the entire foundry output.

LM 4 and a recent alternative LM 21 contain approximately 3% copper and 5% silicon and have good fluidity in pouring and resistance to hot-tearing, machine well, and are hard and strong. They also possess adequate corrosion resistance. LM 6 contains 12% silicon and has high fluidity.

Cast aluminium alloys without heat-treatment range in tensile strengths from 120 to 180 MN/m^2; after heat-treatment, alloys reach a tensile strength of 230–280 MN/m^2.

1.9 Copper

Copper *sources* today are all mixed ores and the commonest is chalcopyrite or 'yellow ore'. Mines occur in the USA, Chile, Zambia, USSR, Canada and the Republic of Zaire.

Production Copper ores rarely contain as much as 4% of the metal, therefore in the production of copper enormous quantities of waste rock must be removed. The ore is first crushed and then ground to fine powder. To separate the valuable dust, 'flotation' is employed. This method depends on the grains of copper ore being carried in a froth to the surface of the liquid used. The product removed is known as copper concentrate, which together with lime or other suitable flux is subjected within a reverberatory smelting furnace to an intense heat and reduced to a molten state. A mixture or 'matte' of copper and iron sulphides is taken to a converter (similar to Bessemer) where the iron is oxidised and forms a slag; the sulphur is blown out as a gas. The 'blister' copper is then cast into cakes or slabs.

There are two methods of refining copper:

(1) In a refining furnace the molten charge is first saturated with oxygen to reduce impurities, and after removing the slag, poles of green wood are thrust into the bath to remove most of the oxygen by combustion.

(2) Electrolytic refining is carried out in tanks with warm diluted sulphuric acid and copper sulphate. Copper slabs are used as anodes and thin sheets of pure copper as starting cathodes.

The copper produced is manufactured in the following *forms*: wire, plates, sheets, strip, tubes, rods, sections, castings and powder.

Properties Pure copper (melting point 1083°C) is red, malleable, ductile, highly conductive to heat and electricity and corrosion-resistant.

Hot or cold *working* is possible with copper, but when cold-worked the hardness and strength increases and it requires frequent annealing. To anneal, heat to a dull red and either leave to cool or quench in water. (*Note:* High conductivity (oxygen-containing) copper should not be annealed in a reducing atmosphere or it will become embrittled.)

Uses Typical uses of copper and its alloys are in the windings of electrical machines, switchgear parts, cables for transmitting electricity, radiators for internal combustion engines and for heating houses, locomotive fire-boxes, chemical plant, water-cooled air blast tuyeres for blast furnaces, copper roofing, tubing for water and gas distribution, and also soldering-iron bits.

The most important copper alloys are brasses and bronzes.

1.10 Brass

Brass is an alloy of copper and zinc. There are many different grades employed for special purposes; the properties and colour depend upon the proportions of the two elements.

(1) *Brass Rod, Sheet, Tube and Wire*
Gilding metal, copper/zinc ratio varies from 90/10 to 80/20. It is used for architectural metalwork and imitation jewellery on account of its golden colour, corrosion resistance and ability to be brazed and enamelled. It may be worked cold and annealed as for copper.

Cartridge brass, 70/30 ratio. A very ductile type of brass particularly suitable for deep pressing and drawing work such as cartridge cases, containers of all kinds, and headlamp reflectors. By adding 1% of tin, *Admiralty brass* (70/29/1) is produced, which has good corrosion resistance and is used for condenser tubes.

Yellow or muntz metal 60/40 ratio. A good hot-working alloy which can also be cold-worked to a limited extent. The addition of 2–3% of lead results in free-cutting brass, such as (58/39/3), suitable for high-speed machining.

(2) *Brass Castings*
General purpose brasses contain between 62 and 80% copper, 10 to 37% zinc, 1 to 6% lead and perhaps between 1 and 4% tin;

there have been many diverse applications, for example in parts of machinery, ornamental uses, valves, etc.

High tensile brasses These alloys contain small amounts of manganese (manganese bronze), iron, tin, nickel and aluminium, and are extensively employed in hydraulic valve bodies, ships' propellers, water turbine runners, etc., where resistance to corrosion is important. Smaller castings are used for applications such as gear wheels and pinions, brackets and non-sparking tools.

1.11 Bronze

'Bronze' strictly means an alloy of copper and tin, but the term is also used commercially for a wide range of copper-base alloys, some of which contain no tin at all.

Bronze coinage British 'copper' coinage is a copper alloy containing 3% tin, and 1·5% zinc.

Phosphor bronze Copper plus 4 to 12% tin, and 0·1 to 0·5% phosphorus. The wrought phosphor bronzes owe the majority of their applications to their good elastic properties, combined with resistance to corrosion and corrosion fatigue. This accounts for their wide use as springs and instrument components. The cast alloys of high tin content have a low coefficient of friction and are popular bearing materials.

Gunmetal Copper, plus 3 to 10% tin, 2 to 9% zinc and perhaps 2 to 5% lead. Gunmetal is widely employed for pumps, valves and miscellaneous castings which need to be corrosion-resistant. The leaded alloys are used when pressure-tightness is required.

Aluminium bronze Copper plus 4 to 12% aluminium and possibly up to 10% iron plus nickel and manganese. The alloys offer good retention of strength and resist oxidation at moderately elevated temperatures; they also have good resistance to corrosion. Alloys of high aluminium content are fabricated by casting and hot-working processes, including forging, and may be cold-worked to a limited extent only. They are suitable for chemical engineering applications, especially at moderately elevated temperatures, and for components such as pump rods, pickling crates, beater bars for paper-making, and numerous marine applications from valve fittings to anchors and chains. The alloys containing 4 to 7% aluminium are cold-working alloys and are used as condenser tubes or as sheet and strip material.

1.12 Lead

Lead is present in the earth's crust to the extent of only about 0·002%, but has been concentrated by natural processes into rich deposits.

The principal *sources* are the USA, Mexico, Australia and Canada, and the most important lead ore is galena (lead sulphide).

Production In the production process, the galena is concentrated by 'flotation' and then smelted to give an impure lead. The lead is refined by one of several methods. A widely employed method is first to melt the metal in a reverberatory furnace and agitate with air, when some impurities are oxidised and skimmed off. To extract any silver and gold, the molten lead is agitated with molten zinc in which the impurities are preferentially soluble. The zinc, carrying these metals, rises to the top in the form of a crust and is skimmed off. An alternative method is by electrolytic refining.

Lead is available in several *forms*: sheet, pipe, foil, extrusions, shot and castings.

Properties Lead (melting point 327°C) is bright and lustrous when freshly cut, but soon oxidises to a dull grey; it is heavy, soft, malleable, corrosion-resistant, immune to attack by many chemicals and has valuable electrical properties.

The *working* of lead is extremely easy, as it is always soft and malleable.

Uses The principal uses of lead are as unalloyed metal, as alloys and as compounds, e.g. coverings for power and telephone cables, lead sheet and pipe in plumbing, lead sheet for X-ray protection, lead bricks and containers in atomic energy, lead in solders (see 4.4), as a principal or secondary ingredient in bearing metals (see 1.14), the main constituent in type metals and lead pigments for paints.

1.13 Tin

Tin is one of the rarest of the base metals, and the principal *sources* are Malaysia, Bolivia and Indonesia. The only important mineral is cassiterite or tinstone (stannic oxide).

Production In the production of tin, tinstone is first concentrated by washing and screening. Special treatment is then given to the tin concentrates from each locality, before smelting to give a crude tin.

The first step in the thermal method of refining tin is in a special furnace where the temperature is kept just above the melting point of tin. The tin runs to an open tap hole and the remaining residue is resmelted. Further impurities are oxidised as described for copper (1.9). The tin is then held just above the melting point and a lead-rich layer forms at the bottom, which can be drained away leaving refined tin, to be cast into pigs.

The second method is by electrolytic refining which produces extremely pure tin.

The *forms* of supply of tin are limited, e.g. castings, foil and collapsible tubes.

Properties Tin (melting point 232°C) is white, soft and when polished has a high light reflectivity, and is corrosion-resistant in moist atmospheric conditions. When a bar of tin is bent, a sound called the 'cry' of tin is heard.

Cold-*working* with a hammer slightly hardens the metal.

Uses The main uses of tin are for tinplate, bronze (1.11), soft solders (4.4), Babbitt alloys (1.14), tinning and type metal (1.14).

Tinplate is made by rolling mild steel in strip or sheet form to a finished gauge of about 0·3 mm, and then applying a coating of pure tin either by dipping in molten metal or by electrodeposition. The thickness of the tin coating is usually less than 0·003 mm.

For standard thickness of sheet and strip see Appendix A, Table 20.

Properties The mild steel base is very ductile and strong, and the tin coating which is soft and very adherent, follows the movement of the steel base when forming. The tin coating protects the steel from corrosion and is resistant to the wide range of processed foods and other merchandise which is packed in tinplate; tin and iron are also non-toxic.

1.14 White Metal

White metal includes bearing metals, printer's alloys, solders and pewter.

There are today, in current use throughout the world, more than a thousand specifications for the tin and lead-base white metal alloys used for lining *bearings*.

The term Babbitt is generally used to include alloys ranging in composition from 90% or more of tin with no lead to 80% of lead and less than 5% of tin. Antimony is always present as a hardening element, and the addition of copper prevents the segregation of the lighter tin-antimony particles which provide the wear-resistance. The *properties* common to all Babbitt alloys are: sufficiently soft to give excellent conformability and embeddability, easily cast, bonds rigidly to steel or bronze, runs satisfactorily against a soft steel shaft, and corrosion troubles practically non-existent. The limitations are spreading under high steady loads or cracking under high fluctuating loads.

Tin base alloys with high tin content are used for the most demanding service, such as high speed aero, diesel, and petrol engine main and connecting rod bearings.

Lead base alloys, the lowest in price, are often preferred for a pounding type of loading and generally intended for the vast field of moderately and lightly loaded bearings.

The *printing metal* used for ordinary books, has somewhere between 6 and 10% of tin and the remainder is of lead, hardened with antimony, usually between 13 and 18%.

Soft Solders See 4.4.

Pewter was originally an alloy of 80% tin and 20% lead. A modern form of pewter is *Britannia metal*, which contains approximately 92% tin, 6% antimony and 2% copper. The alloying elements are added to increase the hardness and mechanical strength and articles are made either by casting in permanent moulds, or by rolling the metal to sheet and then forming it. Care must be taken when soldering to use a low melting point soft solder and to localise the heat.

Pewter is one of relatively few metallic materials which soften when mechanically worked. Hardness can be increased by heat-treatment.

The finish may be obtained with a metal polish or by nickel- or silver-plating.

Uses include tankards, plates, beakers, vases, coffee and tea pots, and plaques.

1.15 Zinc

The chief *source* is zinc blende, a sulphide ore. The principle deposits are in Canada, USA, Mexico, Central Europe and Australia.

The ore is first concentrated by gravity or flotation. The sulphur is removed by roasting in air and in sintering machines, leaving zinc oxide. The sulphur is manufactured into sulphuric acid.

Production The production of zinc may be by either thermal or electrolytic methods. In the thermal process, brickettes of roasted ore and coal are fed from the top into a heated vertical retort; here the zinc metal formed by reduction is distilled off as a vapour and caught as a liquid in external condensers.

The electrolytic process requires the roasted ore to be dissolved in sulphuric acid and the resulting zinc sulphate solution is then freed of impurities. The zinc is then deposited electrolytically on aluminium cathodes from which it can be finally stripped off.

One of the most widely used *forms* of zinc is as an alloy (brass); others include compounds, dust, die castings, sheet, strip and plate.

Properties Pure zinc (melting point 419°C), is bluish-white, ductile and is covered with a protective film of oxide.

The *working* of zinc is easy at or above normal temperatures. In the workshop, this can be achieved by immersing in hot water.

The uses of zinc include compounds, e.g. zinc chloride as soldering flux, wood preservative and disinfectant. Zinc sulphate is used in calico printing and in varnish making. Zinc and copper are alloyed to form brass, see 1.10. Of great importance is the coating of steel with zinc, e.g. hot-dip galvanising for hardware and roofing-sheets, electro-galvanising for finer work, sheradising (small steel parts and zinc dust subjected to a temperature just below the melting point of zinc, resulting in a relatively cheap abrasion-resistant zinc coating—sheradising is also applicable to other metals and alloys), zinc spraying and paint. Die castings for quantity production, e.g. carburettors. The uses of rolled zinc include roofing, rainwater goods, engraving plates and battery cans.

1.16 Heat Treatment

Heat treatment of metals involves a combination of heating, holding and cooling at controlled rates to produce the desired conditions. For non-ferrous metals, see 1.7 to 1.15.

The heat treatment of steel first requires a knowledge of the structure of steel. Pure iron is built up of crystals of the same composition, named 'ferrite', see Fig. 8.

The addition of carbon results in a structure consisting of ferrite and seemingly darker parts called pearlite, see Fig. 9. Pearlite is an intimate mixture of flat plates of ferrite and 'cementite', see Fig. 10. Cementite is a compound of iron and carbon, which is hard, brittle and brilliantly white. A 0·87% carbon steel will consist of 100% pearlite.

Any further increase in carbon gives rise to free cementite at the grain boundaries, see Fig. 11.

Fig. 8. Pure iron (microsection)

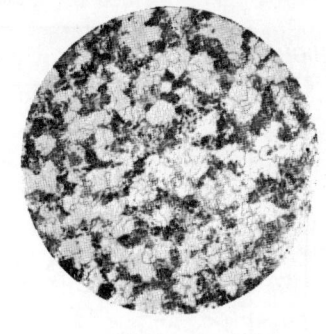

Fig. 9. Steel containing under 0·87% carbon

Fig. 10. Steel containing 0·87% carbon

Fig. 11. Steel containing over 0·87% carbon

Allotropy is the property of some elements to exist in different physical forms, and is characterised by a change in atomic structure at a definite temperature. Iron changes to a different form at 910°C, loses its magnetism and if cooled will revert to its original form.

The high temperature form of iron can hold carbon in solid solution, and is an allotrope known as 'Austenite'. On cooling, the austenite breaks down and precipitates the carbon (cementite). The temperature at which the change takes place varies with the carbon content.

By altering the rate at which the steel cools, different structures may be 'frozen'. Cooling more and more rapidly makes available three methods of heat treatment of carbon steel, i.e. annealing, normalising and hardening.

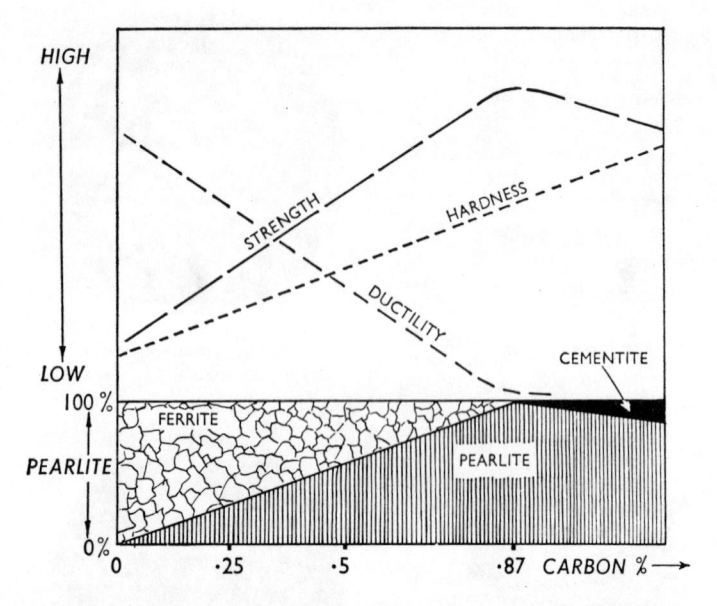

Fig. 12. Effect of carbon content on mechanical properties and microconstituents

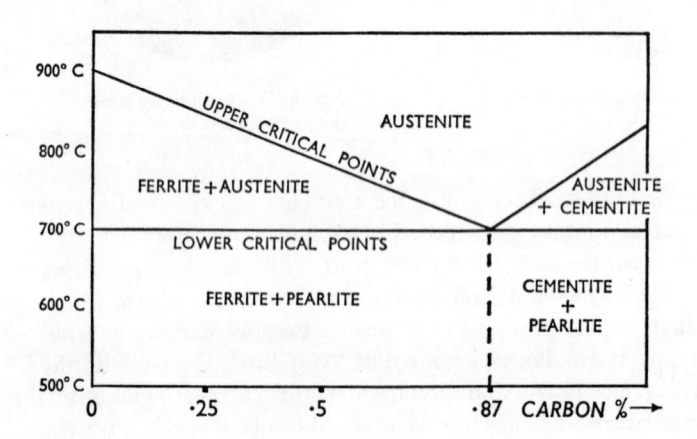

Fig. 13. Heat treatment panel

Annealing To soften and relieve internal stresses. Cold-worked steel may be 'process' or 'close' annealed by heating to 650°C for several hours to cause re-crystallisation. To anneal fully, heat to

25–50°C above the upper critical point for steel of less than 0·87% carbon, and to 50°C above the lower critical point for steels over 0·87% carbon. Avoid higher temperatures and prolonged soaking time which will cause grain growth. When all the carbon has been absorbed into austenite, cool slowly in the furnace to ensure the complete separation into ferrite and pearlite, see Fig. 14.

Normalising Similar to annealing except that the metal cools more quickly, by removing from the furnace and cooling in still air. This increases the strength, toughness and hardness, see Fig. 15.

Hardening To cut other metals and resist wear. The steel is heated, as for annealing, and quenched. The metal is 'frozen' in an intermediate and unstable condition, known as 'martensite', which is hard and brittle and has few uses.

Tempering To relieve extreme hardness and toughen. When 'quenched steel' is heated to some temperature below the lower critical point, some carbon comes out of solution.

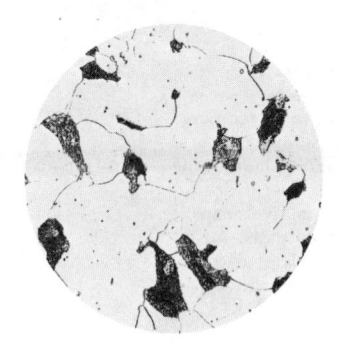

Fig. 14. 0·20% carbon steel. Annealed

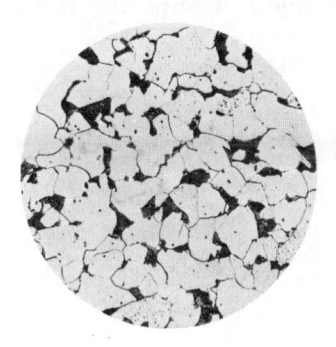

Fig. 15. 0·20% carbon steel. Normalised

Carbon steel is usually quenched in water whilst alloy steels are often oil or air quenched. Long articles should be quenched vertically and flat sections edgeways, agitating to promote rapid cooling, and uniform hardness.

Methods of Heat Treatment
The most accurate method for annealing, normalising and hardening, is to use a furnace with a pyrometer and for tempering, an oil, salt or lead bath, also with pyrometric control.

If a furnace and pyrometer are not available, the blacksmith's forge or gas blowpipe can be used. The temperature of the steel must be judged by its colour; a commonly accepted comparison is that 'Cherry Red' is about 800–820°C. This is in average daylight; in direct sunlight or under an electric light bulb 800°C may only appear dull red. As can be seen from Fig. 13 'Cherry Red' is approximately correct for carbon steel. After heating as evenly as possible, to anneal, cover with coke, firebricks or asbestos, to normalise, place on one side out of draughts, and to harden, quench.

If the article is a punch, chisel or similar tool and is to be tempered using a gas blowpipe, the cutting edge only need be hardened. This is then cleaned with emery cloth or a carborundum stone and heat applied, say 50 mm back from the cutting edge. Coloured films of oxide will appear, first pale straw and then darkening. When the correct temperature (tempering colour) reaches the cutting edge, quench.

Table 1. Tempering Temperatures

Temper Colour	Temperature °C	Articles
Pale straw	230	Turning tools, scrapers
Dark straw	240	Drills, milling cutters
Brown	250	Taps, shear blades
Brownish-purple	260	Punches, twist drills, reamers, rivet snaps
Purple	270	Axes, press tools
Dark purple	280	Cold chisels
Blue	300	Springs, screwdrivers

Hardening and tempering a punch or chisel in the forge must be completed at one heat. The cutting end is heated to a dull red, and only the tip quenched. The hardened tip is quickly cleaned with a stone and the remaining heat in the shank will temper the edge, when the whole tool is quenched.

To harden and temper more complicated articles than punches and chisels, using only the forge or blowpipe, great ingenuity is often required. A large bar of iron is sometimes heated and the tool turned on it until the tempering colour appears. Another method is to heat a thick iron tube, to heat the article from all sides. Small intricate parts might be immersed in a tray of sand, which is then heated.

A carbon steel cutting tool, if overheated either in use or when re-sharpening, will 'blue', destroying the original temper. The soft cutting edge is soon destroyed and may become red hot.

1.17 Case-Hardening

Some articles require a hard surface to resist wear and a tough core to resist breakage. There are several methods of surface-hardening, and the most common method is case-hardening.

Low carbon steel is heated to 900°C in carbon-rich material, to raise the surface carbon content, which can then be heat-treated. Although there are also liquid and gaseous techniques, the description in this book will be limited to two methods using solid carbon-rich material.

Pack carburising consists of packing the steel articles to be treated in a welded mild steel or nickel chrome box, with about 25-mm layers of chemically impregnated wood-charcoal around each part. The box lid is made airtight with fireclay and the box placed in a furnace and heated to 900–920°C. The carburising action is not due to the contact of the steel with carbon, but the action of carbon monoxide formed in the process. The case may have a carbon content of up to 0·87%, gradually decreasing to the core, in fact there are two steels requiring different treatment.

First the core is refined by heating to 880–920°C and then quenched in oil or water. The case will now be hard, coarse and brittle, but this can be refined by reheating to 760–780°C and again quenching in oil or water, and finally to remove stresses which might cause 'crazing' (fine hair-line cracks) heat uniformly to 200°C and allow to cool slowly. The steel now has a hard refined case and tough core.

Open hearth case-hardening requires only the minimum of equipment. For wrought iron and mild steel, heat uniformly to a bright red and then dip or roll in a carbon-rich powder. The powder will melt and adhere to the surface, forming a shell around the work. Reheat to a bright red and quench in clean, cold water.

For a deeper casing, either repeat the operation before quenching, or allow the work to soak in the powder, in a suitable container, at bright red heat for 5 to 30 minutes before quenching.

Portions to be left soft can be covered during the process, using fireclay, protective collars, copper plating or a special anti-carburiser powder or paste.

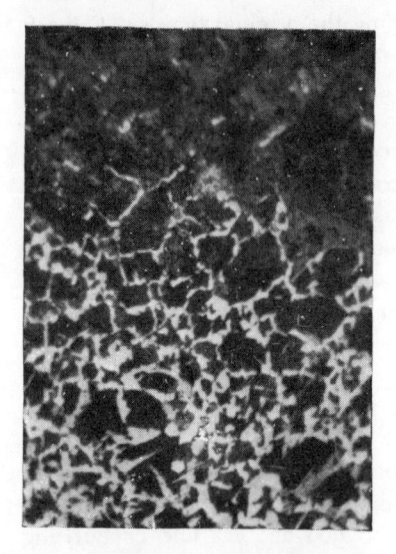

Fig. 16. Micro-photograph of mild steel after carburising and before refinement × 100. (Courtesy: Kasenit Ltd.)

Fig. 17. Micro-photograph of mild steel after refinement showing the case and core gradually merging × 100. (Courtesy: Kasenit Ltd.)

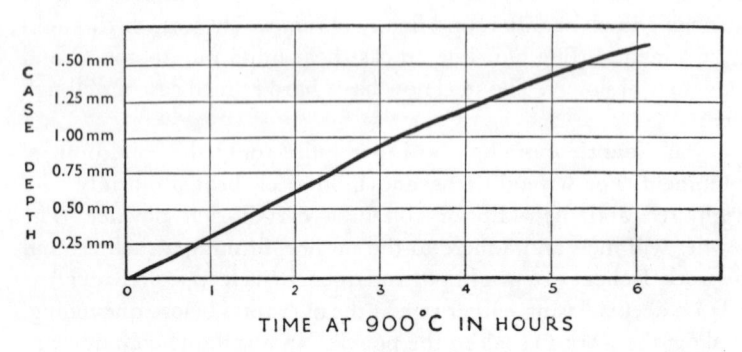

Fig. 18. Chart showing case penetration against time. (Courtesy: Kasenit Ltd.)

Fig. 19. Fracture of a case-hardened specimen. (Courtesy: Kasenit Ltd.)

1.18 Table 2. Workshop Tests and Methods of Identification

Test	Wrought Iron	Mild Steel	Carbon Steel	Cast Iron
1. Appearance	usually brown and scaly	smooth	smooth	grey and textured surface, rounded corners, tapering to flash mark
2. File and turn	whitish, poor finish and slag lines visible	whitish finish, cuts easily	hardness increases with carbon content	hard skin, black crumbly chips
3. Grind	light stream of individual lines	stream of lines with sparks	heavy stream of lines with large sparks	dull red, non-explosive (similar to high speed steel)
4. Drop on ground	dull sound	slight ringing sound	high ringing sound	very dull sound
5. Cut notch and break	bends easily	bends well before breaking	breaks with very little bending	breaks easily
6. Fracture	fibrous	crystalline	crystalline	large crystalline
7. Hammer when red hot	flattens very easily	flattens easily	flattens fairly easily	crumbles
8. Quench from red heat	no change	very slightly harder	much harder (test with edge of file)	cracks, or may fly into pieces

2

Preliminary Considerations

2.1 Safety

Safety is largely dependent upon knowledge and common sense.

The *student* should wear an overall which completely covers all loose ends of clothing. Loose clothing and long hair have both been known to drag the operator into moving machinery. Personal cleanliness is also important to prevent dermatitis (inflammation of the skin). Particular care must be taken to wash before eating, especially after handling poisonous or corrosive materials.

The *workshop* should be large enough to prevent overcrowding. The floor should be in good condition, clear of loose material and kept free from coolants and lubricants, which tend to make the floor slippery. Lighting must be adequate, preferably with individual adjustable lamps on machines requiring precision work. A first-aid case and fire extinguisher must be easily available. Fire drill and the means of escape must be known to all who use the workshop.

All workshop *machines* should be wired to strategically placed cut-out switches for emergency stopping. In training workshops, the rule is 'one student to each machine and a responsible person present'.

All moving parts must be adequately guarded, and certain operations require eye protection. When dry grinding, turning or drilling non-ferrous metals or cast iron, without a coolant, a transparent screen or goggles should be used.

At regular intervals all machines and tools must be thoroughly cleaned, inspected for worn and broken parts, repaired and adjusted where necessary, and lubricated with the correct grease or oil. Over periods when the equipment is not in use, all machined surfaces should be wiped over with a clean cloth soaked in oil. Precision instruments such as micrometers should be given a thin film of

PRELIMINARY CONSIDERATIONS

vaseline on all bright parts. Clean, well-maintained machinery and tools are a vital factor in the safety of the workshop.

Some *dangers* in the workshop are not at once obvious, and care should be taken to remember them. A few of the less obvious dangers are listed below.

Air trapped in an enclosed space will expand when heated and may cause an explosion. Hence, in the design of the hollow handle to a tankard (Fig. 95) one small hole must be drilled to allow the air to escape, and a second one is necessary to prevent an air lock, allowing liquids to drain out after the cleaning operation.

A more serious error is to heat an enclosed space which may contain moisture, perhaps only a very small amount. When bending a tube, the difficulty of preventing flattening is often overcome by plugging one end, loading and ramming tight with sand, and plugging the remaining end. If the sand is not absolutely dry, when the tube is heated one of the plugs will explode outwards. Another example is the danger of moisture on any tools or parts in foundry-work; for example moisture in the mould will explode when trapped by molten metal.

When quenching hot parts, care should be taken to avoid the scalding steam. A red hot tube plunged into water will produce a jet of boiling water and steam, therefore direct the open end away from the body.

When making up the acid pickle for silversmithing, the acid must *always* be added to a volume of water. The reverse causes an explosion.

An underrated danger on machine work is the swarf. It should never be touched with a bare hand nor touched when the machine is in motion. Steel swarf can easily cut the flesh as far as the bone.

A cleaning rag should not be held near moving machinery. A revolving shaft or buffing wheel can easily carry a loose end of material round once and then drag in the operator's hand.

If the student thoroughly understands the process he is about to perform, and acts in a workmanlike manner, the risk of accidents should be very small.

2.2 Design

Before designing an article many necessary facts must be obtained, such as the purpose(s) for which it is required, size and approximate cost (if applicable).

The designer then makes rough sketches of possible alternatives. The most important factor to bear in mind is 'fitness for purpose', for unless the article will fulfil the purpose(s) intended, it is worthless. For example, the purpose of a tankard is to hold say ½ litre of liquid, to be pleasant to drink from, to be stable on its base, and hygienic in use. A garden-gate latch must be easy to open and shut, strong and weather-resistant. In conjunction with 'fitness for purpose' the designer should also consider aesthetic qualities, constructional details, materials and finish.

Aesthetic qualities are those concerned with the beauty of the article, and appreciation of these can only be acquired by personal effort. The beauty of form and shape can be illustrated in nature by flowers and leaves and in art by Greek vases and Chinese porcelain. If a study is made, various points will be noted, such as the interesting contrast between large and small shapes, plain and decorated areas, and curved and straight lines (many curves approximate to conic sections, i.e. ellipse, parabola and hyperbola). Some authorities have suggested a mathematical guide to proportions, known as the *'Golden Section'*, which appears to date from antiquity.

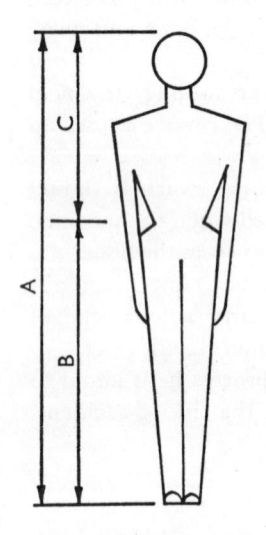

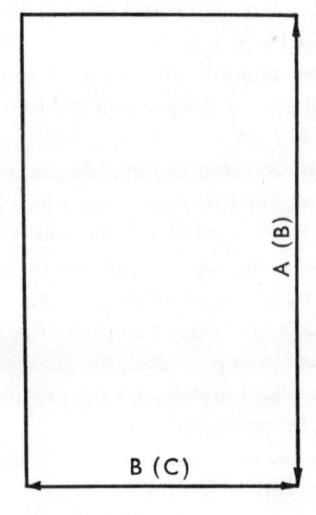

Fig. 20. The Golden Section

The formula can be written A : B = B : C and approximates to 5 : 3.

PRELIMINARY CONSIDERATIONS 31

Constructional details will be modified by the craftsman's ability and the tools and machines available in the workshop.

Materials and finish will normally be those most suitable, although the cost may be a determining factor. Taking the previous examples, the tankard may be made in solid silver or less expensively in gilding metal and silver plated; and the garden-gate latch would be cheaper and just as effective, if made from 'black' rather than 'bright' mild steel.

2.3 Working Drawings

Once finalised, the design is made into a working drawing, giving all necessary information for the craftsman to make the article as intended. To prevent possible misunderstandings, drawings are made to an appropriate British Standard, for example Engineering Drawing Practice is to BS 308: 1972.

Before attempting a working drawing, it is necessary to have a knowledge of geometry, and of machine drawing, which are the subject of complete text-books and no attempt will be made to cover these here.

Sheetmetal development should be full size and include allowances for joints and safe edges, see 5.1; the development can then be copied, marked through or traced on to the metal.

An accepted method of making drawings for silversmithing is to draw half the front elevation in section, usually on the vertical centre line. Small detailed sections such as hinges and bezels are often drawn to a larger scale, to one side of the main drawing. To assist in drawing teapots, bowls and other symmetrical shapes it is helpful to fold a rough drawing down the centre line and to cut out the profile of one side; this can then be opened and used as a template to mark round on the working drawing. To give added effect the section and exterior view can be given a watercolour wash; for silverwork use 'Neutral Tint' (a pale grey). Extra washes can be given to suggest shading, keeping the difference in tones quite subtle.

To prevent buckling of the paper on drying, it is preferable to use special water-colour drawing paper.

Forgework and particularly wrought ironwork, is often drawn full size on squared paper, with 25-mm squares. The drawing can then be transferred to a sheet of metal using chalk for the squares and outline. The red hot metal can then be offered for comparison, without risk of burning the original drawing.

Working drawings used in industry are almost invariably copies from an original. The original drawing is usually in pencil on white paper; tracing cloth or paper is placed over this, and the original copied, using dense black waterproof drawing ink. The tracing is then laid in close contact with light-sensitive paper and exposed to light for a predetermined length of time. The copies are usually black on a white background, or white on blue ('blue-print'). To eliminate the tracing stage, either the pencil or pen drawing can be made direct on to a special translucent material, which is the equivalent of a tracing, or alternatively, for a drawing on opaque paper, a photographic method can be used.

3

Foundrywork

3.1 Patterns
Patterns are used to produce cavities in sand, into which molten metal can be poured (Figs 21 and 26).

The patterns are commonly made of a softwood such as white pine which is easily worked, glued and varnished and is fairly durable. For small patterns a hardwood such as mahogany is often used. Mass production in the foundry necessitates metal patterns to reduce the amount of wear.

The pattern-maker must have a considerable knowledge of foundrywork if the pattern is to produce the desired result. As the hot but solidified casting cools to atmospheric temperature, solid shrinkage or contraction will take place. Therefore to produce a casting to the dimensions of the working drawing, the pattern must be oversize. The extra allowance largely depends upon the metal to be cast, and to facilitate the pattern-maker's work, special contraction rules are used.

Table 3. Pattern-maker's Contraction Allowance

Metal	Metric units (mm/m)
Lead, Zinc	26
Tin	21
Steel (carbon)	16 to 21
Brass	13 to 16
Aluminium alloys gunmetal, phosphor bronze	10 to 16
Cast iron (grey)	8 to 13

Patterns are given a taper called 'draft', to facilitate easy withdrawal from the moulding sand. A general guide is to allow on each vertical side, a taper of 10 mm per metre.

For maximum strength and also ease of withdrawal, all corners should be rounded. Inside corners can be rounded either by glueing in strips of leather fillet, or by using plastic wood. Abrupt changes of thickness weaken the casting.

A finish allowance must be made to allow for machining. This is usually about 3 mm on small castings. Extra metal may also be added to facilitate holding the casting during subsequent machining, such as a central lug for easy chucking in the lathe.

Patterns which cannot be withdrawn in one piece must be made in two or more parts. To make a split pattern the mating surfaces are aligned by pins, pointed at both ends; the surfaces are then joined by paper glued on both sides. The assembly is shaped and then the parts separated; the pin holes are drilled out for the insertion of metal dowels, rounded and tapered at the ends.

The finished wooden pattern is smoothed with glasspaper and painted with varnish or shellac to prevent the adhesion of sand and absorption of moisture. Three coats are usually applied by spraying or using a fine camel hair brush. An accepted foundry practice is to colour the different parts of the pattern, such as surfaces to be left as cast, surfaces to be machined and core-prints, red, yellow and black respectively (BS 467: 1957).

WORKING DRAWING
(✓=MACHINED SURFACE)

SPLIT PATTERN
(---- =OUTLINE OF FINISHED WORK)

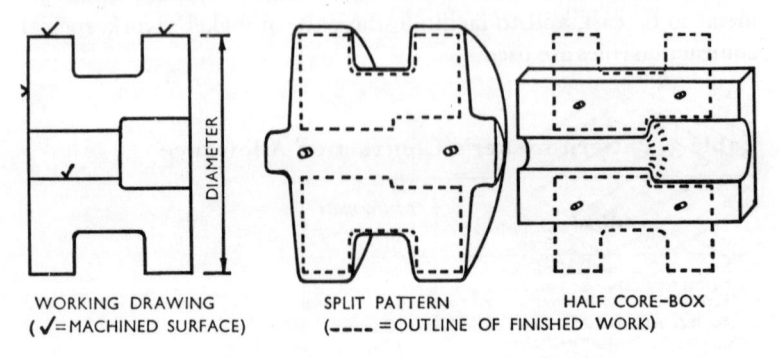

HALF CORE-BOX

Fig. 21. Planning pattern and core-box from working drawing (allowances and draft exaggerated)

3.2 Cores

Cores are used to produce an internal shape in the casting (Figs 21 and 26).

To locate the core relative to the pattern, 'core-prints' are added to the pattern, forming extra hollows in which the core can rest. To give extra support to the core, 'chaplets' can be used (Fig. 26). They remain in the casting and should alloy with the molten metal.

The core is basically silica sand specially bonded (with oil and cereal binders) to give cohesion. It should be strong, yet brittle enough to collapse when the casting contracts, and permeable to permit the escape of gases.

The core is made in a 'core-box' which is usually a split wooden mould (Fig. 21). The two halves are clamped together, stood vertically and rammed full with core sand. To level or 'strickle off', the sand at the top, a steel straight edge is used with a sawing motion. The core is now baked in an oven at approximately 200°C until it begins to turn brown. To give added strength, wire reinforcement can be added to the core, during or after ramming. To increase permeability, a central vent is made with a pointed wire, which should correspond with a vent in the sand mould.

3.3 Castings

Once the pattern(s) and core(s) have been produced, the sand mould is made in the foundry.

The mould is made in a moulding-box or 'flask' comprising an upper box or 'cope' and a lower box or 'drag'. Dowels and sockets align the two halves which are usually made either of steel, cast iron or of aluminium alloy.

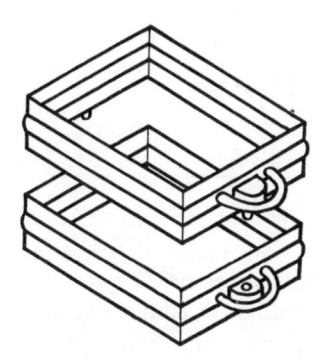

Fig. 22. The flask

The moulding sand is either the traditional 'green sand' which is a mixture of sand grains and clay particles, such as Mansfield or Erith sands, or now more commonly, clean sand with oils or synthetic resins added as binders. The desired properties are a compromise between permeability and smoothness coupled with cohesion. The moisture content should be such that a handful remains unbroken after gripping firmly, but loose enough to break when thrown down. Over-dampness may cause bubbling and a porous finish to the casting, see 2.1 Safety.

Four Stages in Moulding and Pouring
Stage 1
The drag is placed upside down on a firm flat surface. If a split pattern is used, as in the previous example, the half with sockets is placed face down and then dusted with a parting powder. (*Note:* detail is usually better in the bottom half of the castings, as gas and dross will rise.) Handfuls of sifted sand are then thrown at the pattern, effectively covering every detail; this is known as 'sand slinging'. The sand is then lightly rammed either with a small peg rammer or the finger tips. Loose unsifted sand is shovelled in and firmed with a butt rammer. The excess is strickled off and a handful sprinkled over and rubbed across to ensure a flat surface.

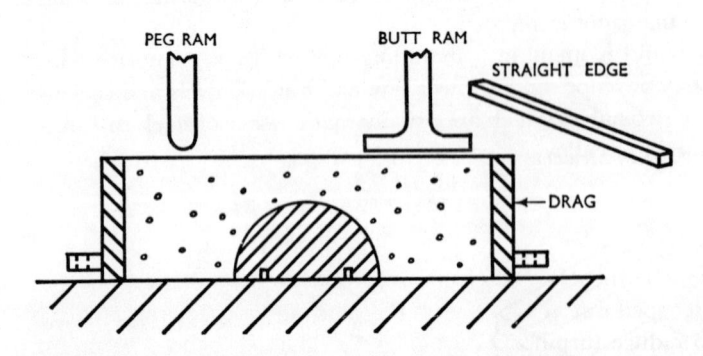

Fig. 23. Stage 1: Moulding

Stage 2
The drag is then turned over in one smooth movement. The cope is fitted on to the drag. To prevent the two halves of sand sticking, a parting powder is used, which can be a proprietary make, french

chalk or more conveniently the burnt sand brushed from castings. The powder can be dusted from a cotton bag.

Sprue pins, or 'runner sticks', which are smooth round tapered pegs, are pressed firmly into the sand. The position is determined by considering the flow of metal and the convenience of excess metal removal afterwards ('fettling').

The cope is rammed with sand and strickled off, making the top smooth and firm. If a large amount of air will have to be driven through the sand, vent holes should be made within about 10 mm of the pattern. A pouring basin or sprue cup is cut before removing the sprue pins.

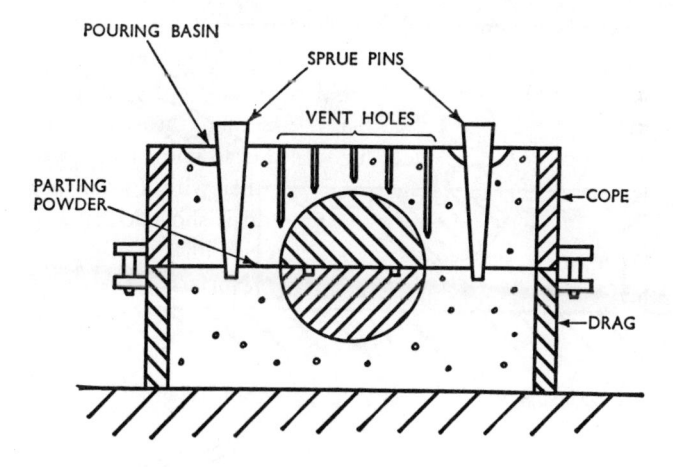

Fig. 24. Stage 2: Moulding

Stage 3

The cope is then carefully removed. A depression or 'skim bob' is often scooped out at the base of the pouring gate, to trap particles and to reduce turbulence. A runner or channel is then cut to link the pouring gate with the mould; this should be slightly smaller than the sprue diameter, to prevent air inclusion and turbulence. One or more fairly large runners join the mould to the riser or feeder head (Fig. 26).

The sand around the edge of the two halves of patterns is moistened to prevent crumbling. A spike or screw is driven into the pattern. This spike is then rapped in all directions before the pattern is lifted vertically.

Loose sand must be removed, for it is better to cast too much metal rather than too little. For a smooth finish the mould can be lightly coated with plumbago or a proprietary product.

The core(s) is (are) now placed in position and the cope carefully replaced, ready for pouring.

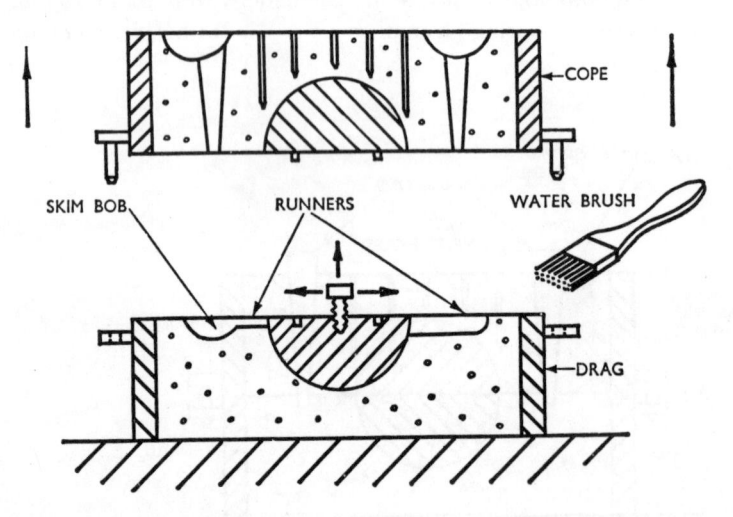

Fig. 25. Stage 3: Moulding

Stage 4

A metal such as aluminium can be melted in a crucible; it is first fluxed to give protection from the atmosphere and to separate metal from dross, and then degassed of hydrogen by plunging a proprietary tablet to the bottom of the melt.

The best means of temperature control is to use a special foundry thermometer protected by a sheath.

The crucible is held about half-way down with special tongs and withdrawn from the furnace. Dross is raked away from the pouring lip with a heated skimmer and the metal poured in one continuous stream until it appears at the head of the riser.

Usually the thickest parts show the greatest shrinkage, therefore either a large feeder head is placed nearby or a sleeve of combustible

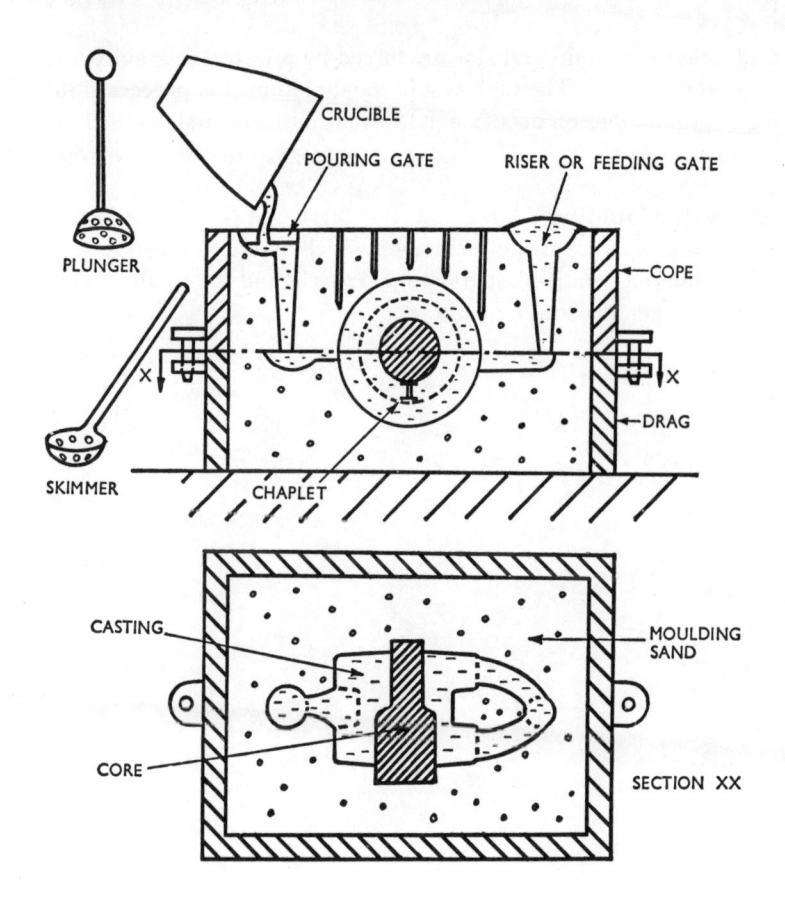

Fig. 26. Stage 4: Pouring

material is placed at the top of the riser to keep the head fluid until the casting has solidified.

To harden the surface of cast iron, metal chill plates are inserted into the mould.

When the casting has solidified and cooled, the sand is knocked out and the casting fettled.

3.4 Die Casting

The fundamental principle of this method is that metallic moulds are used rather than sand. Molten alloys of aluminium, copper, lead, magnesium, tin and zinc are forced by pressure or gravity into preheated moulds. The high cost of the dies limits the process to the mass production of accurate and well-finished small-to-medium castings.

3.5 Shell Moulding

This is a precision casting technique, widely used in industry. Sand with a binder resin is blasted on to a pattern, and the resulting shell is broken open to use as a mould.

4

Joining Processes

4.1 Introduction
Before specifying the joint(s) for a particular article, the designer must consider many factors.

The first consideration may be whether to use a permanent or temporary joint and secondly whether heat can be applied. Other factors include strength required, water or pressure tightness, the melting point of the parent material, corrosion resistance and surface finish. Joints may be conveniently classified as follows:

1 Permanent Joints
(a) Made with heat   *Approx. melting range*
   (1) Soft Soldering   183–255°C
   (2) Hard (or silver) Soldering   600–800°C
   (3) Brazing   800–900°C
   (4) Welding   melting point of metal
(b) Made without heat
   (1) Riveting
   (2) Sheetmetal joints (see 5.11)

2 Temporary Joints
(1) Screws   (2) Bolts   (3) Studs

4.2 Sources of Heat
The most common source of heat in the workshop is from combustion or burning. The fuel, which is a hydrocarbon and may be blacksmiths' coke or breeze, coal-gas or acetylene, is burnt in a stream of air or oxygen. The temperatures vary and depend on the impurities present.

Table 4. Flame Temperatures

Air — Coal-gas	1700–1800°C
Oxy-coal-gas	2000–2200°C
Air — Acetylene	2300–2500°C
Oxy-acetylene	3100–3300°C

Fig. 27. Oxy-acetylene flame

Zone 1 Unburnt mixture of oxygen and acetylene.
Zone 2 C_2H_2 + O_2 = $2CO$ + H_2
(Acetylene) (Oxygen) (Carbon monoxide) (Hydrogen)
Zone 3 Blue reducing zone of carbon monoxide and hydrogen.
Zone 4 $4CO$ + $2H_2$ + $3O_2$ = $4CO_2$ + $2H_2O$
(Carbon monoxide) (Hydrogen) (Oxygen from air) (Carbon dioxide) (Water, steam)

The flame shown has a reducing zone caused by excess acetylene (fuel gas) and is known as either a reducing, carbonising or carburising flame.

Oxygen in excess of that required for complete combustion produces an oxidising flame.

Usually a neutral flame is required, which is neither reducing nor oxidising.

Steel which is heated with an oxidising flame or placed too near to the air blast in the forge fire, see 7.1, will oxidise on the surface to form iron oxide or 'scale'.

Electricity as a source of heat in the average workshop is mainly confined to high-resistance heating wires used in soldering irons and furnaces.

4.3 Fluxes

To join two surfaces by soldering, brazing or welding, the joining metal alloys with the parent metal.

Before heat is applied, the surfaces must be cleaned mechanically, e.g. wire brushing, scraping, filing, etc. Although apparently clean,

Fig. 28. Magnified section through a soldered joint showing compound layers.
(Courtesy: Tin Research Institute)

the surfaces must now be chemically cleaned with a flux, to remove the remaining thin film of grease and oxides.

Once the flux has been applied it will prevent further oxidation during the joining process. Additional properties are to float oxides and other impurities to the surface where they can easily be removed and to reduce the surface tension of the solder.

The following are the more important fluxes for soft soldering:

Zinc chloride (killed spirits of salts) is made by adding zinc to hydrochloric acid until the effervescing action ceases, but normally zinc chloride is nowadays obtained as a ready-made chemical. Zinc chloride, often combined with ammonium chloride (sal ammoniac) forms the active basis of most fluxes for brass, bronze, copper, iron, steel and tinplate.

Hydrochloric acid (spirits of salts) is used as an additive to zinc chloride flux for the soldering of zinc and galvanised iron.

Ammonium chloride (sal ammoniac) is rarely used as a flux by itself except as an aid to pre-tinning soldering irons. However, ordinary killed spirits fluxes are equally useful for this purpose.

Tallow is used for the soldering of lead and pewter (Britannia metal).

Aluminium fluxes are nowadays almost exclusively proprietary products which are more satisfactory and effective than some of the home-made preparations which were sometimes used and which are not always reliable.

Resin is particularly valuable as a flux for the soldering of electric assemblies where the flux residue cannot be removed and therefore has to be absolutely free from any corrosive action whatever. In most cases proprietary resin-based fluxes which contain an activator are used. These activators are so chosen that they enhance the fluxing action of the resin without imparting corrosive properties to the flux residue.

Active fluxes, such as zinc chloride, must be thoroughly washed away to prevent subsequent corrosion.

Borax is a flux for hard soldering and brazing.

For convenience and improved fluxing it is now common practice to use proprietary fluxes in preference to those named above.

4.4 Soft Solders

The lowest temperature method of joining is by soft soldering, using an alloy mainly of lead and tin.

Table 5. Soft Solders

% Tin	% Lead	Melting characteristics	Typical applications
60 (60–65)	40 (40–35)	Lowest melting point of series	Components liable to damage by heat or requiring free running solder, e.g. electrical radio and instrument assemblies
50 (44–50)	50 (56–50)	Moderately low m.p. short pasty range	Coppersmith's and tinsmith's bit soldering; general machine soldering
40 (39–40)	60 (60–61)	Moderate pasty range	Blowpipe soldering, soldering of side seams on high-speed body-forming machines
30 (29–35)	70 (65–71)	Long pasty range	Plumber's solder, wiping of cable and lead pipe joints. Dipping baths

JOINING PROCESSES 45

Note: Up to 3% antimony is added to some solders, mainly to reduce costs. Antimonial solder is not recommended for zinc and galvanised work.

When designing articles to be soldered, the surfaces should engage or interlock for strength, leaving the solder to seal and solidify the joint.

CROSS SECTION OF CAN SIDE SEAM

Fig. 29. Solder unites the interlocking joint members. (Courtesy: Tin Research Institute)

Parts should fit closely enough to draw solder in by capillary force. The clearance varies from 0·02 mm for tinned surfaces to 0·1 mm for untinned.

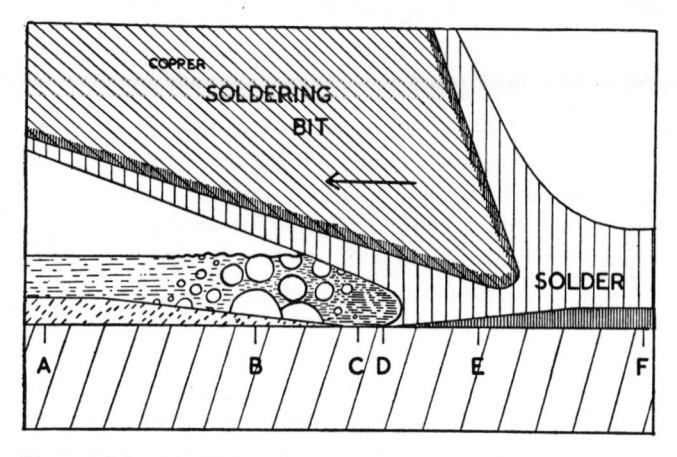

Fig. 30. Diagrammatic representation of the displacement of flux by molten solder. (Courtesy: Tin Research Institute)

A Flux solution lying above oxidised metal surface
B Boiling flux solution removing the film of oxide (e.g. as chloride)
C Bare metal in contact with fused flux
D Liquid solder displacing fused flux
E Tin reacting with the basis metal to form compound
F Solder solidifying

The surfaces to be joined are next mechanically and sometimes chemically cleaned before fluxing. It is often an advantage to pre-tin parts with the solder to be used, unless already tinned, as tin-plate.

Methods of Soldering

(1) The most common method of soldering is to use a soldering iron with a copper bit which stores and then delivers the heat and solder to the metal, finally withdrawing surplus molten solder. Copper has a high heat capacity and conductivity and is readily wetted with molten solder. The shank is made of steel which is strong and inexpensive and not a good conductor of heat; the handle is usually wooden for cheapness and again a poor heat conductor.

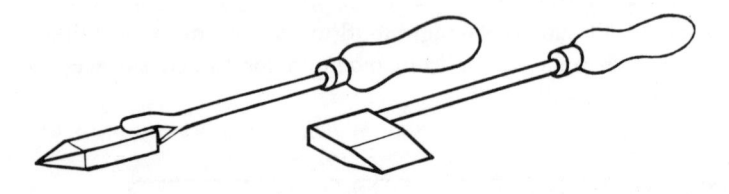

Fig. 31. Straight and hatchet soldering irons

The soldering irons shown in Fig. 31 are heated in a stove (usually gas heated). When the green flame appears the copper is at the correct temperature. For quantity work the iron could be heated by an internal gas flame. Electrically heated irons are more suitable for small work, e.g. electrical and radio.

Before soldering, the copper bit must have a bright tinned surface which can be achieved by filing smooth and then rubbing the hot fluxed-bit on a piece of solder in a shallow tin lid.

When soldering a new tinplate article, assemble first, then flux and 'tack' solder before fluxing and soldering all the joints. To ensure a good joint, sufficient heat must be applied by using an ample size copper bit raised to the correct temperature and held in close contact with the metal joint. The bit is then drawn along slowly. At the end of the joint, surplus solder can be picked up with the copper bit. The article is then washed and dried.

(2) Where the article must be kept as cool as possible, a small localised flame (e.g. blowpipe flame) is applied for a short time.

JOINING PROCESSES 47

The solder is applied from a fine cored wire or as a flux and solder paste.

(3) For maximum neatness many parts are fluxed and tinned on the mating surfaces, held together and then 'sweated' together by applying a clean iron or holding in a flame.

(4) Industrial techniques include painting with a solder and flux paste, and then either heating in an oven, or using electrical induction heating.

(5) Work such as automobile radiators are cleaned, fluxed and dipped into molten solder.

(6) Lead work is soldered using 'Plumbers' solder' which acquires a pasty consistency as it cools, allowing the plumber to manipulate and mould the joint by the wiping process. The solder is applied either in a molten state by a ladle, or as a stick in conjunction with a blowlamp, and is then wiped to a smooth contour using a buckskin cloth.

Special work such as aluminium and parts subject to higher temperatures should be soldered using prepared proprietary solders and fluxes.

4.5 Hard Solders

For high-strength joints, higher temperatures must be used. Brazing, one of the oldest metal joining methods, uses brass as the joining material and requires high temperatures which may be a disadvantage particularly with copper and its alloys. By adding silver to the brass a low temperature silver brazing alloy is produced. This alloy is often known as hard or silver solder and is an alloy of silver, copper and zinc.

Hard soldering is therefore an intermediate stage between low temperature soft soldering and high temperature brazing. Hard solders may be divided into two groups:

Low temperature silver brazing alloys which are quaternary silver, copper, zinc, cadmium with up to 50% silver, have a melting point ranging from 600–800°C. These alloys are used for most general engineering applications where strength coupled with low melting point is required.

Silver solders which are predominantly silver, are used in silverwork where colour match and the ability to pass the 'hallmark' test are required.

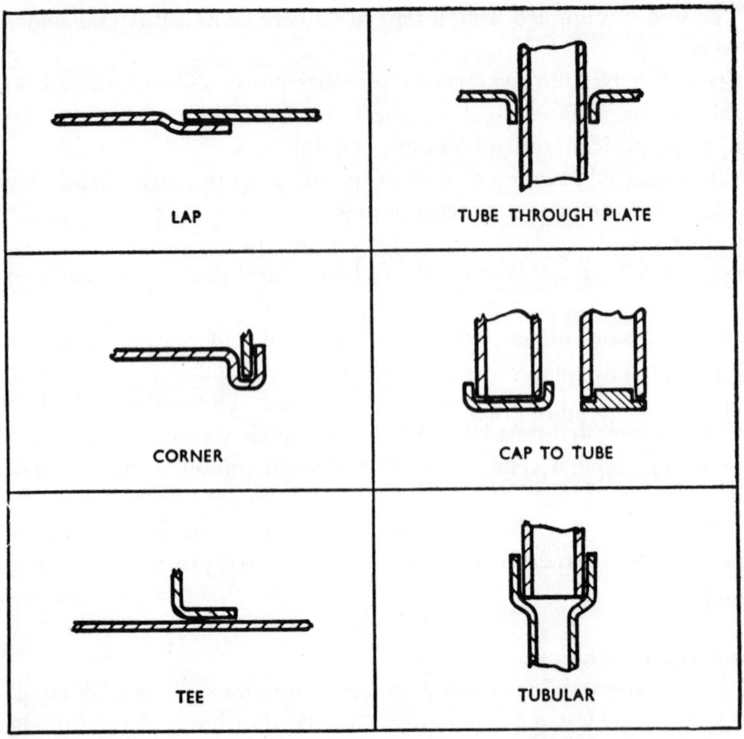
LAP
TUBE THROUGH PLATE
CORNER
CAP TO TUBE
TEE
TUBULAR

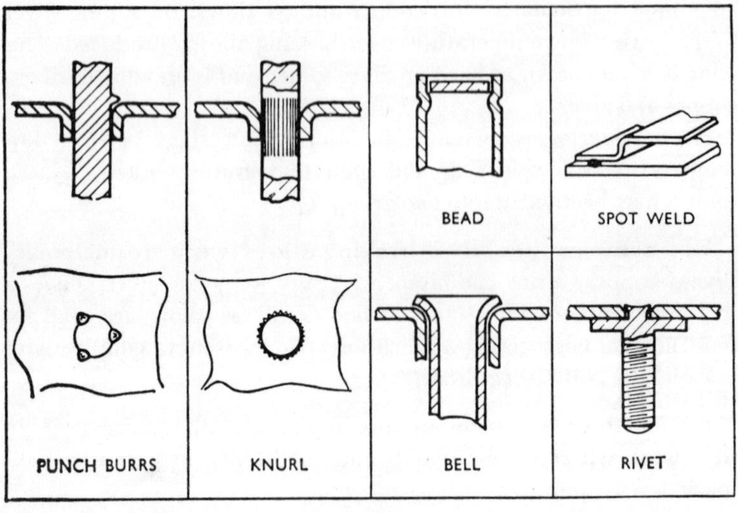
BEAD
SPOT WELD
PUNCH BURRS
KNURL
BELL
RIVET

JOINING PROCESSES

Fig. 32 (opposite, above). Fundamental joint designs for silver brazing. (Courtesy: Johnson, Matthey & Co. Ltd.)

Fig. 33 (opposite, below). Methods of locating without using external jigs. (Courtesy: Johnson, Matthey & Co. Ltd.)

The joint gaps for silver brazing should be between 0·05 and 0·15 of a millimetre. The easiest joints to braze are those which are self-locating, see Figs 32 and 33.

Silver brazing alloys are obtainable for a wide range of applications and in a variety of forms: rod, strip, wire, washers, discs, powder, powder and flux, and paint.

For built-up work in silversmithing (see 6.8) more than one joint is usually required. To avoid melting the previous joints, high melting point joints are made first.

Table 6. Silver Solders

Grade	Silver	Copper	Zinc	Approximate melting points
Hard	80	20		778–825°C
Medium	75	20	5	750–775°C
Easy	50	30	20	690–740°C

As all silver solders appear very much alike, it is common practice to mark with a file or punch along the whole length of the solder before issuing for general use in the workshop.

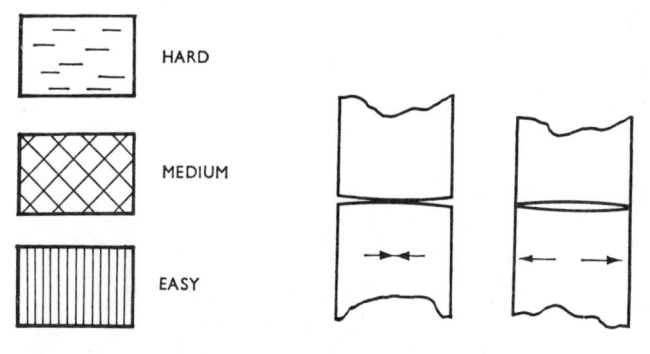

Fig. 34. Marking silver solder

Fig. 35. Capillary attraction in joint design

'Easy silver' solder should not be used on a seamed joint because on annealing the zinc will volatilise, leaving the solder porous and spongy. This is called 'fretting' and can be partially overcome by thinly painting the joint with borax and water. Another form of fretting is caused by the action of the acid pickle on the copper and zinc content.

When the joints are cut, it is important to ensure a good fit at the edges; capillary attraction will then draw the solder to the edges.

Due to the high coefficient of expansion of silver and copper, use an iron binding wire of a size that will stretch, usually between 0·5 mm and 0·8 mm.

Silver Soldering Procedure

(1) The parts must *fit* and be *clean*.
(2) *Secure* and *flux* the parts.
(3) *Heat* slowly and evenly for parts to be of the *same temperature*.
(4) Apply the *solder* as strip, panels (or paillons) or filings (or grain). The heat of the metal must melt the solder.
(5) Allow to *cool* (cut binding wire).
(6) Remove binding wire and *pickle*.

Although proprietary fluxes are more commonly used for low-temperature silver brazing, borax cones are often used for silver soldering. The cone is rubbed on a slate with water, and applied as a cream using a small camel hair brush, called a 'pencil'.

To prevent solder flowing into adjacent parts such as alternate knuckles of a hinge, paint with a mixture of water and either loam or jewellers' rouge.

4.6 Brazing

Brazing using an alloy of copper and zinc, is the highest melting point process which does not actually melt the parent metal.

Table 7. Brazing Alloys

Metal to be brazed	Approximate % copper	Approximate % zinc	Approximate melting points
Brass	40	60	840°C
Copper	50	50	880°C
Iron and steel	60	40	890°C

JOINING PROCESSES

The brazing alloy is often called 'spelter' and can be a plain brass as listed above, or a proprietary metal. A popular and quite suitable rod for brazing is that sold under proprietary names for bronze-welding. The term 'bronze-welding' is rather misleading as the rod contains approximately 60% copper and 40% zinc with additional elements such as silicon.

The technique of brazing is similar to hard soldering, requiring a clean, well-fitting joint, flux and the heat applied to the work, which in turn melts the brazing rod.

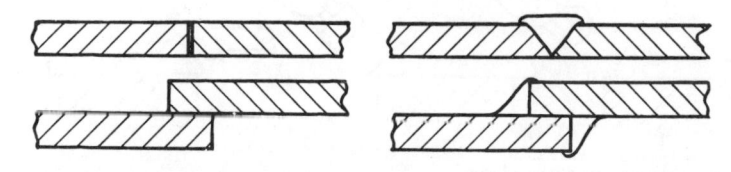

Fig. 36. Brazing and bronze-welding

Bronze-welding is similar; both rely on adhesive strength and not fusion. The difference is in the technique and application.

The technique of bronze-welding is to clean and vee the metal if the thickness exceeds 3 mm and then apply a fluxed rod using a concentrated heating flame, such as oxy-acetylene. Providing the work is clean and at the correct temperature, the bronze-welding rod will melt in the flame and flow forward on to the joint. This technique enables several layers to be built up if desired, and applied in any position (vertical, overhead, etc.).

4.7 Welding

The more common welding processes may be listed according to heat generation used:

(1) Blacksmith's fire   Blacksmith's forge welding
(2) Gas   Oxy-acetylene welding
(3) Electric arc   Metal arc and carbon arc welding
(4) Electric resistance   Spot, seam and butt welding

Blacksmith's forge welding is for wrought iron and steel only. Forge or fire welding is carried out by hammering the metal parts together whilst in a plastic (i.e. almost molten) state.

The technique is as follows:
(1) Make a clean, clinker-free fire with a good heat.
(2) The ends to be joined are upset (thickened), see 7.4, and shaped to a scarf. The scarfed ends must touch in the centre; this forces out the molten scale during welding.

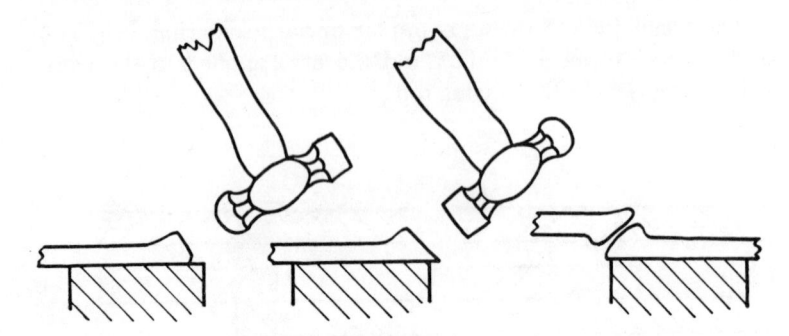

Fig. 37. Preparation of scarfed ends

(3) Heat work in fire and flux as follows, either (*a*) at dull red, remove and place a proprietary fire welding compound (e.g. 'Laffite' plate) between scarfs and lightly hammer before returning to the fire; or (*b*) with the scarfs face down; heat to near welding heat and then withdraw to sprinkle on either silver sand or burnt borax. (Heat borax to red heat to drive off water and then reduce to a powder.)
(4) At welding heat (a creamy white), remove from fire, tap on edge of anvil to shake off dirt and scale and deliver the first blow to the centre of the weld. Work from the centre of the weld to drive the flux and molten scale out.
If necessary re-heat for final welding.

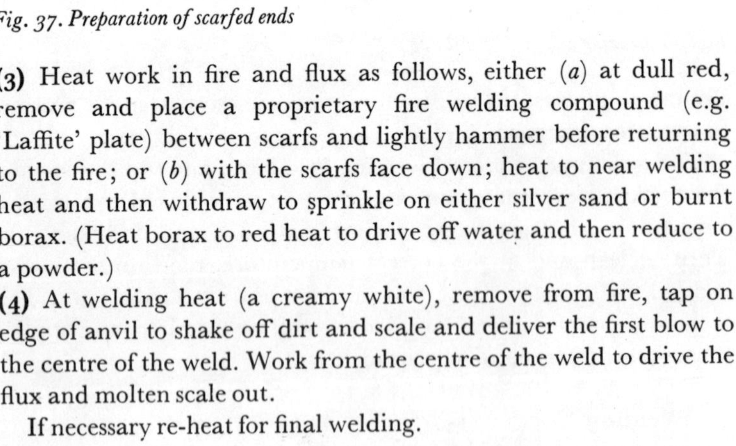

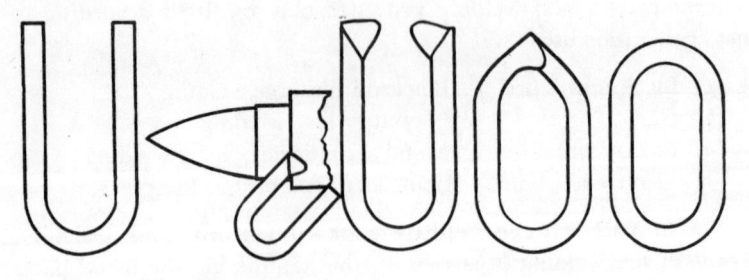

Fig. 38. Stages in making a chain link

JOINING PROCESSES

Oxy-acetylene welding for ferrous and non-ferrous metals.
The intense heat of the oxy-acetylene flame melts a pool of molten metal, and usually a filler rod of the same composition is added.

Before attempting to use this process, the care and use of equipment should be thoroughly understood. (*See* Safety Precautions, Form 1704 HMSO.)

Electric Arc and Resistance Welding techniques are used in industry where the size and/or quantity of work is sufficiently large.

4.8 Rivets

Riveted joints are made by holding the machine-forged head and inserting the shank through a punched or drilled hole and forming a second head either by machine or by hand. Where possible, rivets are 'closed' when red hot and under hydraulic pressure. For hand riveting see 8.7. A practical formula for calculating rivet size is:

$$\text{Diameter of rivet} = 1\cdot 2 \sqrt{\text{thickness of plate}} \text{ (approx.)}$$

The minimum distance between the centres of two rivets in the same row ('pitch') is 2 × diameter of rivet, and the minimum distance between the centre of the rivet and the edge of the metal is $1\frac{1}{2}$ × diameter of rivet.

To rivet up a snap head allow an extra $1\frac{1}{2}$ × diameter of rivet, and for a countersunk head allow an extra 1 × diameter of rivet.

Table 8. Rivets

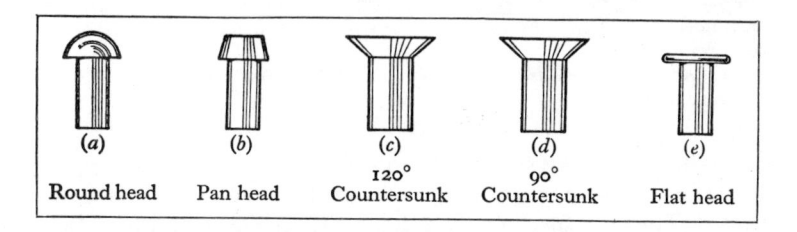

(a)	(b)	(c)	(d)	(e)
Round head	Pan head	120° Countersunk	90° Countersunk	Flat head

Rivets are obtainable in a wide range of sizes, and in the more common metals such as aluminium, brass, copper and steel.

4.9 Screws, Bolts, Studs and Nuts

Cap Screws are chiefly used to hold two or more pieces together.

Fig. 39. Hexagon socket head cap screw.
(Courtesy: G.K.N. Screws and Fasteners Ltd.)

CUP POINT   CONE   HALF DOG

Fig. 40. Hexagon socket set screw. (Courtesy: G.K.N. Screws and Fasteners Ltd.)

Set and Grub Screws are chiefly used to prevent relative movement between two parts.

The method of tightening the screw may be either by a hexagon socket and wrench as above; by a hexagon and spanner, see 8.9; by a Pozidriv (formerly Philip's Recess) (socket, shape of a cross) and driver; or by a slot and screwdriver.

C — C'sunk Head   R — Round Head   O — Raised Head   B — Pan Head   M — Mush. Head

Fig. 41. Additional screw heads with screwdriver slots. (Courtesy: G.K.N. Screws and Fasteners Ltd.)

Easy removal is obtained by using thumb screws.

Bolts for engineering work are usually either square or hexagonal headed. They are specified by a diameter, type of thread (e.g. ISO Metric coarse), length to underside of head and in special cases the threaded length is also given.

Studs When joining two pieces together, if it is preferable not to have a nut or bolt projecting, either a tap bolt or stud may be used. The stud is used in preference when the two pieces are frequently parted.

Fig. 42. Thumb screws. (Courtesy: G.K.N. Screws and Fasteners Ltd.)

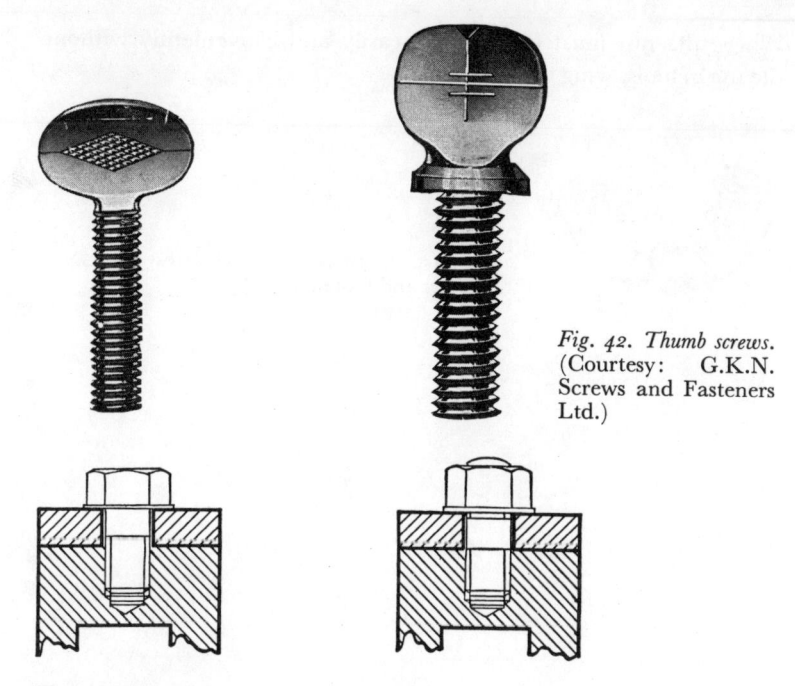

Fig. 43. Tap bolt and stud and nut

Nuts are made to suit all threads and are usually either plain (square or hexagonal) nuts or special locking nuts.

Locking may consist of two thin lock nuts acting together, or a slotted nut acting in conjunction with a cotter pin (split pin). Other locking methods include special nuts with fibre or nylon inserts, and special washers such as coil spring and tooth lock washers.

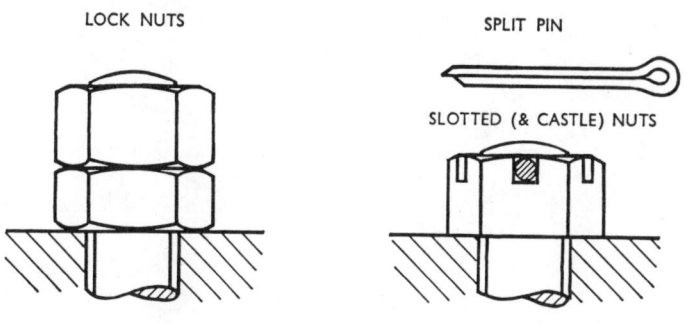

LOCK NUTS

SPLIT PIN

SLOTTED (& CASTLE) NUTS

Fig. 44. Locking devices

C

55

Where the nut must be removed easily and conveniently without the use of tools, wing nuts are used.

Fig. 45. Diecast wing nuts. (Courtesy: G.K.N. Screws and Fasteners Ltd.)

5

Sheetmetalwork

5.1 Developments

Developments are the shapes which must be cut from flat metal, before bending and folding can begin.

Before attempting pattern development (or drafting), an adequate knowledge of geometry and sheetmetalwork is required.

The geometrical methods of development may be divided into three classes:

(a) Parallel lines (e.g. cylinder and square prism)
(b) Radial lines (e.g. cones)
(c) Triangulation (complex surfaces which cannot be developed by (a) or (b), e.g. square to circle transformer).

A full description of these methods can be found in geometry textbooks.

When making the initial surface development the positioning of seams must receive practical consideration. If the article is to have a longitudinal seam, either position the seam for it to be as short as possible, or if the appearance is important, to be in the least conspicuous position. Many articles can be developed in one piece, but this often makes the shaping and joining more difficult, for example a box with a hexagonal base would be much easier to construct with the bottom separate from the sides.

Once the surface development has been made, the various edge and joint allowances must be added. The methods of making the edges and joints are described later, see 5.10 and 5.11.

Before the pattern is complete, mark parts to be cut away at the corners (called 'notching'). This allows edges and joints to fit closely without overlapping or leaving a gap.

5.2 Marking Out

Simple developments can be made direct on to the metal, whilst the more complicated ones are drawn on paper and then transferred by carbon paper or marking through with a dot punch. If the development is to be repeated, the first one is cut out and used as a pattern.

When marking out tinplate, mark with a scriber those lines which are either to be cut or hidden inside an edge or joint, and use a sharp pencil for lines which will remain visible.

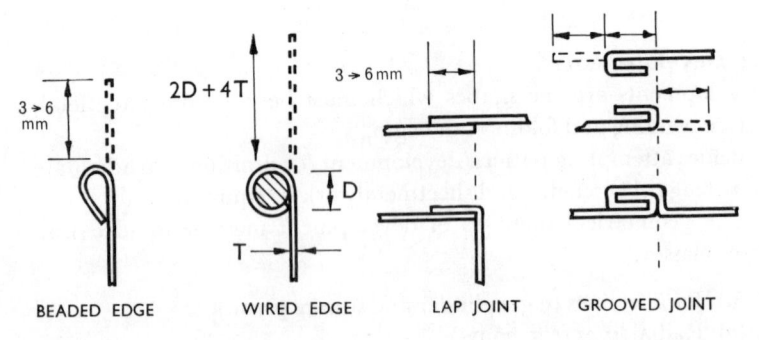

Fig. 46. Edge and seam allowances

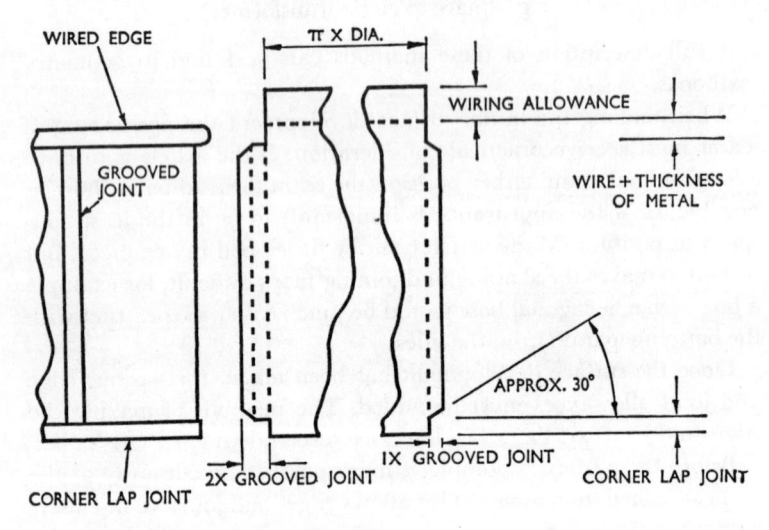

Fig. 47. Notching a wired circular container

SHEETMETALWORK

5.3 Wire and Sheet Gauges

The working drawing should indicate not only the metal to be used but also the thickness. The thickness for wire and sheet is given in *Recommendations for Metric Basic Sizes for Metal Wire, Sheet and Strip* BS 4391 : 1969, see Appendix A.

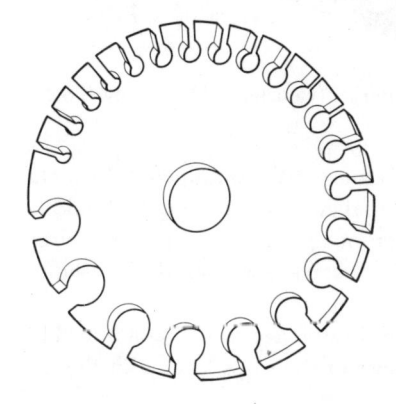

Fig. 48. Wire gauge

5.4 Snips

The most popular method of cutting light sheetmetal by hand is using straight and bent snips. Straight snips are to cut straight lines or outside curves and bent snips to cut inside curves.

(Courtesy: The Gilbow Tool & Steel Co. Ltd.)

STRAIGHT SNIPS

CURVED SNIPS

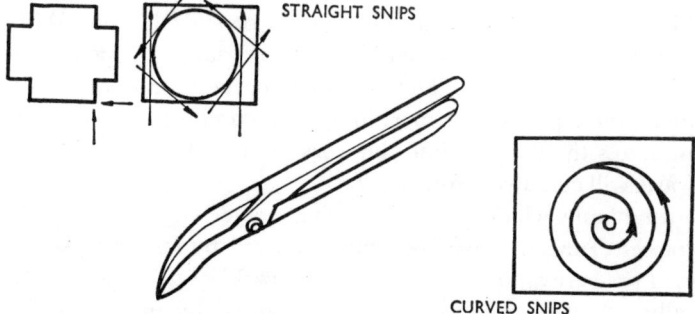

Fig. 49. Straight and curved snips

Universal snips are designed to cut straight lines and both outside and inside curves.

Fig. 50. Universal snips (anti-clockwise cutting). (Courtesy: The Gilbow Tool & Steel Co. Ltd.)

When using snips, accurate work is more easily obtained if the metal is cut roughly to shape before the final cutting, i.e. a circle should be cut to an oversize square and then octagonal, and an inside circle requires a hole in the centre to give a start, and then the cut should spiral out to full size.

Notching often requires the snips to stop accurately at a line. This can be achieved by holding the nose of the snips level with the line

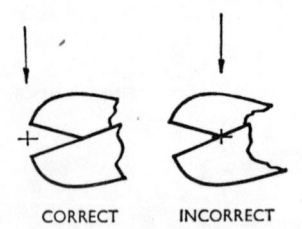

CORRECT   INCORRECT   *Fig. 51. Cutting accurately to a line*

before cutting, as opposed to regulating the length of cut by partially closing the blades.

Many snips are supplied for either right or left hand use. When attempting to cut to a line consider before starting which is the correct direction to work. This is most important for work such as trimming the top of a container; in one direction the snips will tend to cut across the line and into the work, and in the other direction the waste will curl away easily.

Cutting faults which sometimes occur include edges with needle-like pieces of metal remaining (this is caused by failing to keep a forward pressure on the snips); and edges with one side rounded and the other torn at right angles (this is caused by snips requiring tightening and/or sharpening).

SHEETMETALWORK

5.5 Bench Shearing Machines

These machines are available over a wide range of capacities, and will make a straight cut on a sheet of any width or length and are generally provided with means for shearing round rods.

The blade is curved in order to present the same angle to the work for all positions of the blade.

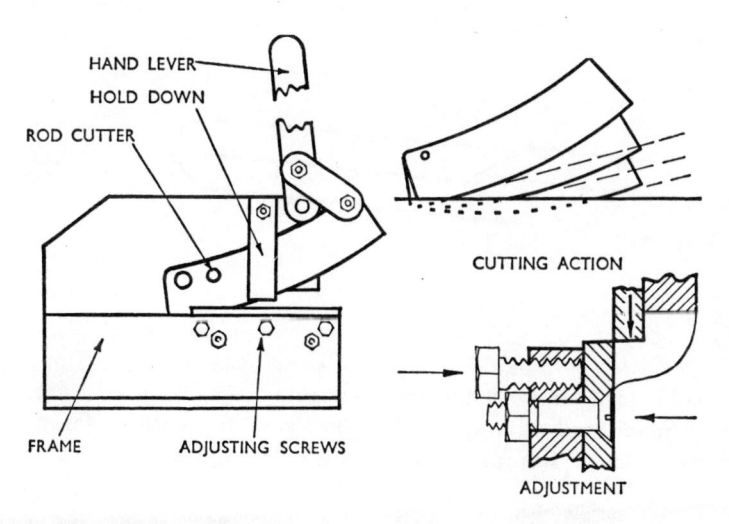

Fig. 52. Bench shearing machine

5.6 Punches

Tinmen's hollow punches are for cutting circular holes out of sheet-metal and usually range from 3 to 60 mm diameter.

To avoid damage to the cutting edge whilst giving support to the sheet, use either a block of lead or the end grain of a piece of hardwood.

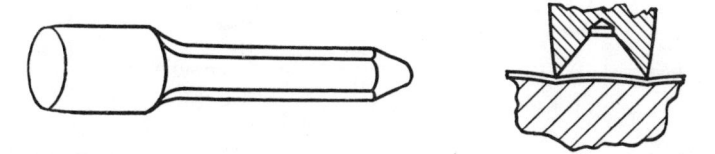

Fig. 53. Tinmen's hollow punch

5.7 Stakes

To support work and for bending purposes the sheetmetal worker uses a number of bench stakes. Probably the most useful for larger work is the cast-iron *mandrel*, 1 to 1½ m long with rounded and flat upper surfaces, and a square hole for small heads of shaped metal, see Fig. 85.

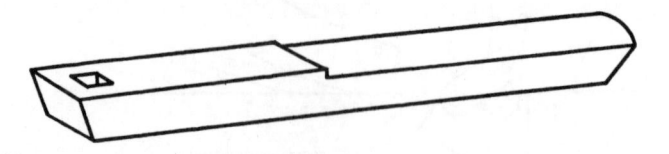

Fig. 54. Mandrel

For small to medium work, the *tinmen's anvil* and *bick (or beck) iron* are most useful, either held in special bench sockets, in squared holes in the surface of a tree stump, or in the hardie hole of the anvil, see 7.2.

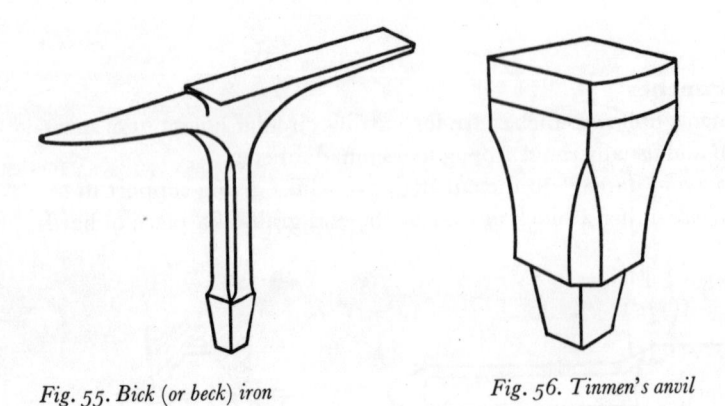

Fig. 55. Bick (or beck) iron *Fig. 56. Tinmen's anvil*

To bend edges beyond a right angle, the *hatchet stake* is used for straight edges and the *half-moon stake* for curved edges.

SHEETMETALWORK

Creasing irons are primarily for creasing pan and tray corners. If this stake is used to finish wired edges, care must be taken to avoid damaging the surface of the article on the groove edges.

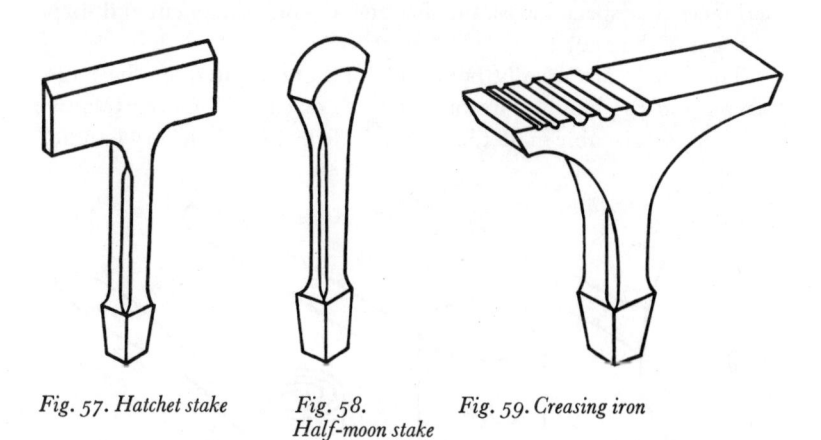

Fig. 57. Hatchet stake

Fig. 58. Half-moon stake

Fig. 59. Creasing iron

Less common stakes are the *extinguisher stake* which is a smaller edition of the bick iron, the *funnel stake* for larger conical work, and the *side stake* which is often replaced by plain lengths of round bar.

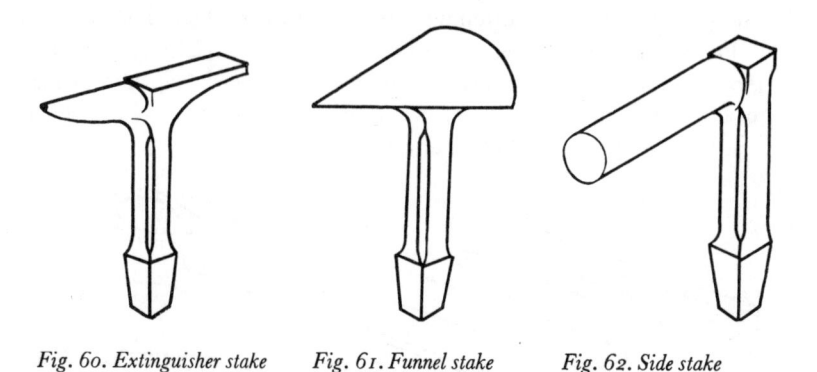

Fig. 60. Extinguisher stake

Fig. 61. Funnel stake

Fig. 62. Side stake

The *round bottom stake* and others, described amongst silversmith's stakes, see 6.6, are often used by the sheetmetal worker.

5.8 Mallets

A mallet is used to deliver a blow without damaging the metal.

There are two main types of mallets, the bossing mallet with rounded ends for hollowing, see 6.4, and the tinmen's mallet with flat faces. For special work the sheetmetal worker may cut and shape the face of the mallet.

The heads are usually boxwood (or lignum vitae for the larger sizes), and the handles are of either ash or cane. A more expensive but very serviceable mallet has a raw hide head and hickory handle.

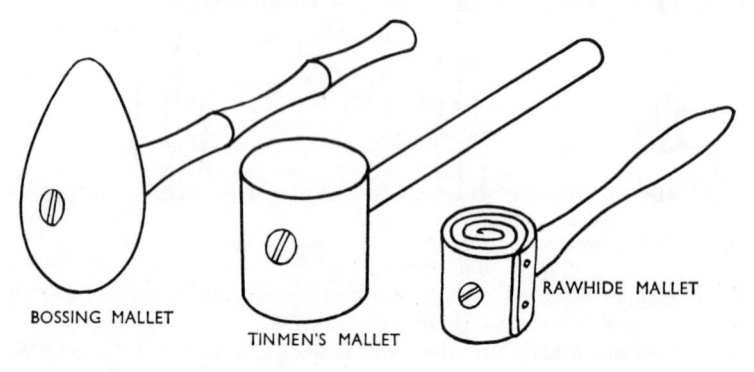

Fig. 63. Mallets

5.9 Bending

In industry, bending and folding are normally machine processes, but good results can be obtained with the simplest of hand tools.

For small work in thin metal such as tinplate, folding bars are most useful. These can easily be made in the workshop by cutting and hot bending. Large work can be held by improvising with lengths of angle, either bolted or cramped together.

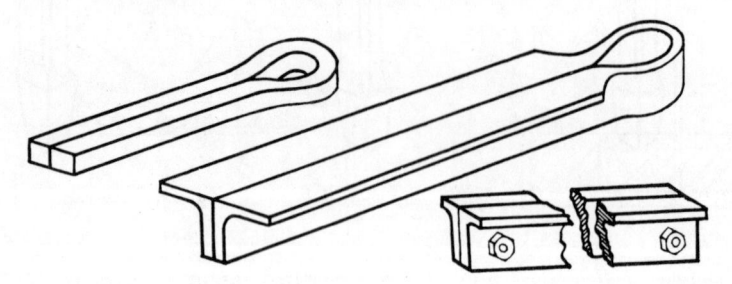

Fig. 64. Folding bars

SHEETMETALWORK

When bending metal to an angle, a neat result is obtained by holding a piece of wood or metal against the projecting metal and forcing over by hand or using a hammer.

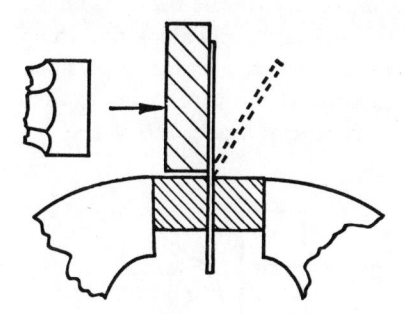

Fig. 65. Bending

If the amount to be bent over is very small (e.g. 3 mm) a tinmen's mallet is used, working evenly along the whole length slightly increasing the angle at each pass. If an attempt is made to bend one portion to a right angle ignoring the adjacent parts, the metal will stretch, and pucker when finally set down.

5.10 Edges

Sheetmetal is rarely strong enough to be self-supporting at the edges. For this reason and for safety, it is common practice to edge all exposed sheetmetalwork.

The simplest is the *beaded edge* which is 3 to 6 mm folded over, and the edge of the metal carefully malleted down to leave a rounded edge to the work.

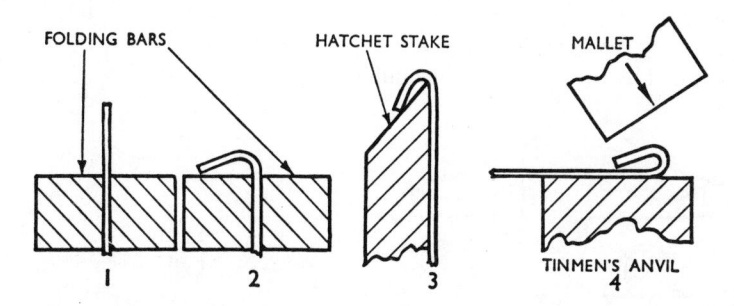

Fig. 66. Beaded edge

For work requiring extra support, the wired edge is used. The wiring allowance, $2D + 4T$ (D = diameter of wire, T = thickness of metal), is malleted over in the folding bar, taking great care to keep the bend as rounded as possible. Take the bend beyond a right angle on the hatchet stake. Insert the wire, and place on the tinmen's anvil; lightly trap the wire in place before working evenly along the whole length. When the metal has been malleted over as far as possible, invert the work and bring the underside of the wired edge against the edge of the anvil, and mallet to force metal neatly into place.

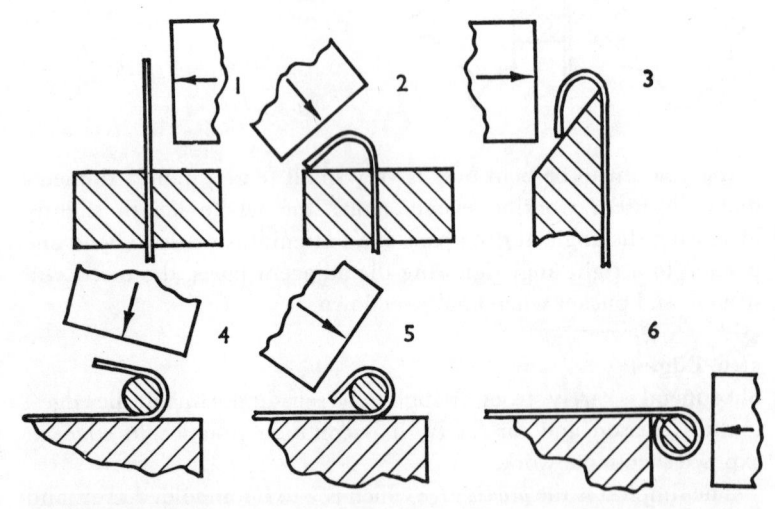

Fig. 67. Wired edge

When this has been completed examine the cut edge which should touch the flat surface. If the allowance was too small or too large, respectively resulting in either a gap or the wire being loose, it can be rectified by dressing with the mallet.

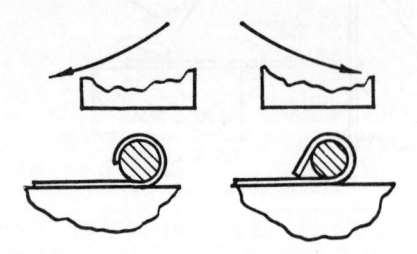

Fig. 68. Dressing with the mallet

SHEETMETALWORK

Heavy gauge sheetmetal may have to be hammered into position using a paning hammer. Unless great care is taken, hammer marks will be left on the face of the metal.

WIRED EDGE

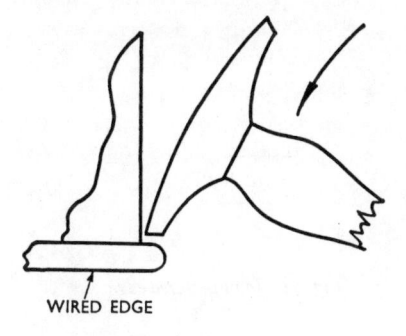

Fig. 69. Using a paning hammer with work resting on a flat surface

As mentioned before the creasing iron may be used with care for finishing or reversing the wire, as below.

Fig. 70. Wiring on creasing stake

To bead or wire a curved edge, the operations are the same in all but the shape of the stakes. The initial right-angle bend must be made on a round stake of the same or slightly smaller radius than the work, using a mallet, and working by eye to a line. To work beyond a right angle either use a half-moon stake or shape a piece of metal to the required curve and angle.

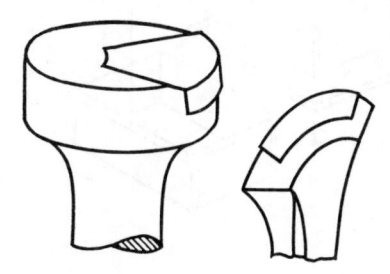

Fig. 71. Bending a curved edge

Where a wired edge is to join up to form a continuous edge, it is better to stagger the wire joint and the sheet joint.

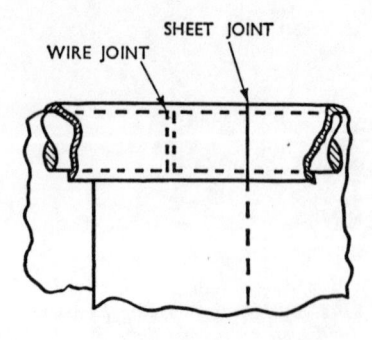

Fig. 72. Joint in wired edge

On small work this can often be achieved by using excess wire, and pulling through to leave one end say 6 mm short and then cutting off with just less than 6 mm protruding. A technique with larger work is to notch the wire with cutting pliers a short distance in from one end and place the notch where the wire must break to provide the recess. The stub end of wire is broken off by twisting, after the edge has been made and prior to joining.

The majority of sheetmetalwork is wired in the flat before bending to shape. An exception to this is a box bent in one piece and wired afterwards.

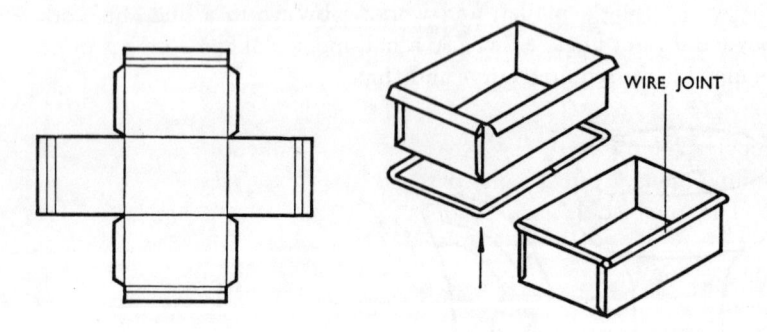

Fig. 73. Wiring a box

SHEETMETALWORK

5.11 Joints

There are many different methods of joining sheetmetal, see Chapter 4; the most common are shown below.

SOLDERED, RIVETED OR SCREWED LAP JOINT

COUNTERSUNK OR FLUSH JOINT

CORNER LAP OR EDGE-OVER JOINT

GROOVED JOINT

PANED DOWN JOINT

KNOCKED UP JOINT

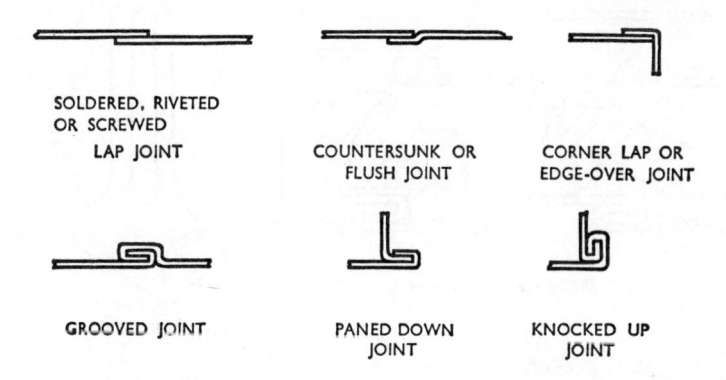

Fig. 74. Common sheetmetal joints

A *grooved joint* may be specified on the working drawing and a definite size given, usually between 3 mm and 6 mm inclusive. As shown in Fig. 47, double the joint size is allowed on one side and only once on the other. Care must be taken to bend slightly less than the joint size in opposite directions usually with the single allowance outwards. Take both edges to a sharp angle and then beyond before malleting down on to a piece of metal, slightly thicker than the thickness of the sheetmetal. Hook together and offer the tinmen's groove punch (or groover) to the joint to ensure that it will cover both edges, as shown in Fig. 75.

Place on a suitable stake, and maintain a pressure against the side of the joint with the groover. This will keep the parts fully interlocking. Hammer the groover as it is brought upright to lock the joint. Finally the top can be malleted flat.

The *paned-down joint* is used in preference to a corner lap where greater strength is required. A small edge 3 mm to 6 mm wide is thrown out at right angles on the sides and the bottom made to fit neatly with an edge which will just fall short of the sides when paned down with a paning hammer. For even greater strength, the whole joint can be malleted up on a suitable stake, to give a *knocked-up joint*.

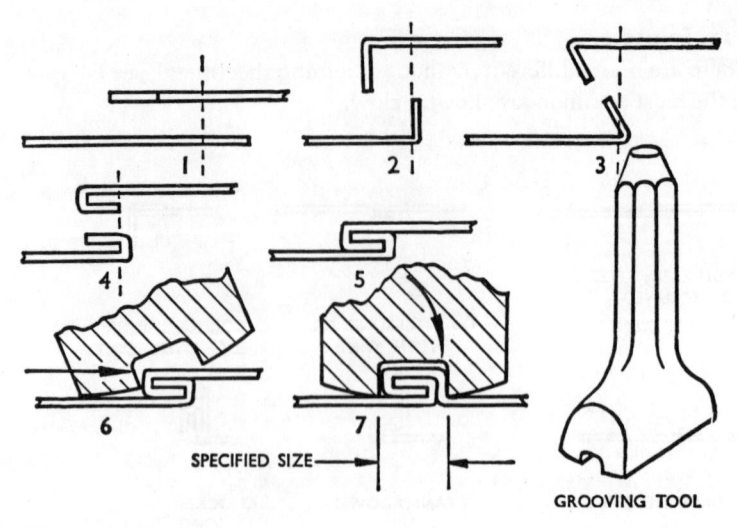

Fig. 75. Making a grooved joint

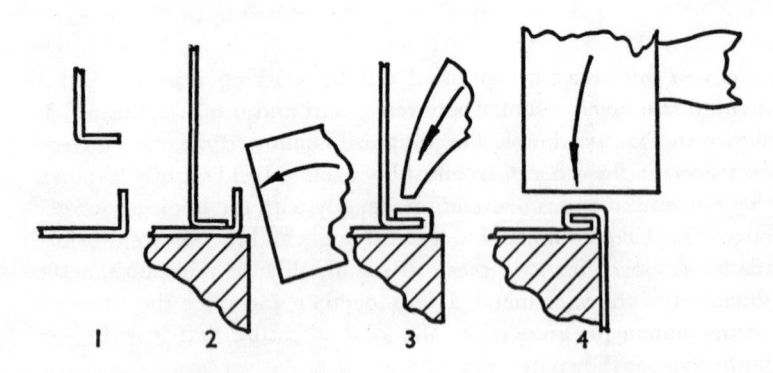

Fig. 76. Making a knocked-up joint

For maximum strength, the grooved, paned-down and knocked-up joints can be soldered. Well-made joints in aluminium can be made watertight by finally planishing firmly down.

6

Silversmithing

6.1 Introduction

The craft of the silversmith is practised in schools under various names such as 'beaten metalwork', 'hammered metalwork' and 'art metalwork'. Whilst work in silver is too expensive for the beginner, the craft and techniques explained in this chapter are those of the silversmith.

The most suitable metals to work with are copper and brass; and of the brasses, gilding metal is the best. Copper is easy to work but is rather soft unless finally work-hardened. Gilding metal is slightly harder than copper, works fairly easily and is suitable for built-up work, which cannot be work-hardened in its final shape. For extra strength a 70/30 brass may be used.

Work which reaches a sufficiently high standard may be silver-plated. It must be emphasised that silver-plating does not hide any defects, and the final finish is largely dependent upon the finish produced by the craftsman.

After some experience the student may decide to work in silver. Extra care should then be taken when annealing and silver soldering, as the colour change is very slight. Direct light on the silver should be excluded and as heat is applied the colour will change to a dull red, which is the maximum desired.

Before the final cleaning and polishing, the work should be hallmarked to denote that the metal is of the legal standard of purity. The assay offices for hallmarking are situated in Birmingham, Edinburgh, London and Sheffield.

6.2 Cleaning

For the best finish to the final article, it is essential to work cleanly from the start. The work bench and tools should be clean and tidy, and the material absolutely clean. Dirt which is left on the work in the initial stages becomes more and more difficult to remove as the work proceeds.

To clean brass, copper and silver thoroughly, a *pickle* is used. This is a lead vat on a stand, heated by a gas ring, and containing dilute sulphuric acid. The most effective technique is to add acid to water in the proportion of 1 : 20 respectively, and use the pickle hot. For infrequent work the pickle may be used cold and the work left in for a longer period, or the strength of the pickle may be increased. It is better to use copper tongs and not allow iron to be immersed, which will cause a reaction which coats silver with copper. For *Safety* see 2.1.

After removing the article from the pickle, it should be washed thoroughly in running water. It may then be handled and given a final clean with pumice powder and a little water, using a bristle brush or a piece of clean cloth. To dry intricate or delicate work, use warm dry boxwood sawdust.

Hollow shapes may be produced without joints, either by thinning the centre of the metal, i.e. sinking and hollowing, or by thickening the edge of the metal, i.e. raising. In the following text it will be assumed that the final article is to be circular in plan, although the principle is exactly the same for oval or irregular-shaped articles.

For sinking and hollowing, the final diameter approximates to the diameter of blank required; and for raising the average diameter of the article added to the height, also approximates to the required diameter. The blank is cut out carefully and rough edges removed; if necessary it is then annealed and cleaned.

6.3 Sinking

This is a method of thinning metal to form a shallow tray with the edge of the metal virtually untouched.

First draw a pencil circle marking the width of the lip. There are two methods of sinking, using a shaped hardwood block and guide pins, which is possibly the easiest, and working by eye which is the most adaptable. The tray hammer should be slightly more radiused than the tray itself both in elevation and plan. Starting at a point just inside the pencil circle, the sinking should be a very gradual depression worked all the way around the tray to the start; this is repeated as many times as necessary with frequent annealing and cleaning.

SILVERSMITHING

Although a tray is quite shallow, sinking is not easy and the planishing, see 6.7, requires a lot of care to produce a circular flat tray.

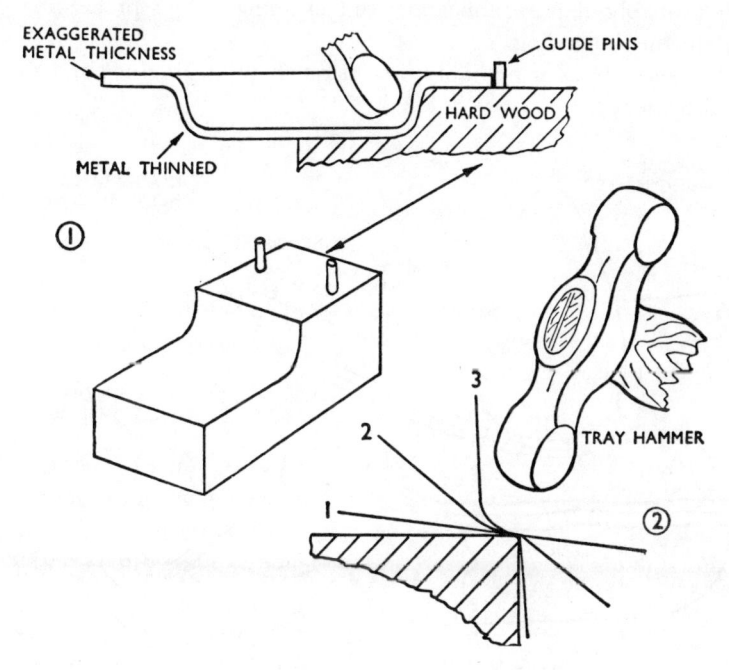

Fig. 77. Two methods of sinking

6.4 Hollowing
This is a method of thinning metal to form a bowl shape.

The centre mark made by the dividers when marking out the blank should always be on the convex side of the work. Using pencil compasses, find the centre on the other side and draw concentric circles between 10 and 20 mm apart, where the thinning is required.

There are two main methods of hollowing. For shallow hollowing a bossing mallet, which has a large diameter face, may be used in conjunction with a leather sandbag. Work which is more difficult to hollow, e.g. hard or thick metal, or a small blank difficult to hold, may be worked using a blocking hammer on depressions in the end grain of a tree trunk. Some work demands combinations of both methods.

Draw a radial pencil line to indicate the start and work round keeping to one circular mark. After one circuit around the bowl, the edge will be a series of waves; these should be dressed out by very light blows, about 10 mm in from the edge. At this stage the work will probably require annealing and cleaning before proceeding with further hollowing.

A shallow bowl is probably the easiest shape to produce and to planish, see 6.7.

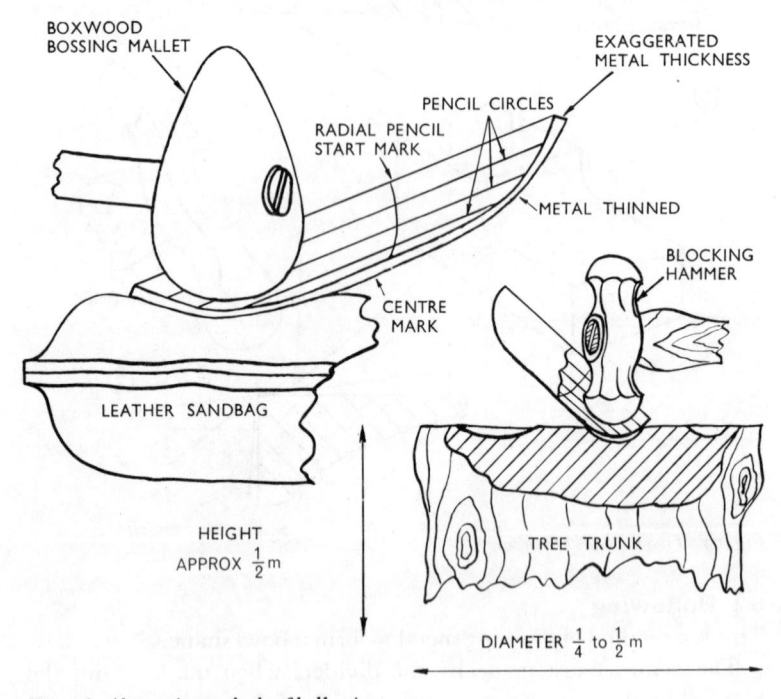

Fig. 78. Alternative methods of hollowing

6.5 Raising
This is a method of reducing the diameter of circular work, which causes the thickness of the metal to be increased. To raise the sides of a bowl the blank is first hollowed, to help stiffen the edge. After annealing and cleaning, a series of pencil circles are marked out on the convex side, about 10 mm apart, and a radial pencil mark made to indicate the start.

SILVERSMITHING 75

Before attempting to raise, the theory of the process should be understood. A hammer or boxwood mallet, with a flat face and rounded corners, is used to force an area of metal downwards, on to a stake and into a smaller area. Providing the force of the blow is stopped when the metal reaches the stake, the metal will have increased in thickness. If however, the blow is not stopped, the metal trapped between the hammer face and the stake will be thinned and little or no progress will be made. This is the reason why beginners are often advised to use a specially shaped mallet.

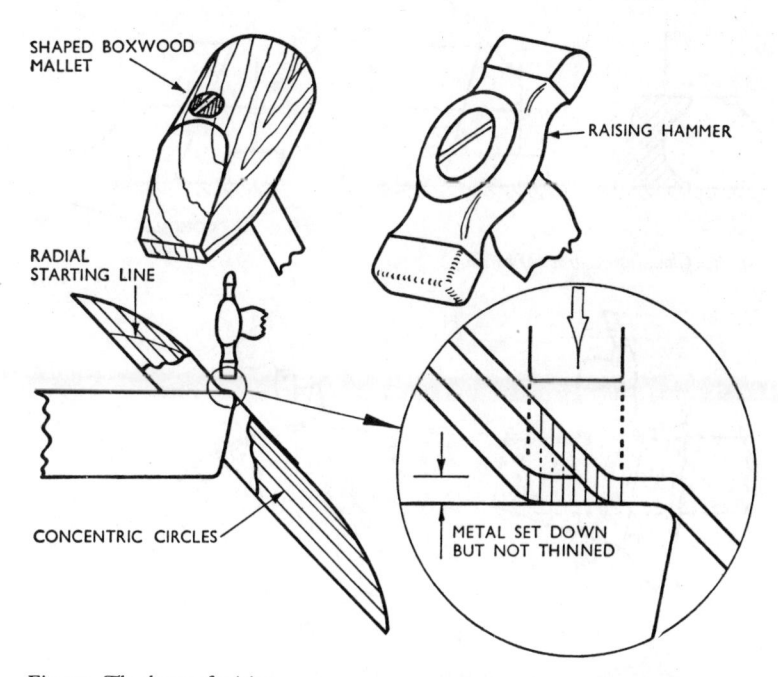

Fig. 79. The theory of raising

The stake to be used for raising should approximate to the shape required, and the working surface polished to a good finish.

The base circle is held in line with the edge of the stake, and the starting line uppermost. The first blow should take a step between 5 to 10 mm deep and about 20 mm wide; this is repeated around the base circle to complete a continuous step. For the second circle aim between 5 and 10 mm in and complete as before; as the work proceeds the raising becomes increasingly difficult and the student may find that steps between 3 and 5 mm deep are more suitable. The last 10 mm will be a series of crinkles, and may be dressed out by using the raising hammer very carefully, or preferably using a mallet. At this stage the work must be annealed and cleaned, before marking out, for another course of raising. As the work proceeds, it should be checked, either by a surface plate with a shaped template, or by a surface gauge and a compass.

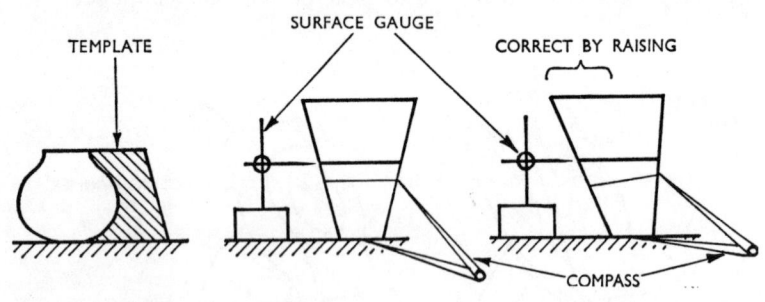

Fig. 80. Checking accuracy of raising

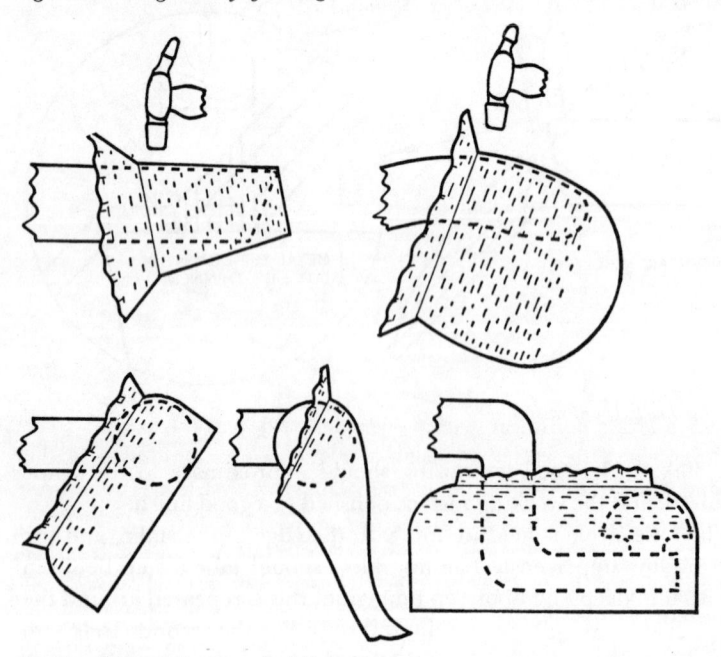

Fig. 81. Some applications of raising

SILVERSMITHING

Irregular work may often be corrected by raising only part of the surface, as shown in Fig. 80.

The work should be raised to a slightly smaller diameter than required, because the planishing operation, see 6.7, will thin the metal slightly.

The top edge of vessels may be thickened and therefore strengthened by *caulking*.

The work is held firmly on a sandbag and the rounded face of the raising hammer is used. The length of the hammer face is at right angles to the edge of the work, and the blow should be delivered exactly in line with the wall of the vessel. Caulking should be carried out at the end of each course of raising. If the top edge is very thin it may be thickened by creasing, see Fig. 83, and then raising.

Fig. 82. Caulking

Fig. 83. Creasing

6.6 Stakes

The materials commonly used are malleable cast iron and steel. Although a wide range of stakes are available commercially, for special work, the craftsman may make his own wooden pattern for a casting, or shape a piece of steel. The working surface should be as true and perfect as possible. A mirror finish on the stake will reproduce a high finish on clean material, whereas a blemish is reproduced hundreds of times all over the work.

Bottom stakes have a long stem to enable the working surface to reach the bottom of deep vessels.

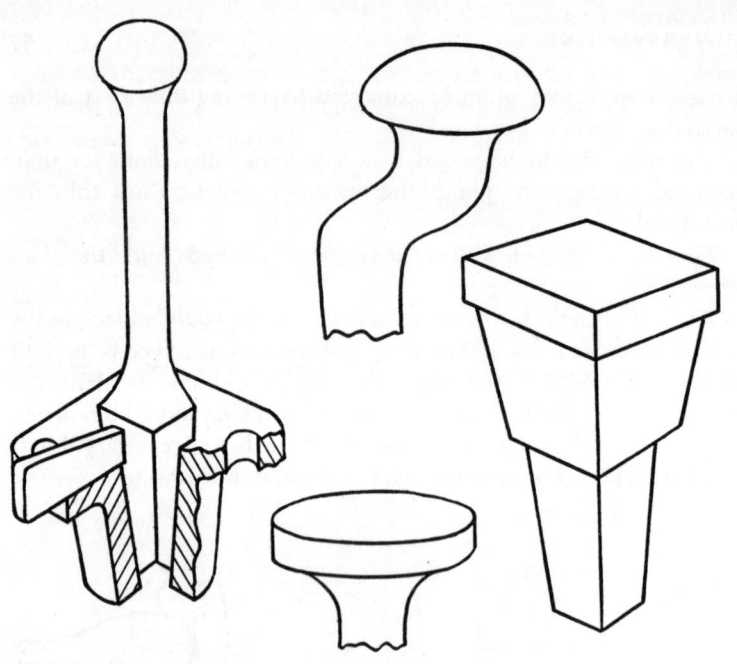

Fig. 84. Bottom stakes (¼ *scale*)

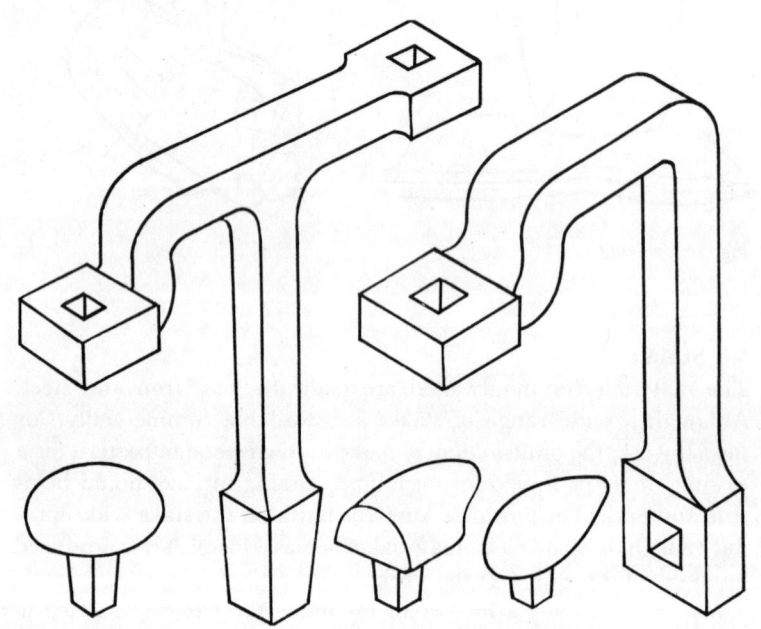

Fig. 85. Horse, crank and heads (¼ *scale*)

SILVERSMITHING

Heads may be held in the vice or in a *horse* or *crank* and are particularly useful for unusually-shaped work, Fig. 85.

Other useful stakes include two-, three- and four-arm stakes, Fig. 86. For truing circular rings, either the round treblet or a mandrel will be found most useful, Fig. 87.

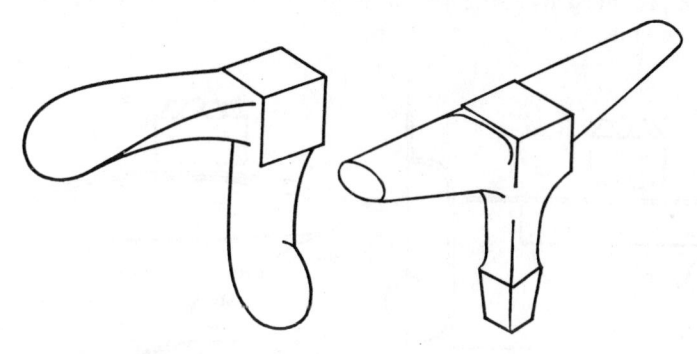

Fig. 86. Two-arm stakes

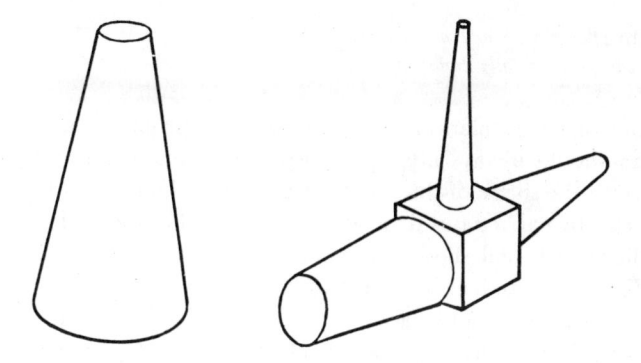

Fig. 87. Treblet and three-arm mandrel

6.7 Planishing

Planishing by carefully hammering the metal on a stake, is necessary for several reasons:

(1) To remove any small marks or indentations left by a previous process, such as raising.
(2) To true the shape of the work.
(3) To work-harden the surface.

The article is annealed and cleaned, and concentric circles 10 mm apart are marked out on the convex side, with a radial starting line.

Next a suitable stake or stakes are offered to the work and the correct hammer(s) selected.

To obtain a high finish, the working face of the stake and planishing hammer must be mirror-bright and without any defects. This may be produced by using several grades of emery cloth or emery sticks, see 11.4.

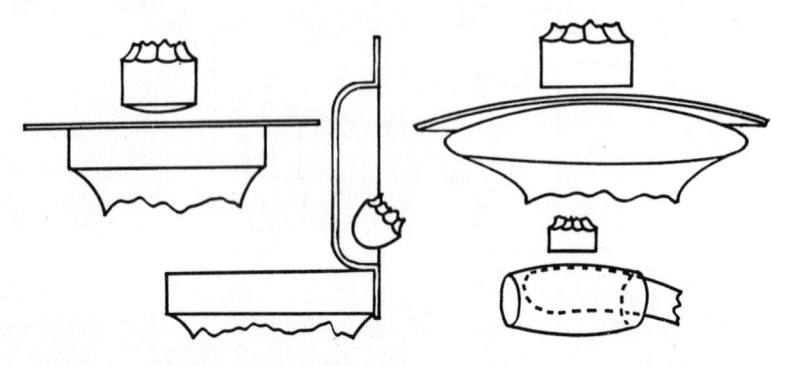

Fig. 88. Planishing flat, concave and convex work
(*Note: hammer edges are normally slightly rounded*)

Each piece of work to be planished presents different problems, and the craftsman should always attempt to work with hammers and stakes as close to the shape of the article as possible. The limit as to how far this can be carried out depends upon the skill of the craftsman. Unskilled work will show half-moon or straight depressions where the edge of the hammer has dug into the metal.

The top of the stake should be about waist high and if possible the worker should stand so that light is reflected from the top of the stake. Positioning himself in this manner, he can easily see every planish mark.

The hammer is held by the end of the handle and the action is from the wrist. Start in the centre and let one blow fall; if the sound is not solid the stake may be too flat or the work not correctly positioned. When a solid blow is heard, then proceed to planish, keeping to the pencil circles. Ideal planishing should be such that each planish mark touches the next but none completely overlap, and each blow should be of exactly the same force.

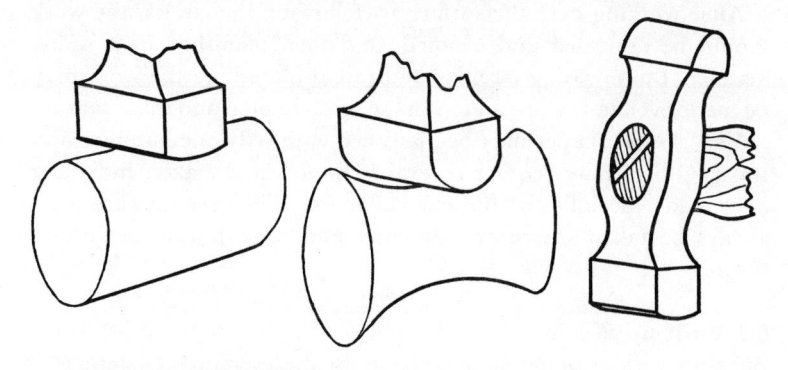

*Fig. 89. Collet hammers for planishing cylindrical work
(Note: hammer edges are normally slightly rounded)*

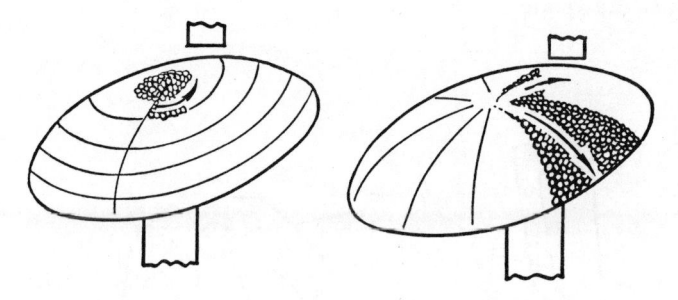

Fig. 90. Marking out for planishing

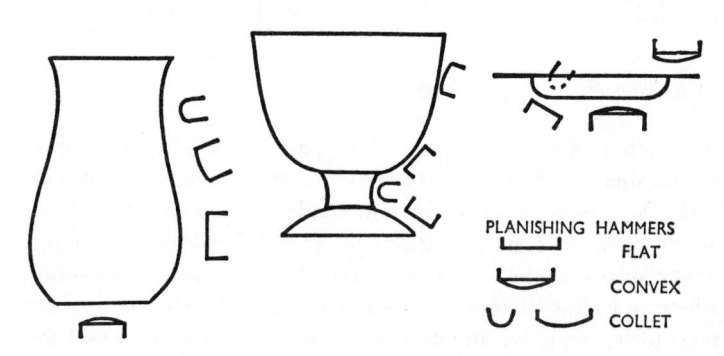

Fig. 91. Planishing

After working over the surface by following the circles, the work should be annealed and cleaned, and then planished in a radial manner. By repeating circular and radial planishing the work may be made even in texture and in shape, both in plan and in elevation.

Very simple shapes may be planished with only one hammer and stake. Others may require several hammers and stakes, including ones made specially for the particular job. The greatest care must always be taken where one hammer and stake finish, and others begin.

6.8 Built-up Work
Built-up work is composed of two or more pieces soldered together.

The individual pieces may be parts already shaped and planished, or they may be pieces of flat sheet, wire, tube, sections or castings.

For hinge joints the tube or chenier can be formed from a flat strip using a drawplate.

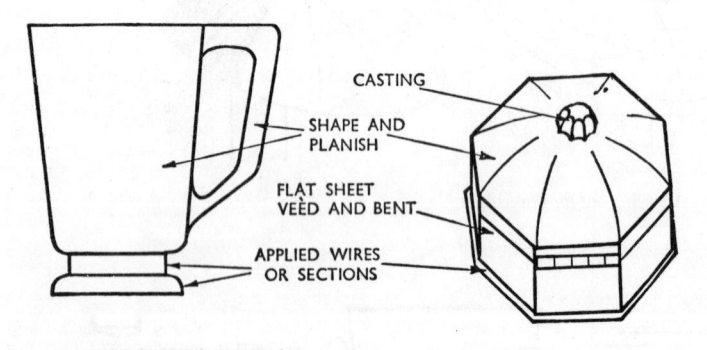

Fig. 92. Built-up work

Articles such as boxes often have all or part of the body developed from a flat sheet; if sharp bends are to be made, 'V' grooves are cut. To make 'V' grooves a scraper can be made from an old file or from a piece of silver steel, hardened and tempered to pale straw; a piece of metal clamped to the work acts as a guide. Other methods include chiselling and filing. The vee should leave only a very small amount of metal to be bent: too much will give a rounded corner, and too little may break.

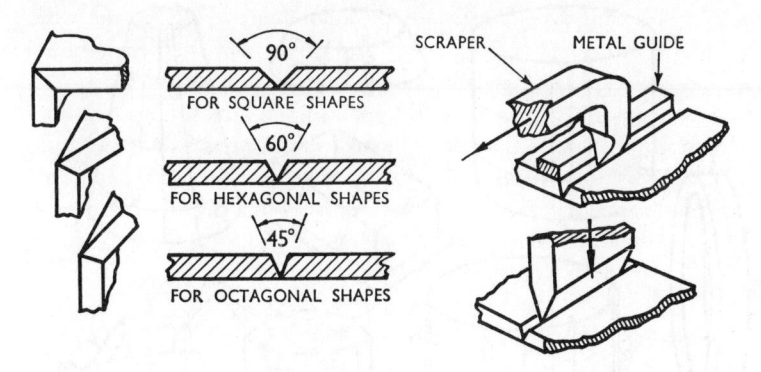

Fig. 93. 'V' grooves

Where two parts meet to make a right angle, and a square corner is required after soldering, the inside edge is bevelled slightly. Bevelling is also necessary on a box lid and bezel to allow them to locate easily.

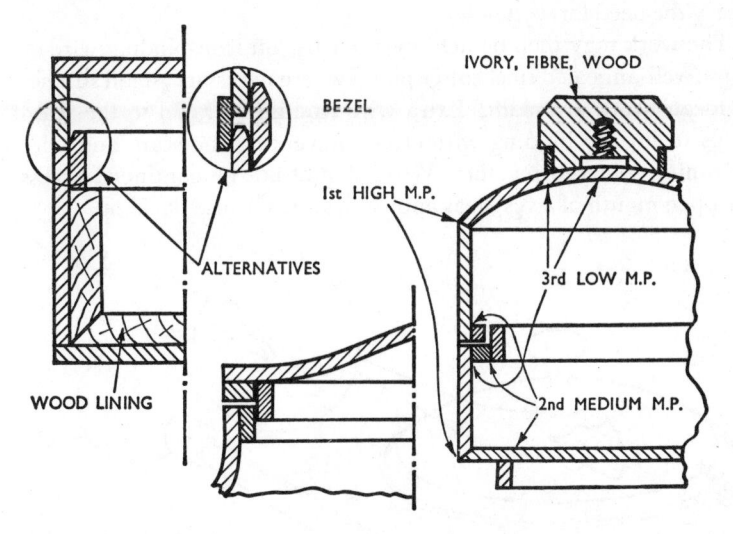

Fig. 94. Box making

Before starting to assemble (see 4.5), the sequence must be carefully thought out. The first joints must use the highest melting point solder and the last the lowest. For most work three solders are sufficient.

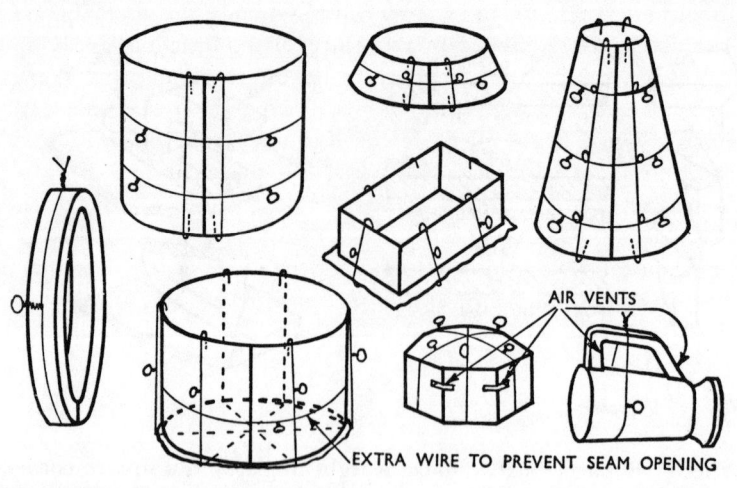

Fig. 95. Wiring

As explained previously (4.5), the joints must be absolutely clean and a good fit. Safety precautions should be observed (2.1), particularly the need for vent holes.

The work may then be held together by soft iron-binding wire or clips (well-annealed steel cotter pins); where necessary, small stitches to locate work are made. Extra wire running parallel to the seam helps to lift the binding wire clear, preventing the seam and wire becoming soldered together. Wires should not be continued across the open mouth of a vessel, as applied heat will cause buckling.

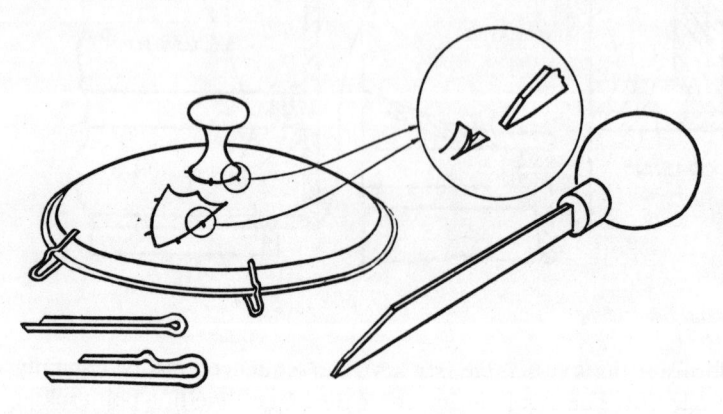

Fig. 96. Stitching

It is most important to heat very evenly with a soft flame before soldering. This is facilitated by using a revolving hearth and leaving air gaps beneath the work to allow the heat to reach all parts. Work which is heated from one side only will expand on that side and distort; a fierce heat will cause the flux to bubble violently, and possibly dislodge or move small parts. For the technique of silver soldering see 4.5.

As soon as the soldering operation is completed, the iron binding wires should be cut to prevent marking the work as they contract. When cool, all iron wire and clips are removed and the article pickled and cleaned. The small stitches can easily be removed with needle files. Any planishing that may be required should be done carefully and kept to a minimum.

6.9 Rolling and Wire Drawing

To reduce cast ingots to the required thickness and width, a rolling mill is used. The rollers are hardened and ground to the desired profile to produce sheet, wire, or sections.

The term rolling covers such wide extremes as power rolling mills handling red hot ingots of steel weighing several tonnes, and hand rolling mills producing wires as small as 1 mm square.

Fig. 97. Hand rolling mill.
(Courtesy: Charles Cooper (Hatton Garden) Ltd.)

Fig. 98. Drawplate and hand draw tongs. (Courtesy: Charles Cooper (Hatton Garden) Ltd.)

If a metal is ductile it may be drawn out as a wire; silver and copper are both very ductile. (Copper may be reduced in the order of 10 : 9 at each pass.) The metal is drawn down, see 7·5, and filed to a long smooth taper. This is inserted through a tapering hole of suitable size in the drawplate.

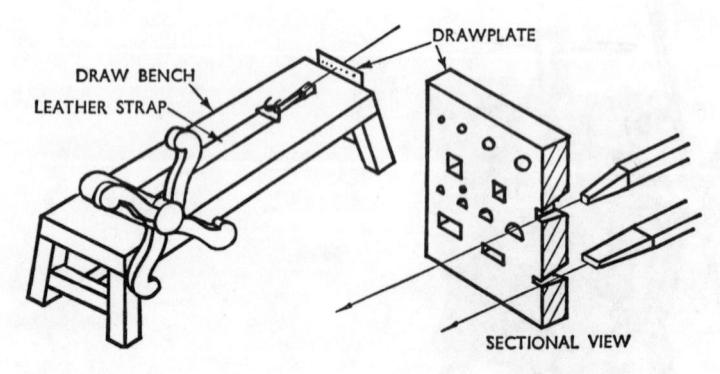

Fig. 99. Wire drawing

The wire is then pulled through by hand or on a special draw bench. Beeswax may be used as a lubricant and the wire will need frequent

SILVERSMITHING

annealing and cleaning. When annealing the wire must be made into a close coil with each strand in intimate contact with the next; failure to do this will result in loose strands being melted before the remainder is at annealing temperature.

6.10 Application of Wires

Base mouldings are often made of square or flat wires. For circular work the circumference is calculated from the mean diameter and sufficient material is bent. If a rectangular wire is to be bent on edge, a groove of the width and depth of the wire is cut on a piece of hard wood. This helps to support the wire as it is malleted over. In Fig. 100 a brass back saw is shown, which is more commonly used by professional craftsmen. After cutting, the ring is then silver soldered, and is approximately to shape. Excess solder is removed by filing and the ring trued to shape by light malleting on a treblet or mandrel, and then on a flat surface. The ring is made exactly circular by heating and dropping on to a suitable taper and allowing it to cool and contract.

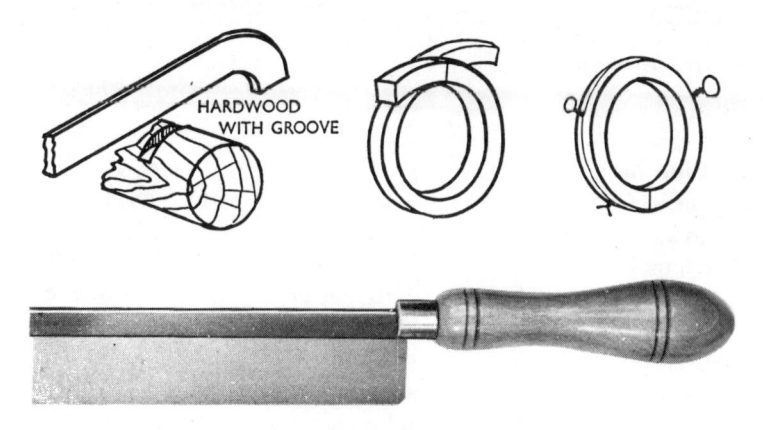

Fig. 100. Making a ring. (Courtesy: Charles Cooper (Hatton Garden) Ltd.)

The ring may be decorated by filing in a vertical direction, or by turning on the lathe. Large section wires may be held in a self-centring chuck, see 10.2. Large diameter rings will require a hardwood block, screwed to a face plate, and turned to receive the ring, and small rings may be held on a steel mandrel, see 10.6.

Straight moulded wires can be obtained by cutting and straightening a turned ring.

Where a more decorative effect is required, the wire may be modelled or several wires used as shown in Fig. 101. The possibilities are almost unlimited; thin wires may be twisted or plaited together and then, if desired, either rolled, hammered or drawn through the drawplate. Bending jigs can be made to give endless patterns.

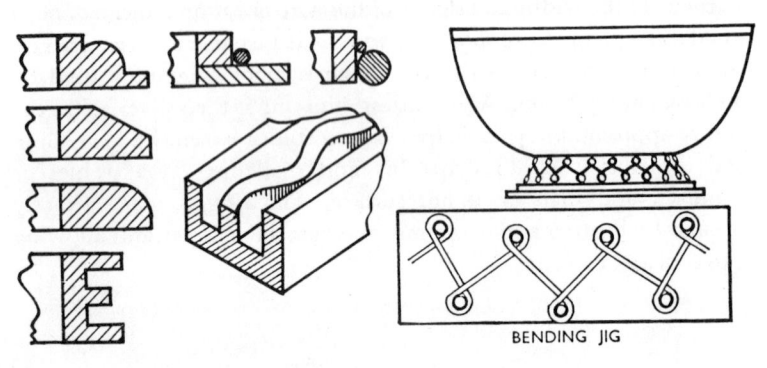

Fig. 101. Applications of wires

6.11 Piercing

Piercing is a technique for removing areas of metal from a sheet, often to an intricate pattern.

It is important when designing for piercing to leave metal of sufficient width, for strength. The pattern may be traced on to a whitened surface, or, with care, scribed through, or the pattern itself pasted on to the metal.

A hardwood board is cut to a vee and supported solidly on the bench; the worker should sit with his chest level with the work. The work has small holes drilled in the pattern to be removed, and the blade is threaded through, with the teeth facing down. By pushing the piercing saw against the bench when tightening the screws, it is possible to tension the blade.

The work must always be held solidly and the saw used carefully and evenly. The saw shown in Fig. 102 is adjustable and can therefore even use broken blades.

Fig. 102. Piercing saw. (Courtesy: James Neill & Co. (Sheffield) Ltd.)

6.12 Chasing

This includes embossing, repoussé work and flat chasing; all are methods of decorative shaping, by punches.

Embossing originated from the practice of forming large bosses in relief, to give strength to the sheet. The work is held face down on to softwood and embossed with domed punches, or if working from inside a vessel, a snarling iron is used.

The snarling iron is held in a vice and the shank is given a sharp blow which causes the working face to rebound upwards.

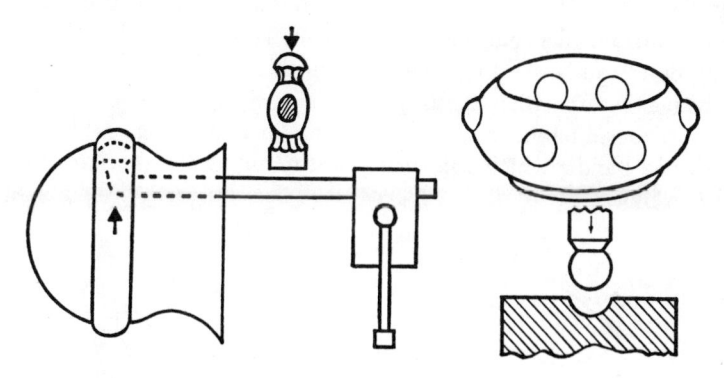

Fig. 103. Embossing

Repoussé is also primarily formed from the back, but is finally worked from the front to give greater detail. The work is mounted on a pitch mixture, which can be made by melting 5 kg of 'Brown Swedish Pitch', adding approximately ½ kg of best tallow and then adding plaster of paris or pumice (up to 8 kg may be required) until difficult to stir. When set and cold it should be just possible to indent the surface with the thumb nail. Flat work is mounted on the warmed surface of the pitch set, in a tray or in a pitch-bowl placed on a leather or rope ring. Before filling a vessel with pitch insert a piece of wood in the centre for holding purposes. (*Note:* this is also the technique for planishing facets on work previously formed and planished to a plain surface.)

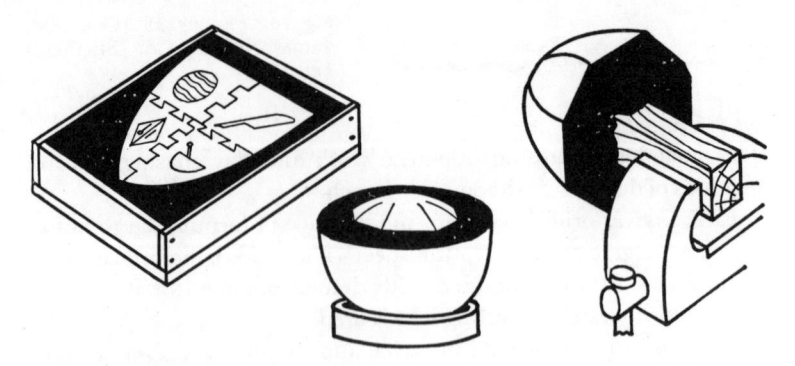

Fig. 104. Mounting on pitch

Flat Chasing The work is mounted on pitch and worked only from the front. The outline is marked in with a 'tracer' and the background can be set down with a 'planishing' tool; parts can also be given a texture with a 'matting' tool.

The repoussé hammer, Fig. 105, is used for all chasing and has a lancewood handle which will spring and minimise the shock of the hammer blows.

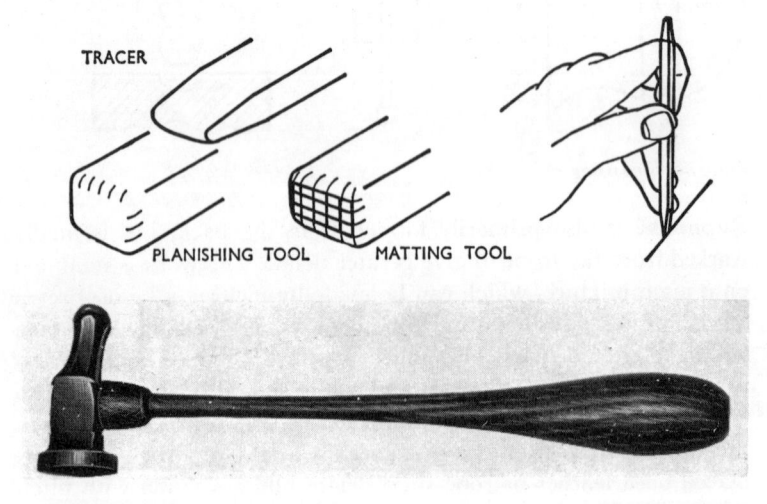

Fig. 105. Tools for chasing. (Courtesy: Charles Cooper (Hatton Garden) Ltd.)

6.13 Further Decorative Techniques

Engraving removes metal by a cutting action.

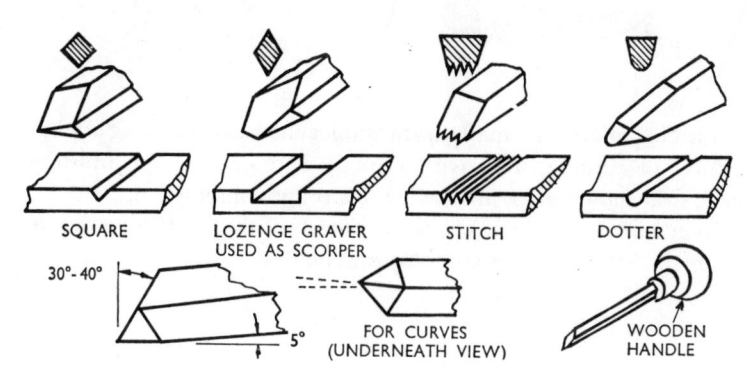

Fig. 106. Engraving tools

The tools should be sharpened on a fine oil stone and may be tested against the thumb nail; when the tip slides over the nail, the tool requires sharpening.

In use, the tool should project 10 to 20 mm beyond the end of the thumb; new tools may require shortening.

Enamelling consists of preparing the surface of the metal and reducing pieces of enamel (essentially glass made with the addition of lead oxide and other metallic particles to give colours) to a powder, which is then applied and fired in a furnace at about 800°C.

6.14 Finishing

The first step is to remove excess solder or metal by filing, progressing down to the finest files. Then various grades of emery, or carborundum stones with water, may be used. After each grade the work must be cleaned to remove any coarse particles.

One of the most useful abrasives (see 11.4) is Water of Ayr or Tam-o'-Shanter Stones used with water. This should be used until all scratches are removed.

Finally the buffing machine may be used. When using this machine, the work should be held with the edge trailing, as shown in Fig. 107, to prevent the work being snatched away from the operator.

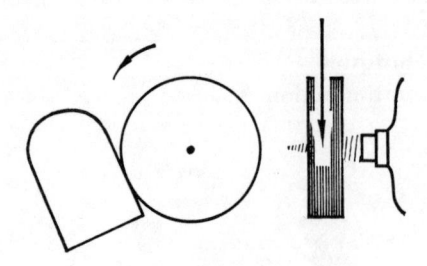

Fig. 107. Buffing

Finishing mops are made from unbleached calico, using a composition of suitable abrasive (Tripoli) and grease. For finishing silver, swansdown mops are used with a rouge composition.

Great care should be taken not to over-buff the work or round the corners, which should remain crisp and bold.

7

Forgework

7.1 Smith's Hearth

The hearth or forge is a shallow open box with a cast-iron nozzle or blast pipe called the 'tuyere' or 'tue iron' projecting from one side. The tuyere may be solid and rely on conductivity to prevent the nose being burnt or on larger forges, water supplied from the water bosh is circulated within.

An alternative arrangement is to place the tuyere in the base and blow from the bottom of a conical cast iron well.

The blast may be produced by either bellows or a hand- or power-driven fan.

Fig. 108. Back blast hearth with water-cooled tuyere and electrically driven fan. (Courtesy: William Allday & Co. Ltd.)

Fig. 109. Fire tools. (Courtesy: William Allday & Co. Ltd.)

Three tools (rake, poker and slice) are used to manage the fire and are kept in or by the hearth.

The fuel for the fire may be either blacksmithing coal or coke breeze. Smithy breeze should be ordered as 'bean size' and be dust-free. To light the fire, either use paper and sticks, or preferably a gas poker. The work should be placed just above the compact centre of a sufficiently large fire with additional fuel above to reduce the heat loss and atmospheric oxidation.

Impurities will collect as 'clinker' and must be removed from the bottom of the fire. For short spells of forging, clinker can be removed after the fire has cooled.

7.2 Anvil

A number of different-pattern anvils are used but the most popular is the 'London Pattern'. The body is of wrought iron or steel with a hardened steel top on the best anvils; others may be cast iron with the working face chilled.

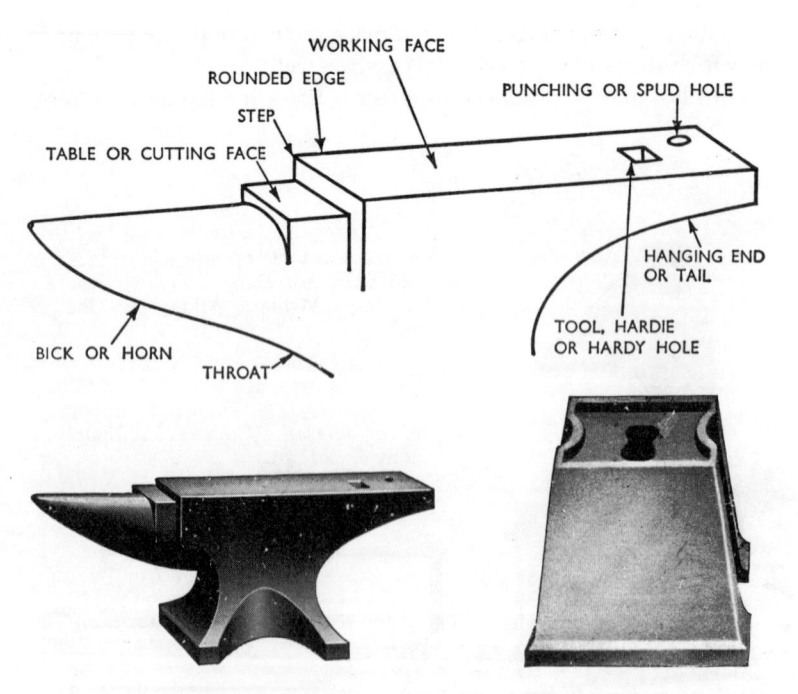

Fig. 110. London Pattern anvil and stand. (Courtesy: William Allday & Co. Ltd.)

FORGEWORK

The stand may be either of cast iron, welded steel sections, or an elm trunk sunk one metre into the ground. As a guide, the height of the anvil should be so that the finger tips just touch the top when standing beside it.

The bick and table are both left soft; all cutting with a chisel should be done on the table to prevent damage to the chisel edge. The edge indicated is usually rounded by the smith, for bending purposes.

A useful companion to the anvil is the cast iron swage block with different half-sectional grooves and holes. Although intended for swaging, see 7.7, it is also useful for bending purposes.

Fig. 111. Swage block and stand. (Courtesy: William Allday & Co. Ltd.)

Fig. 112. Cross pein sledge hammer head. (Courtesy: William Allday & Co. Ltd.)

The blacksmith's hammer is usually a ball pein hammer, see Fig. 153, weighing between $\frac{1}{2}$ and $1\frac{1}{2}$ kg. His assistant, the striker, uses a sledge hammer weighing between 2 and 9 kg, but commonly about 4 kg. The heads may be cross pein, straight pein, ball pein, or double-faced (i.e. flat on either side), and the handle is made of hickory, up to 1 m long.

To hold the hot work, the smith uses a wide variety of tongs, usually made by himself. For ease and safety the tongs must suit the work in hand and for students an elongated ring can be slid over the jaws and up the handles to lock the jaws on to the work. The more common types are shown in Fig. 113.

Close Mouth Tongs

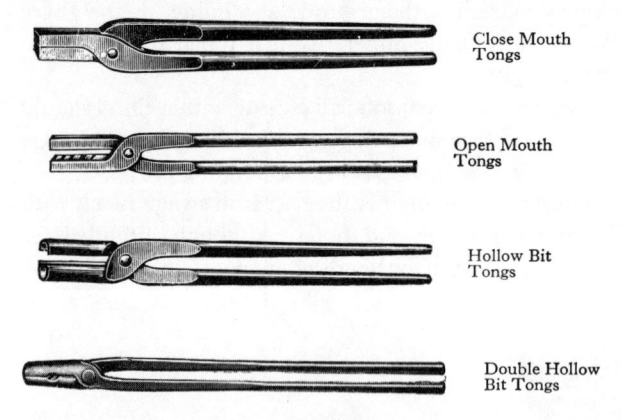

Open Mouth Tongs

Hollow Bit Tongs

Double Hollow Bit Tongs

Fig. 113. Tongs. (Courtesy: William Allday & Co. Ltd.)

Hot bends are usually made over the bick or rounded edge of the working face, depending upon the radius required. For very small circles in eyes, use the bick-iron, see Fig. 55, held in the hardie hole. A rule to remember when hot-bending is that the bend will take place where the metal is red-hot and therefore plastic.

As an example, when making an eye to a poker, bend to a right angle first and then quench the right-angle bend before making the eye.

Fig. 114. Stages in making the eye to a poker

7.3 Leg Vice

The steel or wrought iron leg vice will withstand hammering and heavy bending, and should always be used for such work. The leg vice is let into the floor to take all of the strain. The disadvantage of this vice is that only at one point are the jaws parallel to each other.

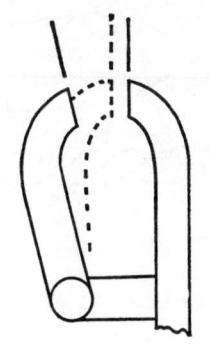

Fig. 115. Leg vice. (Courtesy: William Allday & Co. Ltd.)

Fig. 116. Action of leg vice

Small section work can be bent and formed cold in the leg vice, with the use of bending bars and jigs for accurate and quick work.

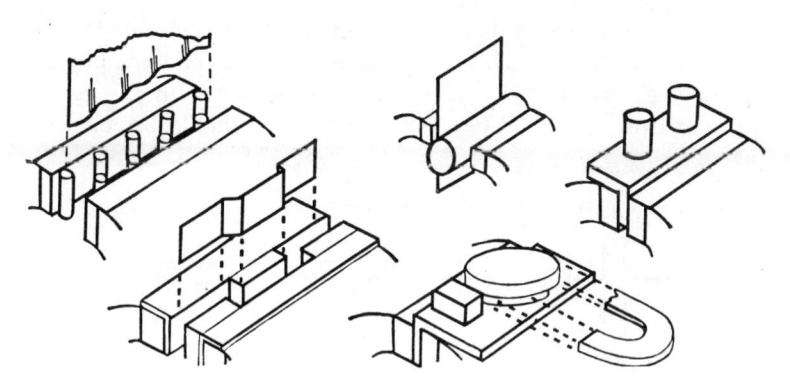

Fig. 117. Bending bars and jigs

Decorative twisted bars can be made from either one or several bars of the same or varying sections. Square bars up to 10 mm can be twisted cold by placing a piece of tube which is a slack fit over the bar, gripping one end in the leg vice and twisting the other with a wrench. Twisting hot metal is easier, but requires more care. The ideal is to heat evenly the portion to be twisted, and then twist at one heat. If the heating is repeated, parts may be over- or under-twisted; this can be overcome by heating and carefully quenching the parts not to be twisted.

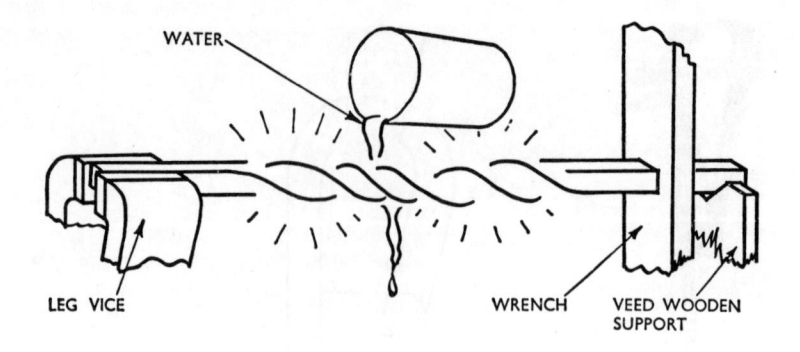

Fig. 118. Correcting an unevenly twisted bar

7.4 Upsetting

Upsetting or jumping-up is to increase the cross-sectional area and decrease the length. This requires considerable skill and can be achieved in a number of ways.

The first essential is that the heat should be concentrated in the portion to be 'upset'. This can be achieved by careful heating and quenching. Secondly the blow must be in line with the bar to prevent bending, but if bending does occur it should be corrected at once.

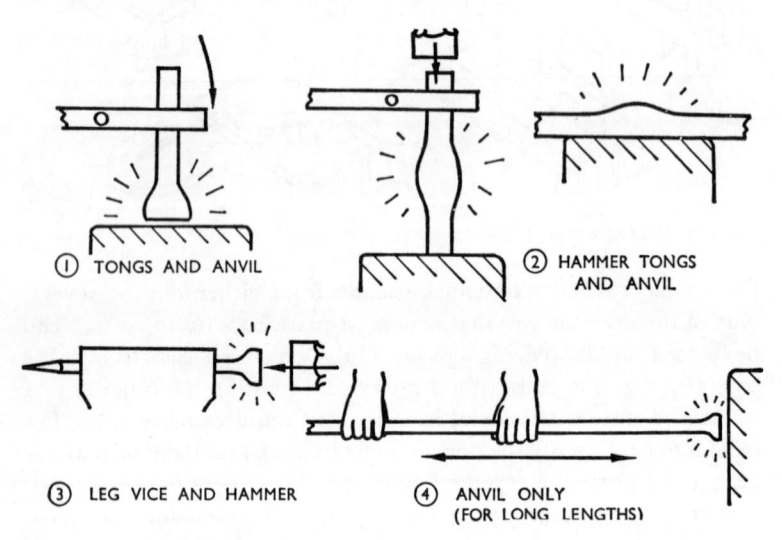

Fig. 119. Methods of upsetting

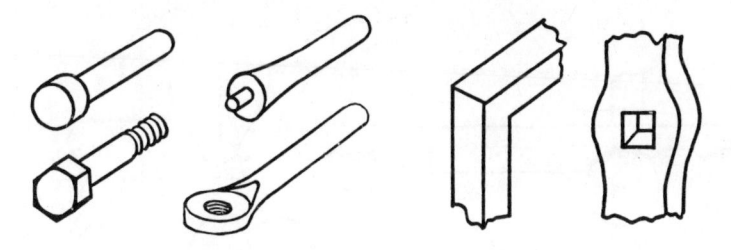

Fig. 120. Examples of work previously upset

7.5 Drawing Down

Drawing down increases the length and decreases the cross-sectional area.

Small section work can be drawn down on the face of the anvil. To produce work evenly tapered on either side, hold the work at an angle and use the hammer face (and shaft) at twice that angle. To prevent a hollow end or pipe shape, known as 'piping', start with a short blunt taper and hammer towards the tongs. If the final section is to be round, work to a square taper first, then octagonal and finally round.

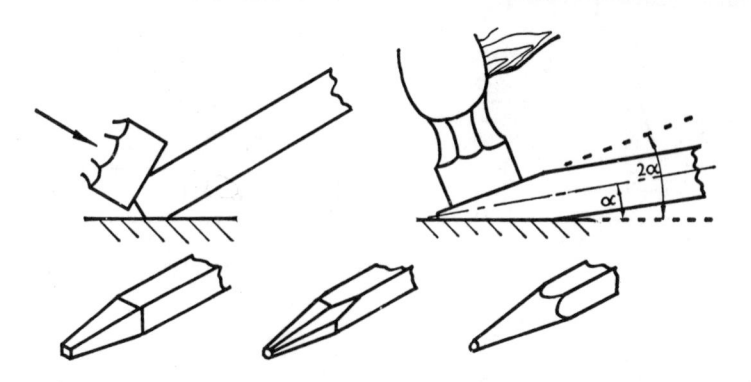

Fig. 121. Drawing down to a taper

To draw down heavier sections, either work on the beak or use top and bottom fullers.

To produce a shoulder use either fullers or the rounded edge of the anvil face.

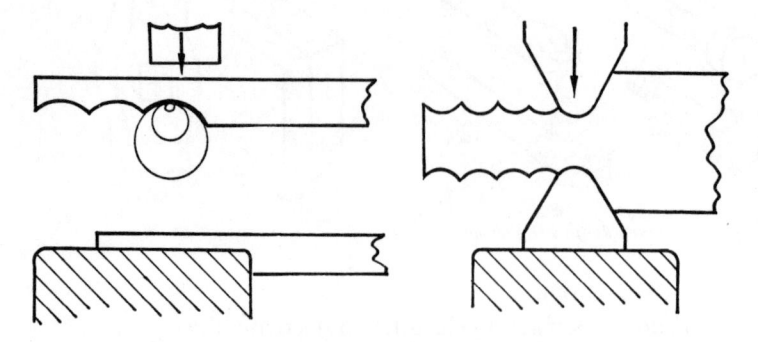

Fig. 122. Drawing down heavier sections and finishing to a shoulder

To finish off surfaces to a good smooth surface, a flatter is used for large areas and a set hammer for restricted areas such as into corners. In both cases they are struck by the sledge.

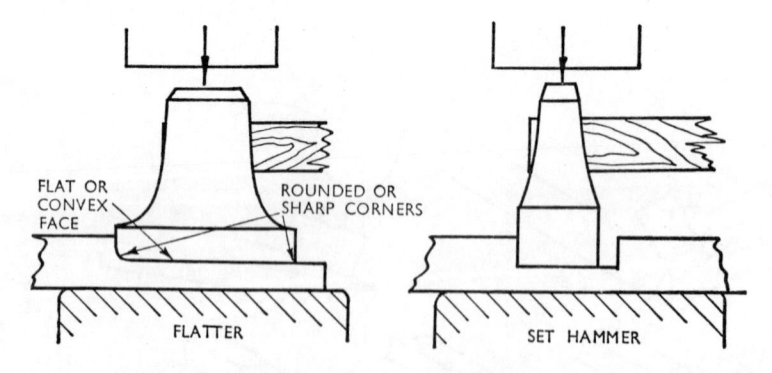

Fig. 123. Flatter and set hammer

7.6 Fullering

Fullering is used to produce a groove across the metal. This can be done by a hand fuller which is like a chisel but rounded on the working end, or by using either both top and bottom fullers as shown, or singly, if the reduction is to be on one side only.

The main use is for making shoulders and drawing down in one particular direction.

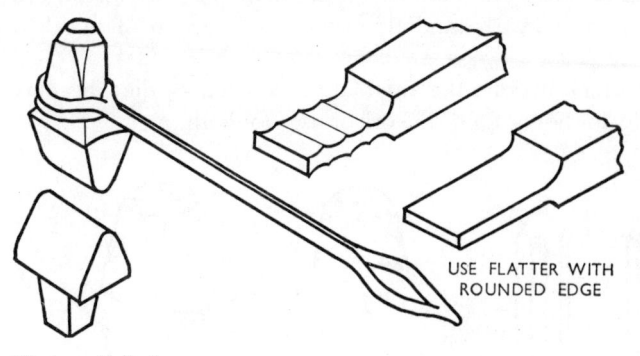

Fig. 124. Fullering

7.7 Swaging
Swaging is to reduce and finish work to size and shape, usually either round or hexagonal.

The most common method is to use top and bottom swages although for large work the swage block can be used, see Fig. 111.

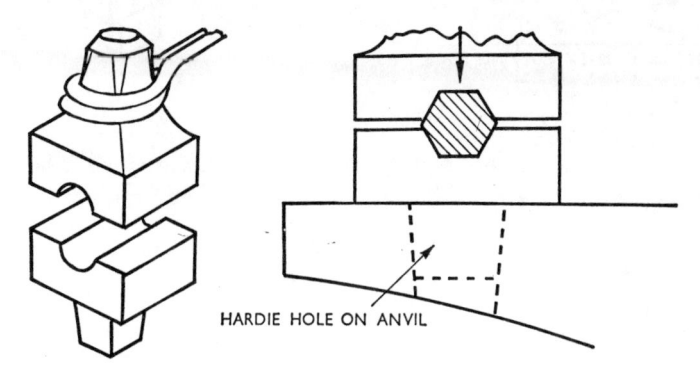

Fig. 125. Swaging

7.8 Cutting Tools
Chisels may be termed hot or cold depending on whether they are to be used to cut hot or cold metal. Hot chisels have a cutting edge of 30° and are not hardened since the heat from the red-hot work would re-soften them. Cold chisels are ground to 60° and are hardened and tempered.

For small or line work hand chisels are used, and for larger work the chisels are fitted with handles in which case they are often called sets, or sates.

A chisel which fits into the anvil face is called a hardie; this may be especially for hot or for cold work or used for both.

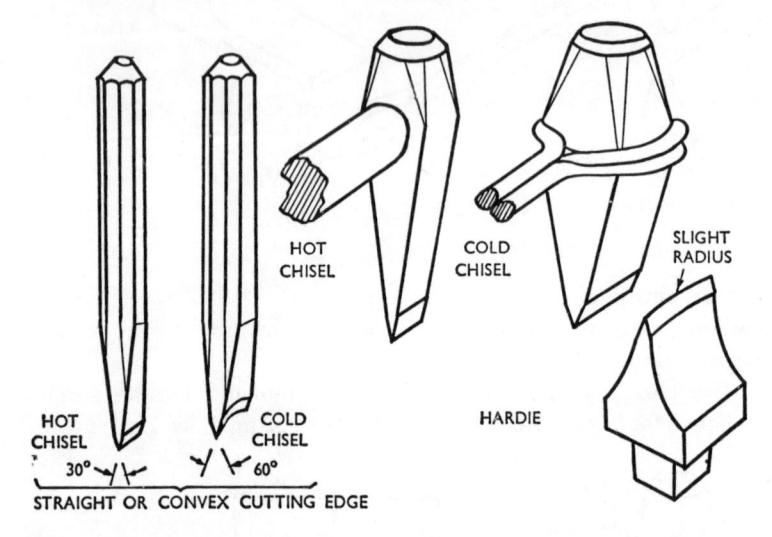

Fig. 126. Cutting tools

For making holes in red-hot metal, punches and drifts are used. The punch can be one of several shapes (round, square, etc.) but for the

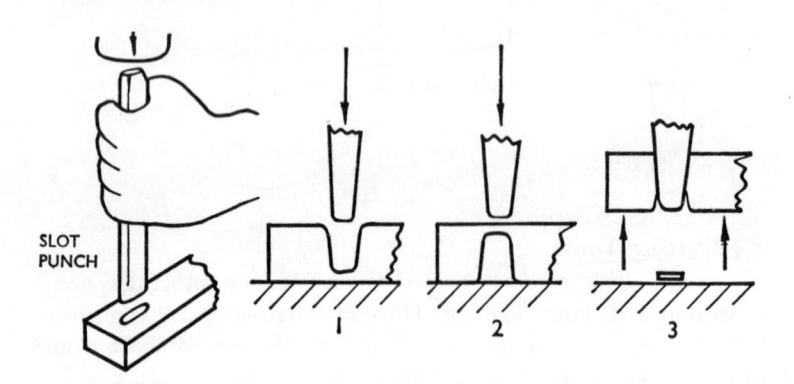

Fig. 127. Punching

minimum removal of metal and maximum strength a slot punch is first used. The punch is driven almost through the red-hot metal, the metal reversed (to eliminate 'drag' on the underside), punch quenched, and the remaining portion of metal is punched through and out the other side.

The hole can now be enlarged to shape and size with a drift of the required cross-section and made parallel with a mandrel.

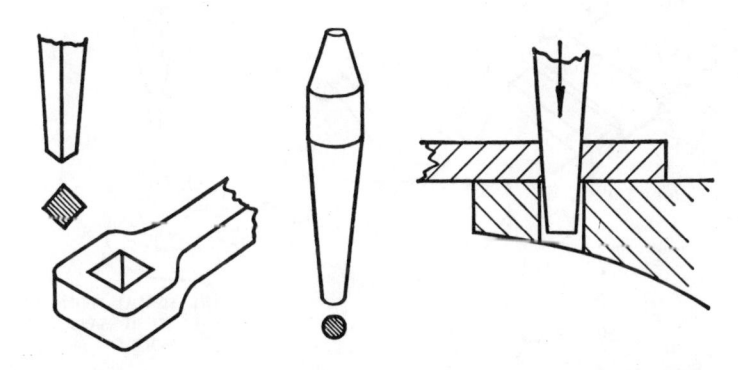

Fig. 128. Drifting

7.9 Flaring and Scrolls

To finish off decorative ironwork particularly as in wrought ironwork the end of the metal may be flared out by hammering on the face of the anvil. The flaring can be left as it is, in which case it is called a fishtail-end, or it can be cut or filed to a decorative shape.

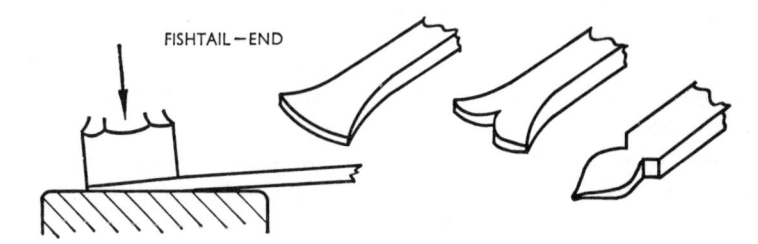

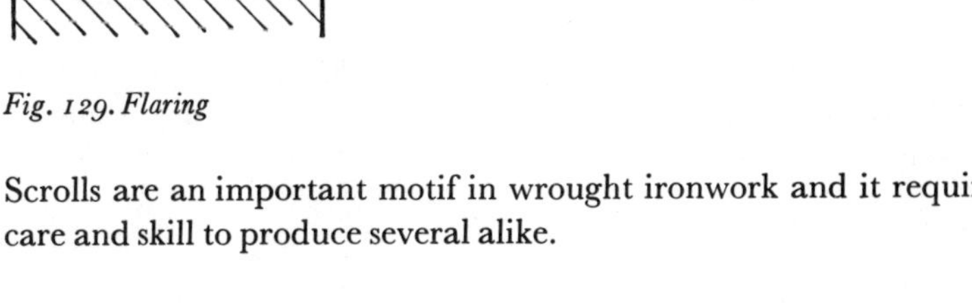

Fig. 129. Flaring

Scrolls are an important motif in wrought ironwork and it requires care and skill to produce several alike.

First draw down, usually to a flared end, then roll the tip on the rounded edge of the anvil. Continue to roll at red heat on the anvil face before holding on the scroll iron with round-nosed pliers, and pulling round. Small scrolls may be bent cold whilst heavier section material may require the help of a scroll wrench. The scroll is then flattened and trued up on the anvil face.

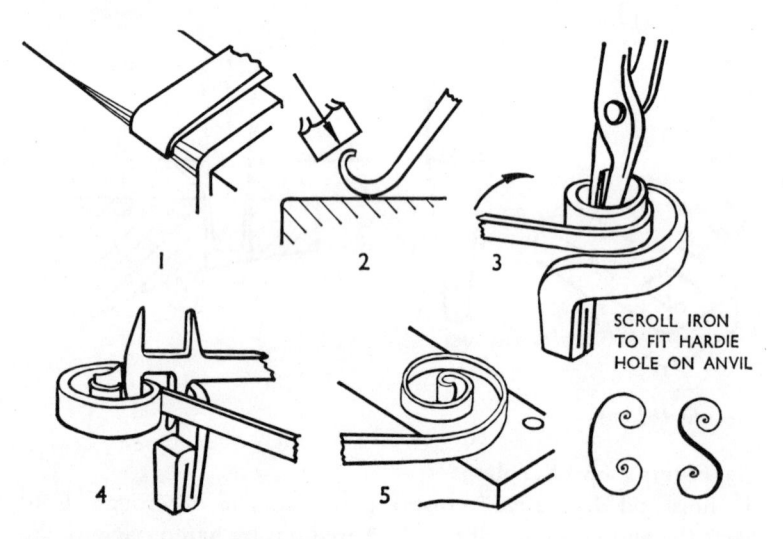

Fig. 130. Making 'C' and 'S' Scrolls

7.10 Drop Forging

For the production of forgings in quantity, forging dies are used. These are made in two halves, one being attached to the rising and falling block (or tup) of the drop forge and the other to the anvil. The hot metal is forced into the impressions which are often of a complex shape.

Drop forged parts include motor car axles, crankshafts and connecting rods, jet engine turbine discs and blades, and crane hooks.

More recent developments include cold forging and cold extrusion which use high cost equipment to produce parts to a high standard of accuracy.

8

Benchwork

8.1 Marking Out

The *rule* is essential to almost all marking out, and accuracy to ½ mm is possible.

The rule is made of hardened and tempered steel, machine-divided down to ½ mm. The length of the rule is usually 150 or 300 mm, but can be obtained in lengths up to 2 m.

Fig. 131. A rule. (Courtesy: Rabone Chesterman Ltd.)

For long and accurate service the edges should never be damaged or used for any other purpose than marking out and measuring. Over long periods when not in use, rules and other equipment with bright unprotected surfaces should be lightly coated with clean oil or smeared lightly with vaseline.

For all marking on metal surfaces, except exposed tinplate, a *scriber* is used. To ensure that the marked line shows up clearly it is common practice to clean the metal and colour with either copper sulphate solution or a proprietary blue marking fluid. The line then shows up as a single bright line. When marking out steel articles, tool rooms often use the oxide film produced by uniform heat tinting to dark brown. Castings are usually painted with a white wash mixture. A variety of patterns of scriber are available with or without removable points, made of tool steel, and the body is usually knurled to provide a firm grip.

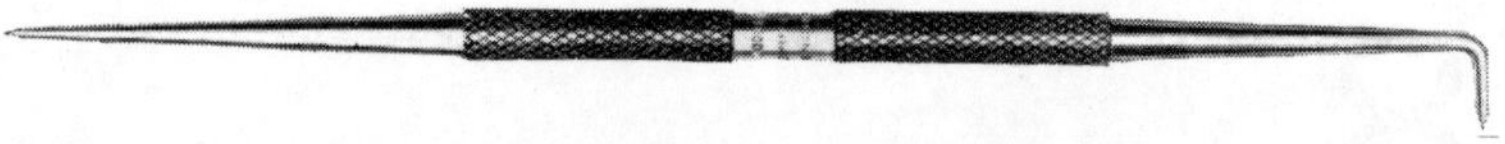

Fig. 132. A scriber. (Courtesy: Moore and Wright (Sheffield) Ltd.)

The scriber should always be placed where it cannot fall and damage the point, which can be protected by a cork when not in use. Should the point become worn or damaged, it can be sharpened on a grinding wheel as shown.

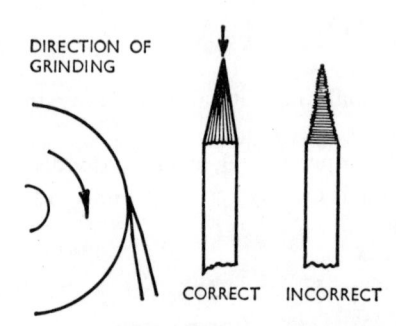

Fig. 133. Sharpening of scriber point

When in use with a straight edge, hold the scriber at an angle to reduce inaccuracies, see below.

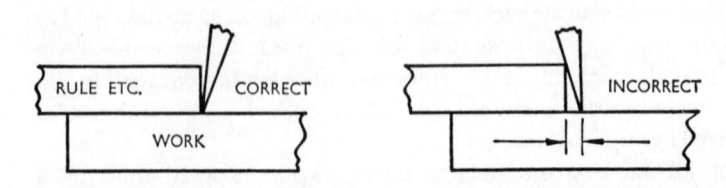

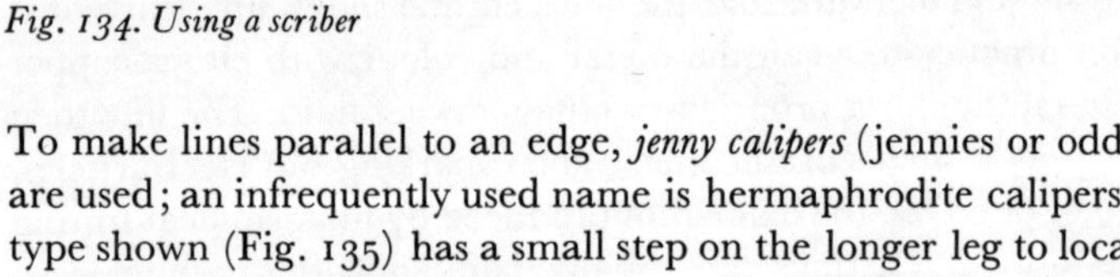

Fig. 134. Using a scriber

To make lines parallel to an edge, *jenny calipers* (jennies or odd-legs) are used; an infrequently used name is hermaphrodite calipers. The type shown (Fig. 135) has a small step on the longer leg to locate on the edge when marking off shoulders. The original type was completely rounded, see Fig. 136, and relied on the skill of the worker to prevent slipping. The point must be sharpened as for a scriber.

Fig. 135. Jenny calipers. (Courtesy: Moore and Wright (Sheffield) Ltd.)

When setting jenny calipers hold the long leg to the end of the rule and set the point in the correct division. Great care should be taken to hold the calipers upright and square to the working edge.

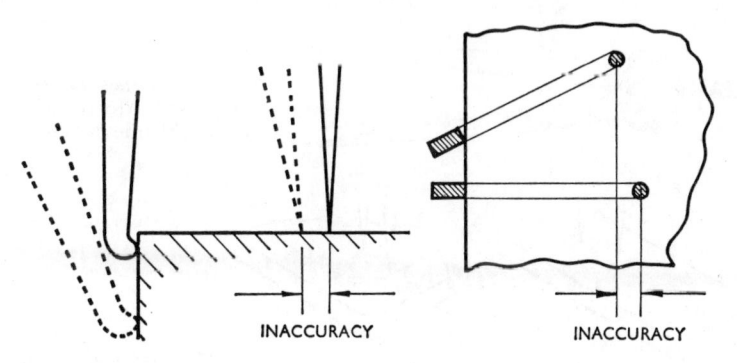

Fig. 136. Use of jenny calipers

A further use of jenny calipers is to find the centre of the end of a bar.

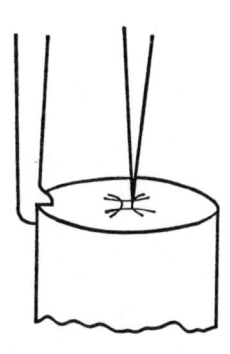

Fig. 137. Centre finding

Dividers are as the name suggests essentially for dividing a length into equal parts, although they are more widely used to draw circles and arcs. They may be plain with a simple riveted joint, or sprung with either a solid nut or a special quick-release type. If sharpened, care should be taken to keep the leg lengths even.

When setting a divider to an accurate length, set the points from and to divisions on the rule, and do not make a guess at the end of the rule. In use the knurled knob is held between the forefinger and thumb.

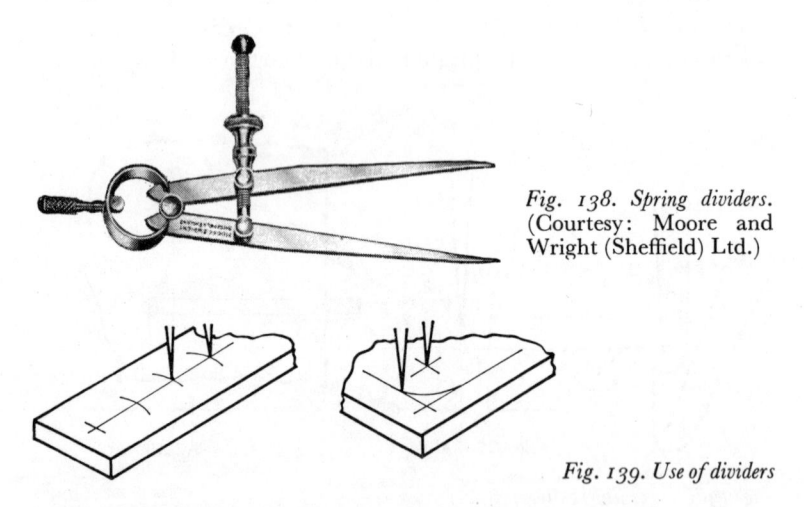

Fig. 138. Spring dividers. (Courtesy: Moore and Wright (Sheffield) Ltd.)

Fig. 139. Use of dividers

Dividers are available up to 300 mm long. For larger work *wing compasses* up to 450 mm in length are used. For even larger work use *trammels*: these are movable heads on a beam at least a metre in length, see Fig. 141.

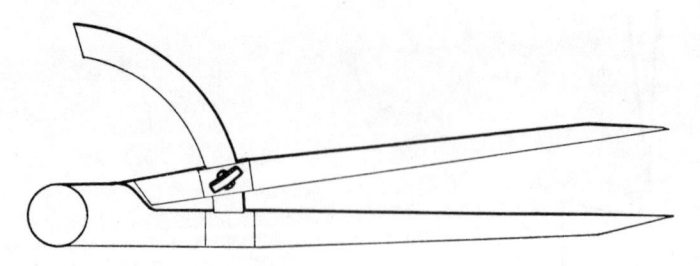

Fig. 140. Wing compasses

Fig. 141. Trammel heads. (Courtesy: James Neill & Co. (Sheffield) Ltd.)

To draw a line at right angles to a straight edge and to check the squareness of an edge, a *try square* is used, see Fig. 142.

The stock is of solid steel and the blade is hardened and tempered. As with all precision equipment, the square should never be dropped or used for any purpose other than that for which it was intended.

Fig. 142. Try square. (Courtesy: Rabone Chesterman Ltd.)

For angles other than right angles a *universal* or *sliding bevel* can be used in conjunction with a *setting protractor*.

Fig. 143. Bevel. (Courtesy: Moore and Wright (Sheffield) Ltd.)

Fig. 144. Setting protractor. (Courtesy: Moore and Wright (Sheffield) Ltd.)

For convenience *combination sets* are available, which comprise a rule 300 or 600 mm long, a centre head (or centre square), to find the centres of the ends of round bars, a protractor and a square head.

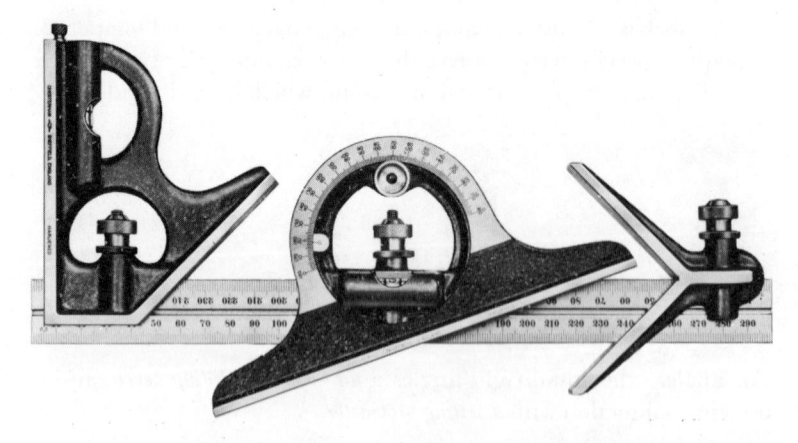

Fig. 145. Combination set. (Courtesy: Rabone Chesterman Ltd.)

For accurate work it is necessary to rest the work either directly or indirectly on a perfectly flat surface, most commonly a *surface plate*.

A surface plate is made of cast iron, of heavy section, strongly ribbed to resist distortion, usually with three feet to ensure stability. The working surface is planed and for very accurate work it is hand scraped, see 8.5; protection when not in use is provided by a wooden cover.

BENCHWORK

For extra-large work, *marking-out tables* are used, which are the equivalent of large surface plates mounted on either four or six legs; the size might be up to 2½ m by 1½ m surface area.

To mark lines parallel to the base of the work, place on the surface plate and use a *surface gauge* (or scribing block). The point could have previously been set to the correct height against a rule held vertically (or rule mounted in the square head of the combination square). The setting can be made accurately by clamping the scriber to the approximate position and using the fine adjustment screw on the base which moves the rocker arm and post.

The base is veed which also allows it to be used on round surfaces. Some models are provided with two frictionally held pins in the base which can be used against the edge of a slot or slideway.

Fig. 146. Surface plate

Fig. 147. Surface gauge. (Courtesy: Moore and Wright (Sheffield) Ltd.)

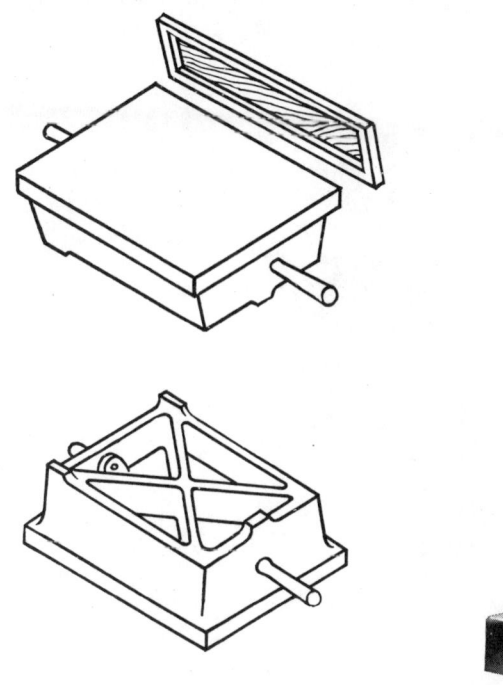

An additional use for the surface gauge is to set work parallel to the surface plate by touching at either end, and for setting work parallel and level, in machine work.

Work which has only been machined true on one side may have to be mounted on an *angle plate*.

Fig. 148. Angle plates. (Courtesy: James Neill & Co. (Sheffield) Ltd.)

Circular work is held in *vee blocks* with or without the use of a *clamp* (stirrup).

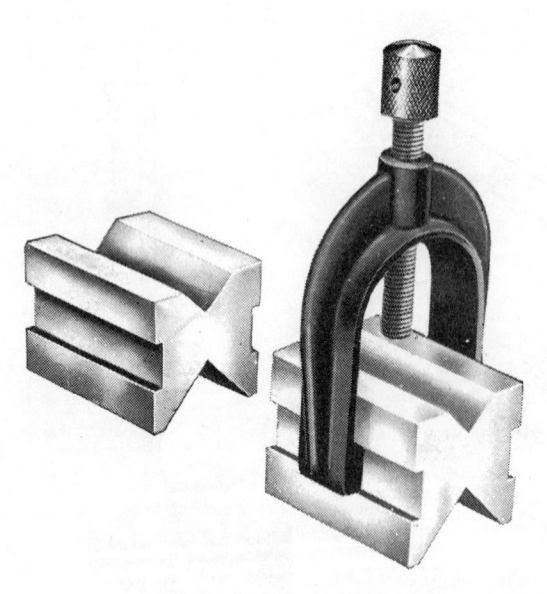

Fig. 149. Vee blocks and clamp. (Courtesy: Moore and Wright (Sheffield) Ltd.)

To set the point of the surface gauge at the centre height of round work, guess the centre height and mark across, then turn the work through 180° and mark again at the same setting. Two parallel lines are produced, and the point is set accurately between the two.

To divide a bar into six equal radial divisions, draw a line across at centre height, as above, and then using a protractor set to 60°, turn the work accurately through 60° and mark across again. Repeat the procedure for the final division. A second method is to mark a pitch circle and use dividers set to the radius.

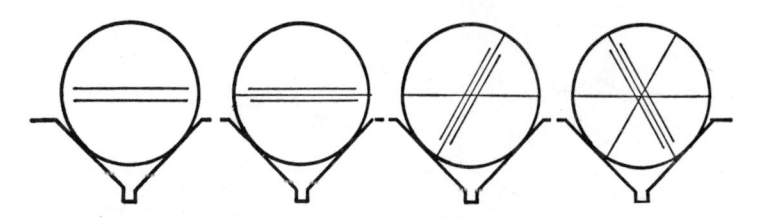

Fig. 150. Dividing a round bar into six radial divisions

Once the lines have been clearly marked by a single line they are made permanent by dot punching. The *dot punch* is ground to 60° by the same method as for the scriber. The work should be supported on a solid surface, and the eye should look along the line as the punch is placed in position. The punch is raised to the vertical position and given a light tap with the hammer. The size of the dot punch mark should be large enough to be seen easily and not likely to be erased accidentally but small enough not to show as an ugly mark on the finished edge.

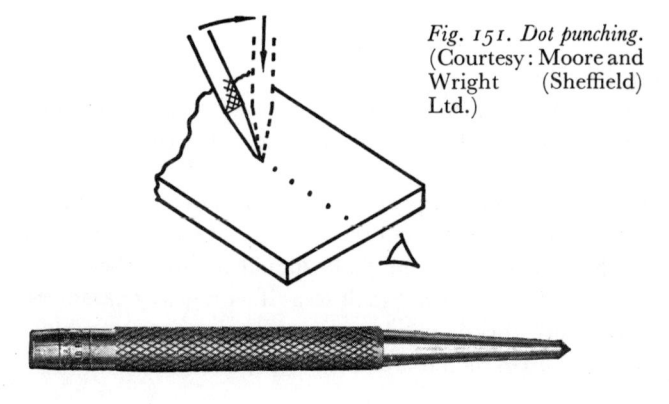

Fig. 151. Dot punching. (Courtesy: Moore and Wright (Sheffield) Ltd.)

Holes which are to be drilled should be marked with a dot punch mark in the centre. If accuracy is required with larger holes the circle is drawn in with dividers and four dot punch marks made on the circumference. These four marks will be visible until the drill is cutting at full diameter and inaccuracies in the drilling can be cured as described in Chapter 9. Before drilling, the dot punch mark is enlarged with a *centre punch* which is similar to a dot punch (sometimes ground to 90°). To offset any slight inaccuracies in the grinding of the point, rotate between the fingers between each hammer blow.

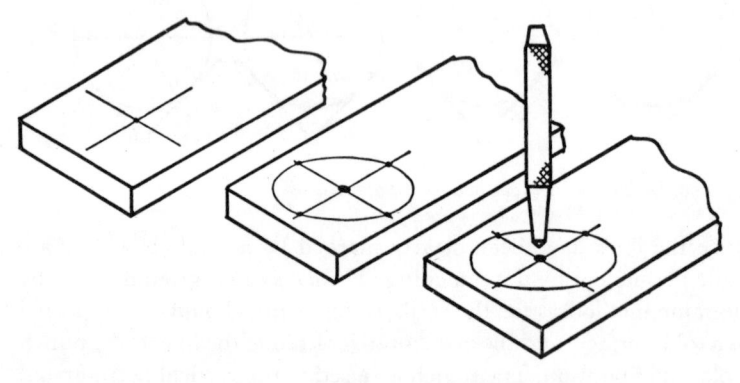

Fig. 152. Marking out and centre punching a hole to be drilled

The three main types of engineers' *hammers* range in weight up to 1½ kg, the popular size for benchwork being about ½ kg. The handles are made of ash or hickory (see Fig. 153).

8.2 Holding Devices

The angle plate and vee block previously described are holding devices, but were considered with marking out equipment for convenience.

The most widely used holding device is the *bench vice* with the body and jaw made of cast iron on all but the engineer's heavy duty vices, which are made of malleable iron. Care should therefore be taken with the popular cast iron vice not to ill-treat it with heavy hammering or bending. Most workshops are equipped with a leg vice which is intended to stand up to such treatment, see 7.3.

BALL PEIN   **CROSS PEIN**   **STRAIGHT PEIN**

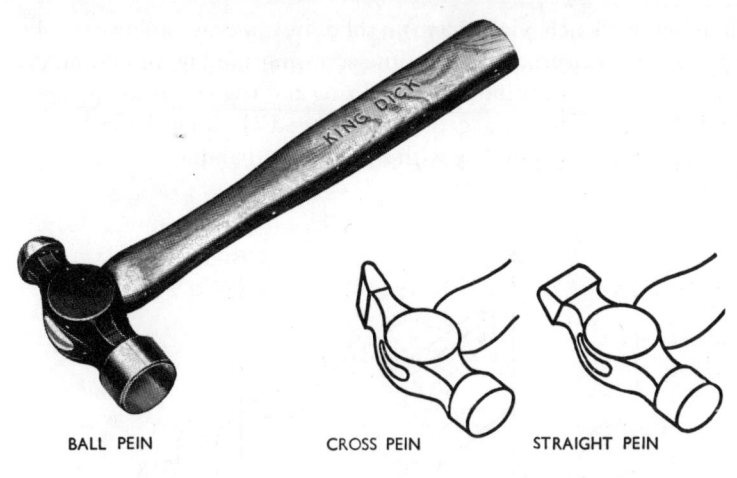

Fig. 153. Hammers. (Courtesy: Abingdon King Dick Ltd.)

Fig. 154. Plain screw bench vice. (Courtesy: C. & J. Hampton Ltd.)

(*a*) *Sectioned*

(*b*) *Sliding jaw removed*

115

Plain screw bench vices have a solid nut which can usually be replaced when worn. To save time screwing the jaw in and out, a quick-grip type is available; by pressing the trigger on to the screw head the nut can be engaged or disengaged allowing the jaw to be positioned before tightening with a turn of the handle.

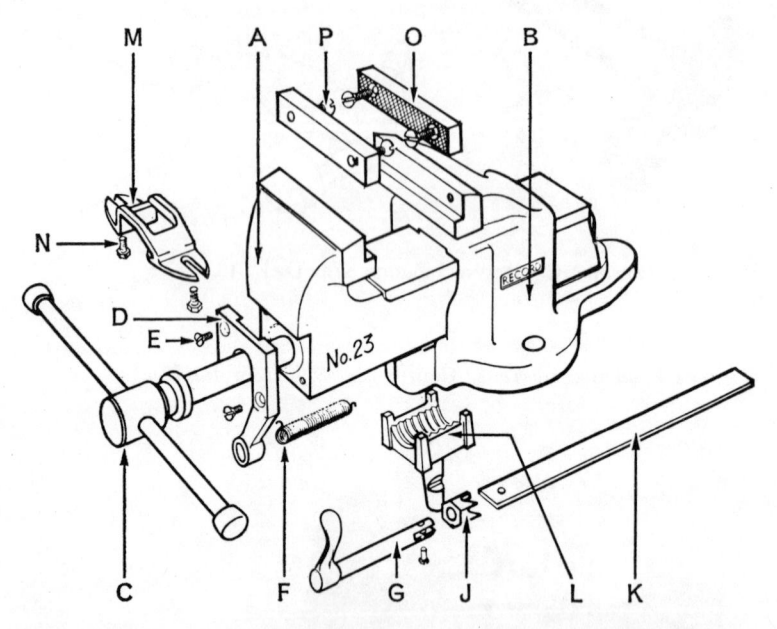

Fig. 155. Quick-grip bench vice (exploded view). (Courtesy: C. & J. Hampton Ltd.)

KEY

A Sliding Jaw
B Vice Body
C Main Screw and Handle
D Front Bracket
E Front Bracket Screws
F Trigger Spring
G Trigger
J Adjusting Nut
K Rocker Bar
L Half Nut
M Nut Guide Bracket
N Nut Bracket Screws
O Jaw Plates
P Jaw Plate Screws

The size of bench vices varies from jaw widths of 60 to 200 mm, opening respectively 60 to 235 mm.

The jaw is made of hardened steel and has a roughened surface to

BENCHWORK 117

grip the work securely. This is a disadvantage with work which may damage, so protective grips or 'clams' are fitted over the jaws. These may be proprietary fibre grips or workshop made, from copper, brass or lead.

Threaded work can be gripped between either lead or fibre grips, or a mating nut can be cut half-way through, to grip over the whole thread.

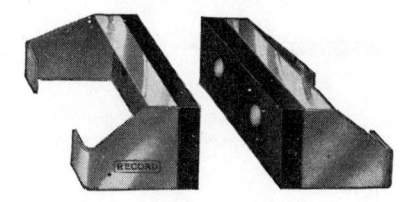

Fig. 156. Fibre grips for vices. (Courtesy: C. & J. Hampton Ltd.)

Small parts on sheetmetal which cannot be gripped in the bench vices can often be held with one or more hand vices. These are sturdily made of drop-forged steel, and range in size from 100 to 150 cm.

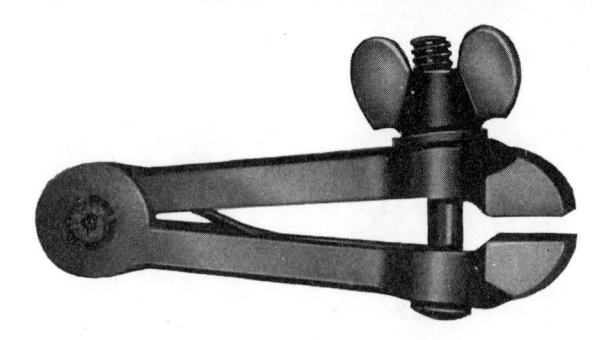

Fig. 157. Hand vice. (Courtesy: Charles Cooper (Hatton Garden) Ltd.)

To hold even smaller work and small tools, *pin vices* and *tongs* are used. The handles are hollow, thus allowing any length of material to be held. Pin vices will hold work up to 5 mm whilst pin tongs range up to $1\frac{1}{2}$ mm capacity.

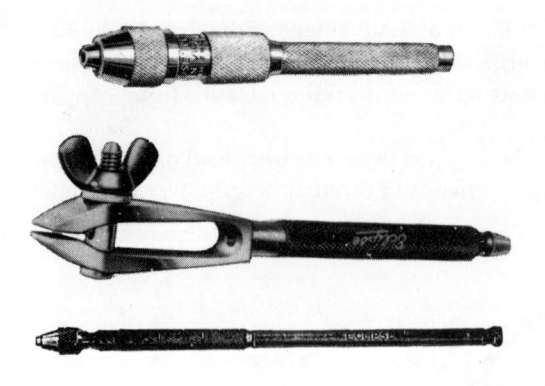

Fig. 158. Pin vices and tongs. (Courtesy: James Neill & Co. (Sheffield) Ltd.)

Toolmakers' clamps are most useful for holding pieces together for either drilling or marking-out from a pattern. The jaws are of case-hardened steel and range in length from 50 mm up to 125 mm. An advantage over other small holding devices is that the jaws may be adjusted to parallel.

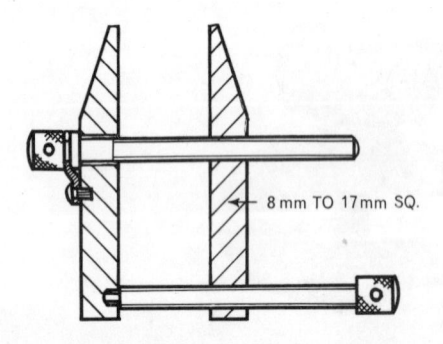

Fig. 159. Toolmakers' clamps

Pliers are available in a multitude of shapes and sizes, and the uses are equally varied. Perhaps the most common types are the combination pliers with or without insulated handles. Other useful workshop pliers include the flat nose, round nose and snipe nose.

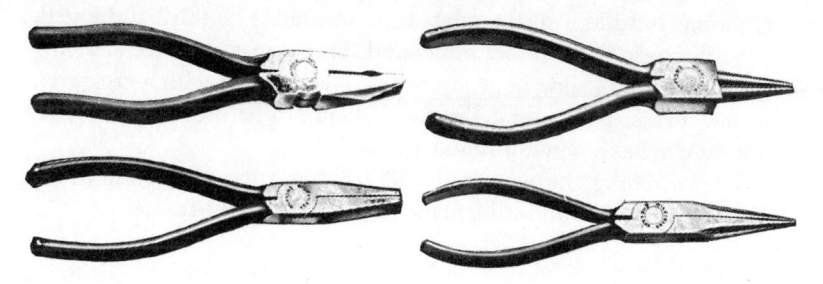

Fig. 160. Pliers. (Courtesy: Wilkinsons Tools Ltd.)

8.3 Cutting

One of the most convenient methods of cutting is to use the hacksaw. The *hand hacksaw* normally takes blades either 250 or 300 mm long, and the frame holding the blade in tension may be one of several designs.

The first type has a tubular frame which can slide through the top of the handle, and is held by a knurled head set screw. The second

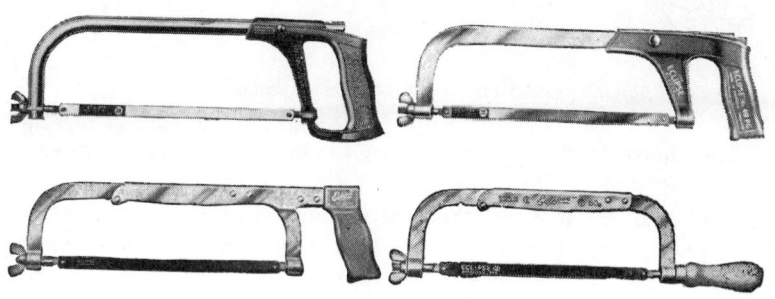

(Courtesy: James Neill & Co. (Sheffield) Ltd.)

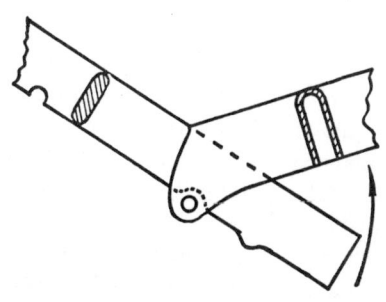

Fig. 161. Hacksaw frames

E

119

is similar but has a rectangular section frame. The third and fourth both dispense with the set screw and 'break' in the centre allowing the outer end to slide in or out until a slot engages with a cross rod, in the correct position for the size of blade to be used. A fifth type, not shown, has a non-adjustable frame.

By slackening the wing nut and removing the blade, the frame can be adjusted to allow the blade to cut at 90° to the frame.

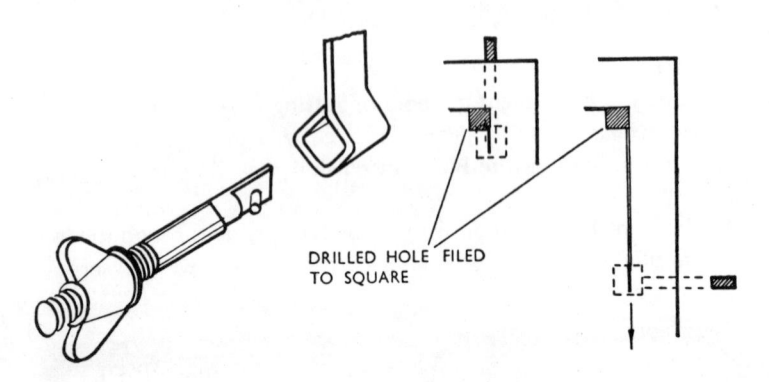

Fig. 162. Adjusting a hacksaw frame to cut to greater depths

The choice of the correct hacksaw blade depends on a number of factors.

The blade may be of either high speed steel which lasts longest and will cut the hardest metals but which costs more, or of low tungsten steel. Low tungsten steel blades are available as either 'Flexible' which are hardened on the cutting edge only and are almost unbreakable, or 'All Hard' which are preferred by skilled workers who find the greater rigidity aids accurate sawing.

The correct tooth size must next be decided upon; this depends on the type and size of material. Soft materials (aluminium and copper) require a greater tooth pitch (i.e. larger teeth) than hard materials (alloy steel). On thin materials there should be at least three teeth in contact to prevent the teeth straddling the metal, which results in the teeth being ripped out.

Once the correct blade has been selected, fit in the frame with the teeth pointing away from the handle. With the wing-nut first take up the slack and then apply three full turns only. The work

Table 9. Tooth Size of Hand Blades

Teeth per 25 mm*	Use
14	Large sections of soft materials
18	Small sections of soft materials, large sections of hard materials (general purpose size)
24	Small sections of hard materials, e.g. 3 to 6 mm tube, sheet and sections
32	Very small sections, e.g. less than 3 mm tube, sheet and sections

* Interim terminology until ISO recommendation to specify tooth pitch is adopted.

(Courtesy: James Neill & Co. (Sheffield) Ltd.)

must be rigid and positioned so that the cutting commences on a flat surface with as many teeth in contact as possible. Use a long steady stroke at the approximate rate of 50 per minute in the case of low tungsten steel blades, and 60 per minute for high speed steel blades, increasing the pressure as more teeth engage. On thin material the pressure should always be light. Remember that the blade only cuts on the forward stroke and the pressure should be removed on the return.

In workshops where a large amount of sawing is necessary, a *power hacksaw* facilitates this work. The machine may be a light duty model with a capacity of about 150 mm × 150 mm or a heavy duty model taking material up to 300 mm × 300 mm.

Relief of pressure on the return stroke is obtained either by an oil pump or, as on the model shown, by an adjustable oil dashpot, in conjunction with the angular setting of the slides, see Fig. 163.

The work should be gripped rigidly as for hand sawing and the frame lowered carefully after starting the machine, relieving the weight during the first stroke.

Never start cutting with a new blade in the old cut, which will be too narrow and therefore cause binding and breakage. If it is essential to use a new blade, the only solution is to turn the work over and start from the opposite side.

Other useful saws for benchwork are *junior hacksaws* using small

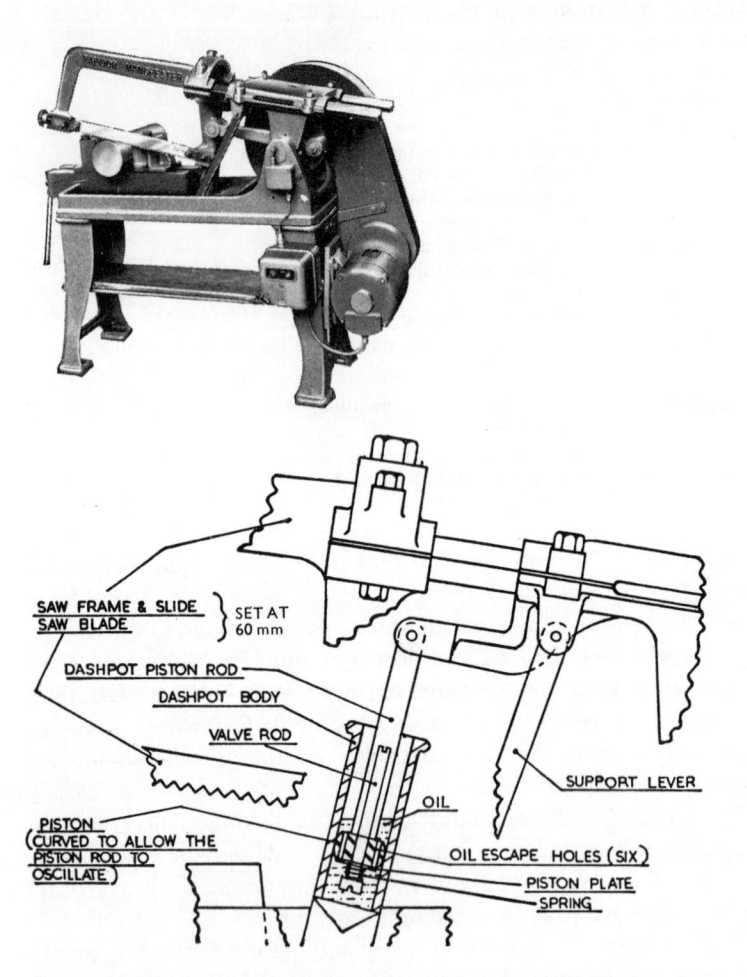

Fig. 163. Light duty hacksaw machine. (Courtesy: Edward G. Herbert Ltd.)

Fig. 164. Junior hacksaw and a pad handle saw. (Courtesy: James Neill & Co. (Sheffield) Ltd.)

BENCHWORK

blades, and *pad handles* to take standard hacksaw blades, see Fig. 164. *Piercing saws* have been described previously, see 6.11.

Nippers are used to cut wire, and may be made to cut from one of two positions.

Fig. 165. Nippers. (Courtesy: Wilkinsons Tools Ltd.)

One of the simplest tools in the workshop is the *chisel*, either forged, hardened and tempered from carbon steel, or purchased ready to use in 'non-temper chrome alloy steel' which can be sharpened with a smooth file when required. Sizes vary from 100 mm to 600 mm long, the popular sizes being 150 mm to 200 mm in length.

The cutting edge is sharpened approximately to the angles given below.

Table 10. Chisel Angles

Metal to be cut	Cutting angle
Iron and Steel	60°
Copper and Brass	45°
Aluminium	30°

Fig. 166. Sharpening a chisel

Probably the most useful is the *flat chisel* which can be used for removing metal where it would be impossible or unnecessary to machine, cutting sheetmetal, and miscellaneous work such as removing the heads of rivets.

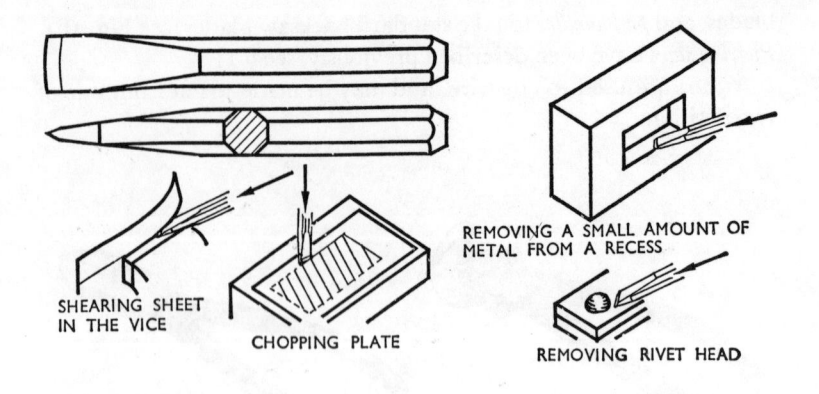

Fig. 167. The flat chisel and uses

The *cross-cut (or cape) chisel* was originally used to cut grooves across the surface of metal, before finally removing the remaining ridges with the flat chisel. The main uses now are for cutting in confined spaces unsuitable for the flat chisel and cutting keyways.

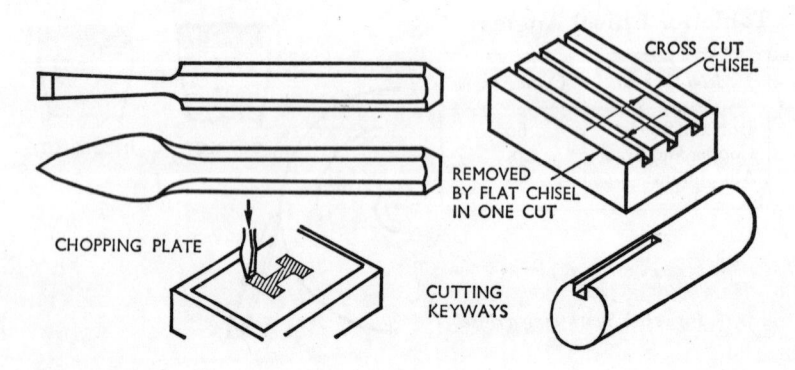

Fig. 168. Cross-cut chisel and uses

The diamond chisel is used to cut corners to a sharp angle and to correct drills starting to drill off-centre, see 9.3.

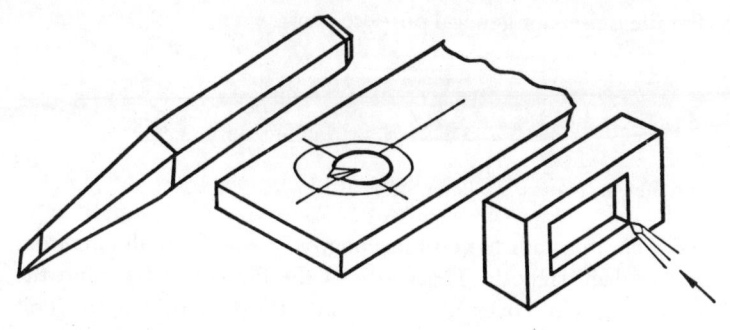

Fig. 169. The diamond chisel and uses

The *half-round chisel* is used to cut oil grooves or to clean up filleted corners.

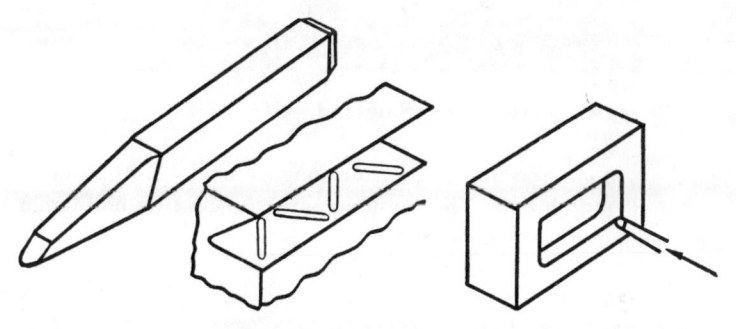

Fig. 170. The half-round chisel and uses

8.4 Filing

The most widely used cutting tool on the bench is the engineer's file, available in different shapes, sizes and cuts.

The *flat (or taper flat) file* is available in lengths from 100 mm to 400 mm, which is the length to the shoulder only, excluding the tang. The available grades of cut, ranging from the roughest to the smoothest are: bastard, second cut, smooth and dead smooth. Soft metal requires the roughest grades of cut, and hard metal the smoothest, whilst a metal such as steel can be worked by all the cuts mentioned here. Brass requires new files for easy working; afterwards they can be used on steel.

The flat file is used for general purpose work.

Fig. 171. Flat file. (Courtesy: Peter Stubs Ltd.)

The *hand file*, 100 mm to 400 mm long, is available in all cuts from bastard to dead smooth. The width of the file is constant, but the thickness tapers off over about the last third of its length. This tapering facilitates filing a surface flat as the convex shape tends to offset the inclination to rock the file as it is pushed forward. One uncut ('safe') edge avoids damage to corners or projections and acts as a guide.

Fig. 172. Hand file. (Courtesy: Peter Stubs Ltd.)

The *half-round file*, 100 mm to 400 mm long, is available in bastard, second and smooth cuts. The rounded side is not a true half-circle and is used to file concave surfaces.

Fig. 173. Half-round file. (Courtesy: Peter Stubs Ltd.)

The *round file*, 100 mm to 400 mm long, is available in bastard, second and smooth cuts. This file is sometimes called a rat-tail file for the medium and larger sizes and a mouse-tail for the smaller. It is used to enlarge holes and for filing fillets and concave surfaces.

Fig. 174. Round file. (Courtesy: Peter Stubs Ltd.)

BENCHWORK

The *square file*, 100 mm to 400 mm long, is available in bastard, second and smooth cuts, and is used to enlarge square or rectangular holes and for slotting and grooving keyways.

Fig. 175. *Square file*. (Courtesy: Peter Stubs Ltd.)

The *three-square file*, 100 mm to 400 mm long, is available in bastard, second and smooth cuts; it is triangular in section and is used especially for cleaning out sharp corners and angles.

Fig. 176. *Three-square file*. (Courtesy: Peter Stubs Ltd.)

The *warding file*, 100 mm to 200 mm long, is available in bastard, second and smooth cuts. It tapers in width but is parallel in thickness. It is used where a thin file is particularly required for grooving and notching, as in locksmith's work, making and repairing keys.

Fig. 177. *Warding file*. (Courtesy: Peter Stubs Ltd.)

The *knife file*, 100 mm to 400 mm long, is available in bastard, second and smooth cuts, and is used to file sharp angles in tool and die work.

Fig. 178. *Knife file*. (Courtesy: Peter Stubs Ltd.)

Other engineer's files not mentioned here are for more specialised purposes.

For more precise work such as silversmithing and die making, the following files are used:

Precision files from 75 mm to 200 mm long and available in much finer cuts than smooth and dead smooth.

Precision needle files from 120 mm to 180 mm long, are available in very fine cuts and in a wide range of shapes including the engineer's file shapes.

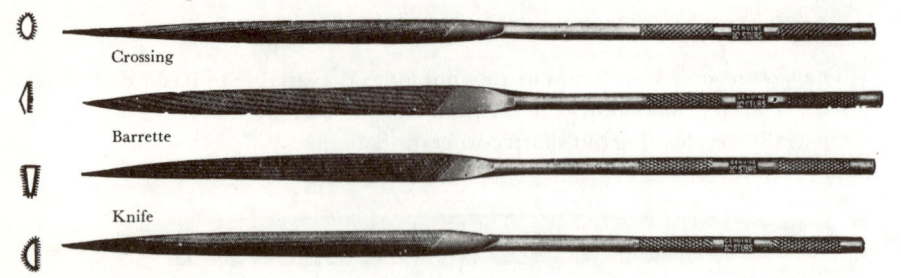

Crossing

Barrette

Knife

Half Round

Fig. 179. Precision needle files. (Courtesy: Peter Stubs Ltd.)

Rifflers are especially made to suit the work of engravers, silversmiths and die makers. The rifflers shown have ends alike and are 175 mm long, see Fig. 180.

A *tension file* is essentially a file 150 mm to 280 mm long, approximately $1\frac{1}{2}$ mm diameter and held in tension either in a special saw frame or by special links in a standard hacksaw frame.

Before an engineer's file is used it must be fitted with a wooden handle. The handles vary in size from 75 to 150 mm long and, for additional strength, are fitted with a steel ferrule. If an attempt is made to force the wooden handle on, it will probably split, therefore heat the point of the tang to a red heat and force into the centre of the handle, taking care to keep the file and handle in line with one another. Ideally it should be possible to force the handle ferrule within say 5 mm of the shoulder of the file, by hand pressure alone; if this is not possible remove the file and reheat before inserting. Should the file tang be too hot, withdraw the tang before the hole has burnt oversize. When within 5 mm, or less for a small file, either bounce the wooden handle on a firm surface, such as the anvil, or use either a hammer or mallet to drive the handle firmly home on the tang and up to the shoulder without any looseness or suggestion of the handle splitting.

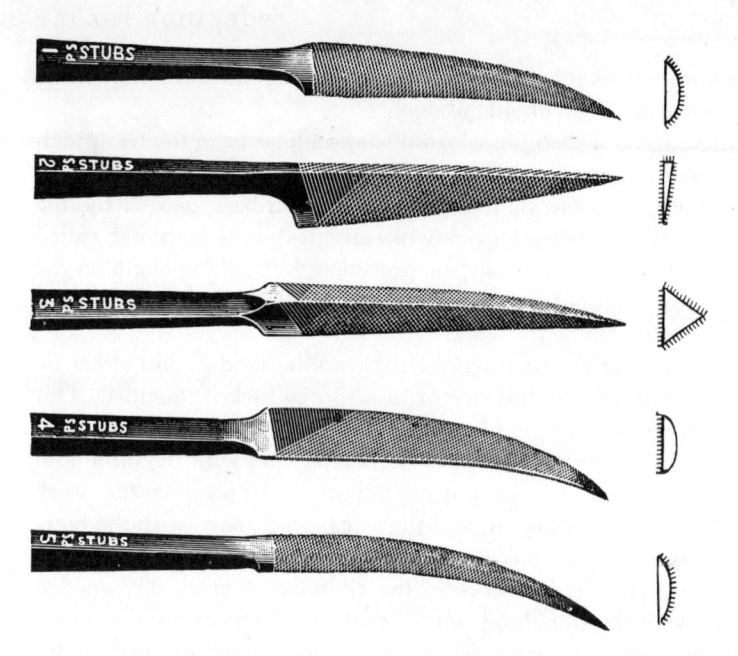

Fig. 180. Silversmith's rifflers (one end only). (Courtesy: Peter Stubs Ltd.)

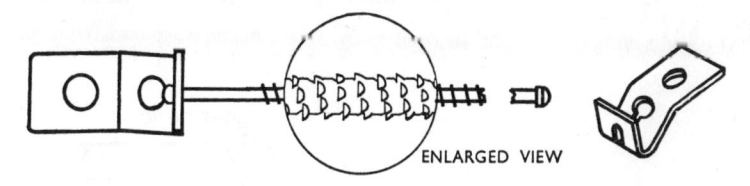

Fig. 181. Tension file with links for hacksaw frame

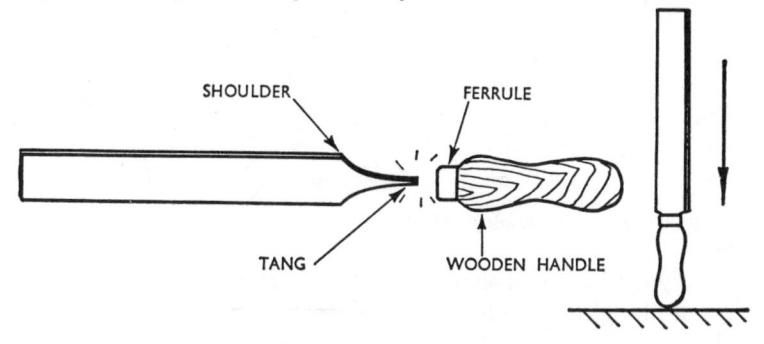

Fig. 182. Fitting a file handle

129

When using files it is better to reserve new files for finishing, taking care not to use them on sharp edges.

Before using a used file, clean dirt and filings from the teeth with a file card (essentially a wire brush with wires approx. 10 mm long). Obstinate pieces can be removed with the scriber point. If the file persistently becomes clogged with minute pieces of metal called 'pins', the fault can partially be prevented by rubbing chalk on the file. Pinning not only reduces the effectiveness of the file, but makes bad 'score' marks on the work.

The files that are required for the work in hand should either be placed separately by the vice or in a special rack if provided. This prevents damage to the file teeth. The work should be held tightly in the vice, the edge to be filed, horizontal, and with the minimum amount unsupported to prevent 'chatter'. If possible the work should be at elbow height, and the feet placed apart, with the body in a good stance, as a boxer.

For a right-handed worker, the right hand grips the wooden handle with the thumb on top. The left hand can be used in one of three positions. For heavy filing the pad of the hand can exert extra pressure, for light filing the fingers and thumb can hold the end, and as an assistance to filing flat, the hand can spread out over the length of the file.

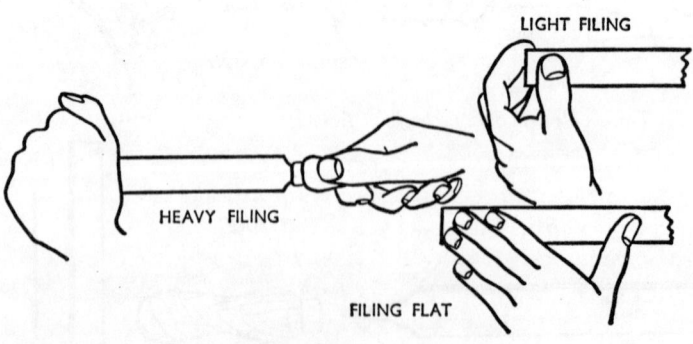

Fig. 183. Positions of the hands for filing

A steady cutting speed should be maintained releasing the pressure but not lifting the file on the return stroke.

To give a good finish, the work can be drawfiled. Always attempt to finish work with the file marks in the long direction only.

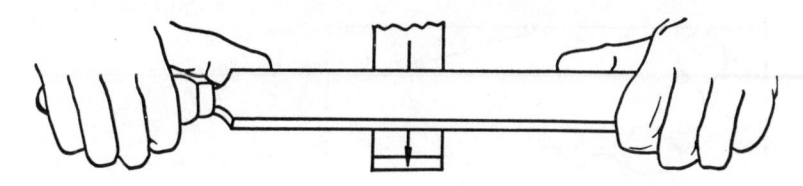

Fig. 184. Drawfiling

If the edge of the work is to be rounded, first reduce to a flat bevelled edge before attempting to round. Accurate work should be checked with a radius gauge, see Fig. 201.

Convex profiles should be cut approximately to shape before filing across the outline. Finally file with the length of the edge, as shown below.

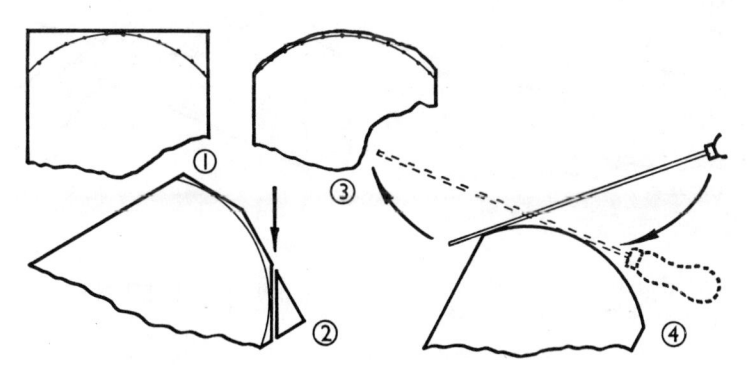

Fig. 185. Filing a convex profile

Concave profiles are cut approximately to shape, by sometimes drilling (mark out carefully first), hacksawing and chiselling (take care not to distort and buckle the work). Either a half-round or round file is then used giving a twisting motion as the file is pushed forward, see Fig. 186. The edge can be drawfiled to finish.

Work which requires a better finish than drawfiling can be finished with emery cloth. Always reduce the surface to a good filed finish first: emery cloth will not remove or cover up faulty filing. Use the appropriate grade or grades of emery, tearing off a strip at least equal to the width of the file. Always back the emery cloth with a file, never attempt to use it in the fingers as this can only lead to

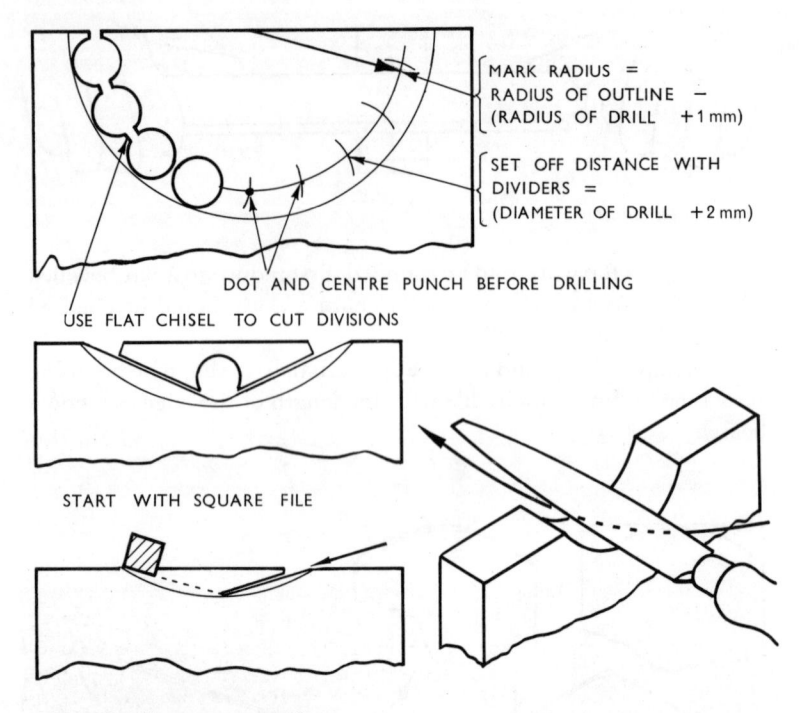

```
                                    ⎡ MARK RADIUS =
                                    ⎢ RADIUS OF OUTLINE  −
                                    ⎣ (RADIUS OF DRILL   +1 mm)

                                    ⎡ SET OFF DISTANCE WITH
                                    ⎢ DIVIDERS =
                                    ⎣ (DIAMETER OF DRILL  +2 mm)

              DOT AND CENTRE PUNCH BEFORE DRILLING
USE FLAT CHISEL TO CUT DIVISIONS

START WITH SQUARE FILE
```

Fig. 186. Filing a concave profile

rounded inaccurate surfaces with a poor, slipshod appearance. To obtain an even higher finish, oil can be applied to the emery cloth after using dry emery as far as possible. If oil is used great care must be taken to prevent any getting on to the file itself. For abrasives and surface finishes, see 11.4 and 11.7.

8.5 Scraping

To remove accurately small amounts of metal, scrapers are used, which have a fine scraping cut.

The finish should first of all be as accurate as can be obtained by the previous process, i.e. filing or machining. The master surface, whether it be a flat surface (and a surface plate is used) or a shaft, is thinly smeared with prussian blue or red lead in oil and the parts rubbed together. The high parts will be marked and should be removed by the scraper until on re-checking the marks are no more than 3 to 5 mm apart (average).

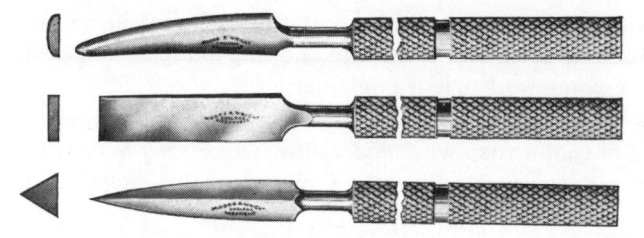

Fig. 187. Scrapers (three-square, flat and flat half-round). (Courtesy: Moore and Wright (Sheffield) Ltd.)

Fig. 188. Hand-scraping a lathe bed. (Courtesy: T. S. Harrison & Sons Ltd.)

8.6 Measurement

The *rule* which is one of the most important bench measuring tools has already been described. With care and in good light it is easily possible to measure work to half a millimetre.

To measure internal measurements, such as the bore of a pipe, the rule is used in conjunction with *inside calipers* which may have either a firm joint or a spring top with either a solid or quick-acting nut.

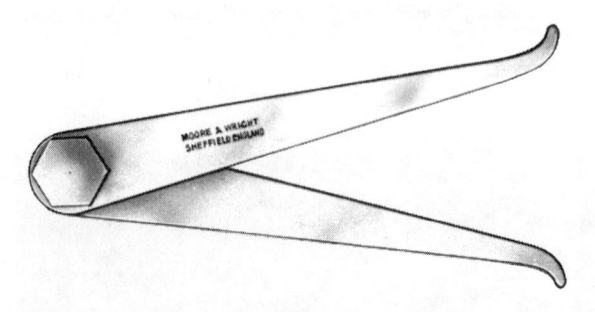

Fig. 189. Firm-joint inside calipers. (Courtesy: Moore and Wright (Sheffield) Ltd.)

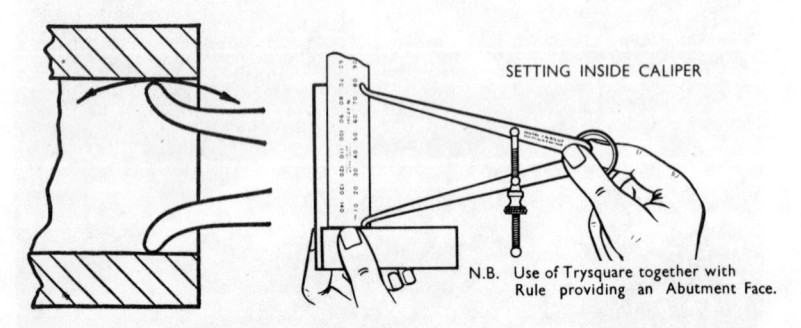

Fig. 190. Use of inside calipers. (Courtesy: Moore and Wright (Sheffield) Ltd.)

External measurements are made with a rule and the assistance of *outside calipers* which may also be either firm jointed or sprung. As the calipers are rocked over the work, the correct 'feel' is that of the pull of a strong magnet.

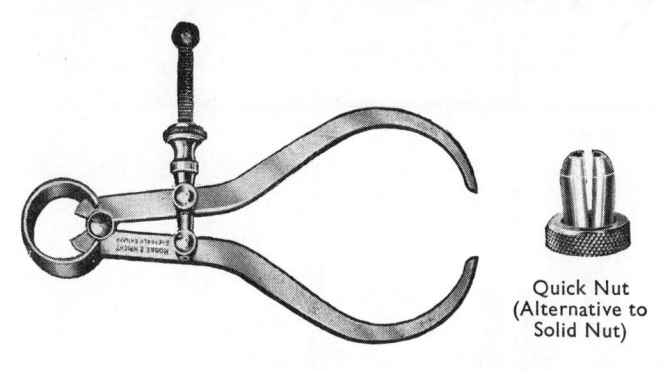

Fig. 191. Spring outside calipers. (Courtesy: Moore and Wright (Sheffield) Ltd.)

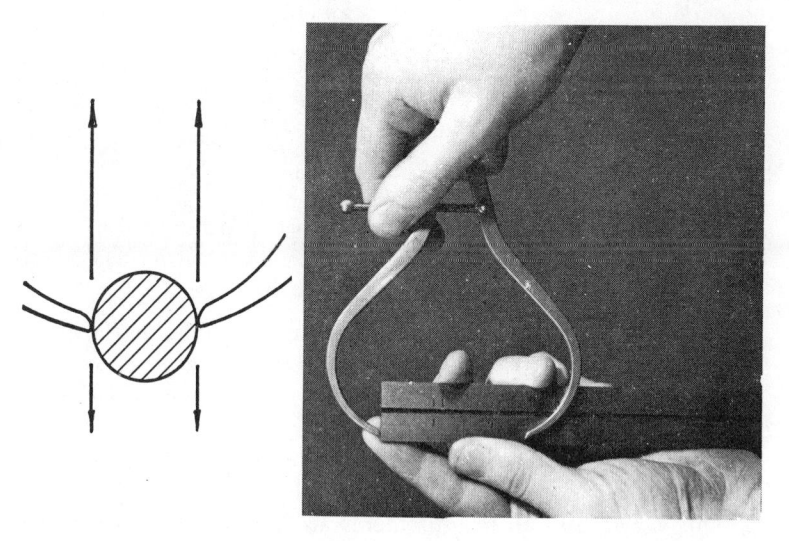

Quick Nut
(Alternative to
Solid Nut)

Fig. 192. Use of outside calipers. (Courtesy: T. S. Harrison & Sons Ltd.)

Depth gauges may either have a plain sliding rod, in which case the depth must be compared with a rule to obtain the measurement, or the depth may be read direct from a narrow steel rule as shown in Fig. 193.

Probably the most widely used precision measuring instrument is the *micrometer* which is essentially a gauge operated by a screw which has a pitch of half a millimetre. In one complete revolution the

135

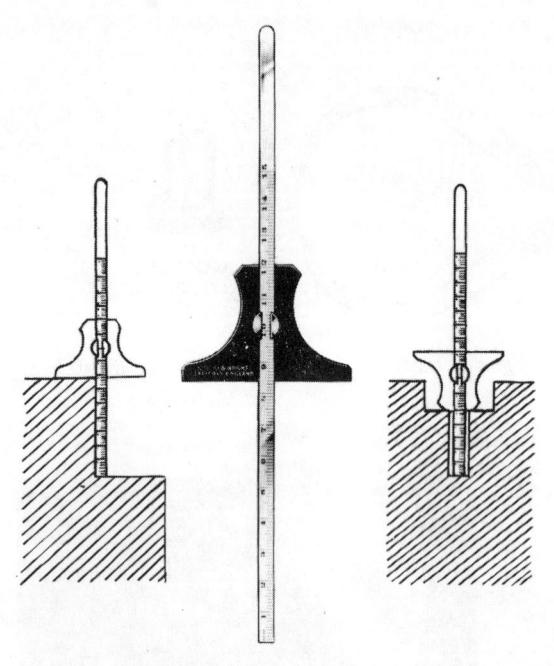

Fig. 193. Depth gauge. (Courtesy: Moore and Wright (Sheffield) Ltd.)

screw advances half a millimetre (0·5 mm). The thimble (labelled 9 in Fig. 194) which is attached to the screw has a bevelled edge divided into 50 equal divisions, each of which represents 0·01 mm (1/100 mm). On the sleeve (4 in Fig. 194) a line parallel to the axis is cut. This is called the datum (or fiducial) line, and when the micrometer is closed the line on the thimble mark 'o' coincides with it. This is zero and all measurements are calculated from it. The sleeve is graduated with two sets of lines — the set below the line reading in millimetres, and the set above in half-millimetres.

Example 1 (*Fig. 195A*)
To read the metric micrometer, first note the whole number of millimetre divisions on the sleeve (MAJOR divisions), then observe whether there is a half-millimetre visible (MINOR divisions), and lastly, read the thimble for hundredths (THIMBLE divisions), i.e. the line on the thimble coinciding with the datum line.

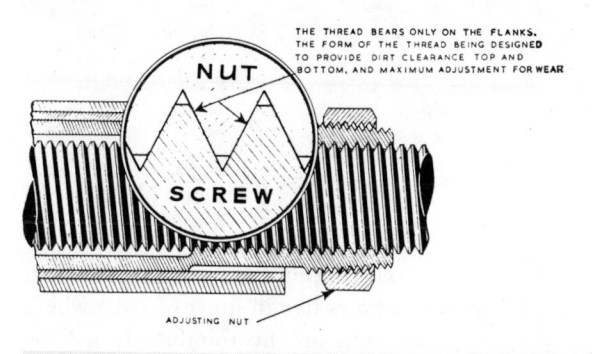

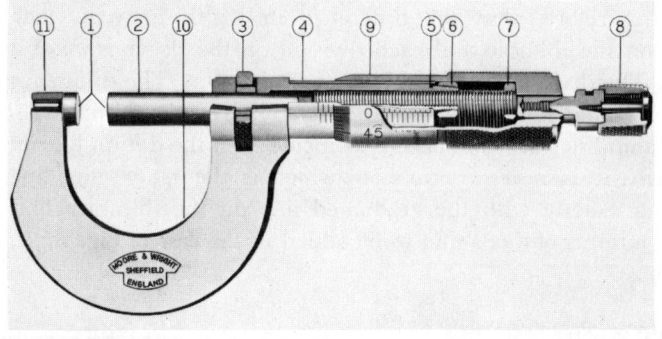

1. Anvil and spindle faces
2. Spindle
3. Locknut
4. Sleeve
5. Main nut
6. Screw adjusting nut
7. Thimble adjusting nut
8. Ratchet stop
9. Thimble
10. Frame
11. Anvil end

Fig. 194. Principal parts of a micrometer. (Courtesy: Moore and Wright (Sheffield) Ltd.)

$$\begin{aligned} \text{MAJOR Divisions} &= 10 \times 1{\cdot}00 \text{ mm} = 10{\cdot}00 \text{ mm} \\ \text{MINOR Divisions} &= 1 \times 0{\cdot}50 \text{ mm} = 0{\cdot}50 \text{ mm} \\ \text{THIMBLE Divisions} &= 16 \times 0{\cdot}01 \text{ mm} = 0{\cdot}16 \text{ mm} \end{aligned}$$

$$\text{Reading} = 10{\cdot}66 \text{ mm}$$

To read to thousandths of a millimetre (0·001 mm), the micrometer has the addition of a vernier on the sleeve, again reading in conjunction with the thimble.

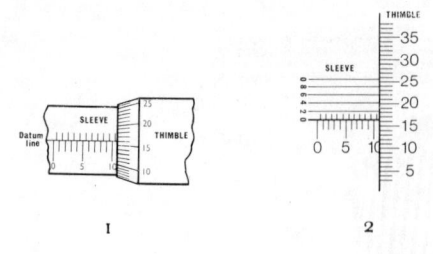

Fig. 195A. Examples 1, 2.
(Courtesy: Moore and Wright (Sheffield) Ltd.)

On the sleeve, parallel to the axis (datum line) are graduated 10 divisions (Fig. 195A, Example 2, shows five in units of two) which occupy the same space as 9 divisions on the thimble. It will be obvious, therefore, that the difference in width between each division on the thimble and each division on the sleeve is $\frac{1}{10}$ of a division. The divisions on the thimble are 0·01 mm. The difference therefore is 0·001 mm. When the graduated line on the thimble (i.e. the 0·01 mm line) does not exactly coincide with the datum line on the sleeve, it is necessary to note which is the 1st vernier line coinciding exactly with the graduated line on the thimble. This gives the number of 0·002 mm to be added in the case of Fig. 195A, Example 2.

Example 2 (*Fig. 195A*)
MAJOR Divisions   = 10 × 1·00 mm = 10·00 mm
MINOR Divisions   = 1 × 0·50 mm = 0·50 mm
THIMBLE Divisions = 16 × 0·01 mm = 0·16 mm
*VERNIER Divisions = 3 × 0·002 mm = 0·006 mm

Reading = 10·666 mm

* VERNIER line coincident with line on thimble, e.g. 3rd Division is marked 6, which can also be read directly as 0·006 mm.

For measurements larger than 13 mm the frame is made correspondingly larger up to 1800 mm, sometimes utilising an interchangeable or sliding anvil to allow a measuring range of 150 mm for each micrometer.

Inside micrometers are made as small as 25–55 mm and extra distance pieces fitted as required. Extension handles allow the measurement to be made within a confined space.

Depth gauge micrometers are made adjustable with extension rods, with a capacity from 0–300 mm.

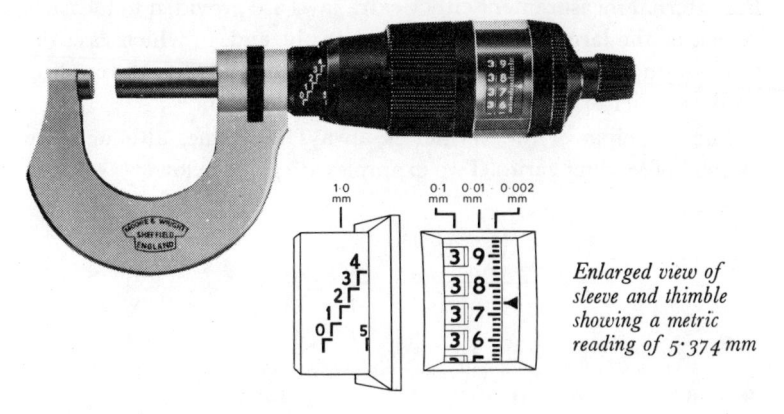

Enlarged view of sleeve and thimble showing a metric reading of 5·374 mm

Fig. 195B. Direct reading micrometer. (Courtesy: Moore and Wright (Sheffield) Ltd.)

Vernier caliper gauges are made to read to 0·05 mm and 0·02 mm, normally up to 300 mm, although 1200-mm models are available.

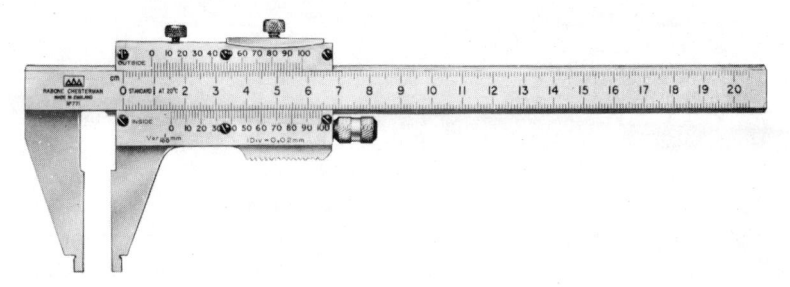

Fig. 196. Vernier caliper gauge 151 mm capacity reading to 0·05 mm. (Courtesy: Rabone Chesterman Ltd.)

Fig. 197. Vernier caliper gauge 155 mm (external) capacity reading to 0·02 mm. (Courtesy: Rabone Chesterman Ltd.)

For internal measurement either extra jaws are provided to measure direct, or the large jaws are rounded on the end, in which case the total width of the closed rounded jaws must be added to the reading on the vernier to give the correct inside measurement.

The principle of the vernier is always the same, although the method of reading varies. Two examples are given below.

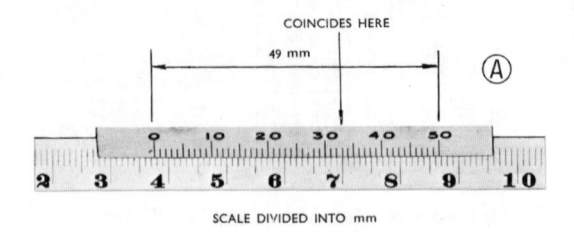

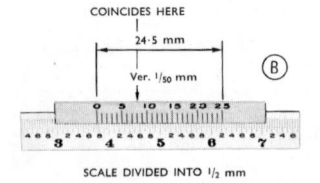

Fig. 198A and B. Vernier Scales. (Courtesy: Rabone Chesterman Ltd.)

Main scale divided into millimetres as at A (Fig. 198A)
The vernier is divided into 50 parts over a length of 49 mm; therefore, each division of the vernier will be 49 mm divided by 50 which equals 0·980 mm or 0·02 mm shorter than each division on the main scale.

The main scale reading to the left of the zero on the vernier indicates the number of whole millimetres and the line on the vernier which coincides with a line on the main scale indicates the additional 0·02 mm.

In the illustration the reading is 37·66 mm (37 mm on the main scale, plus 0·66 mm on the vernier).

Main scale divided into ½ millimetres as at B (Fig. 198B)
In this case the vernier is arranged to read on alternate lines on the main scale to facilitate the reading. It is divided into 25 parts over a length of 24·5 mm, therefore each division will be 24·5 mm divided

by 25, which equals 0·980, or 0·02 mm shorter than two divisions on the main scale.

The reading is as above but the main scale is read to the nearest ½ mm. In the illustration the reading is again 37·66 mm (37·5 mm on the main scale, plus 0·16 mm on the vernier).

Bevel Protractors are similar to the protractor shown in Fig. 145, but intended for more precise work.

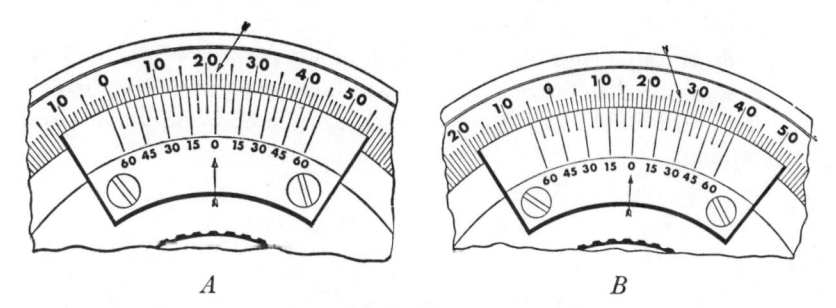

Fig. 199. Reading a vernier on a bevel protractor. (Courtesy: Moore and Wright (Sheffield) Ltd.)

Whole numbers of degrees can be read by simply taking readings with the zero line on the vernier. Where this line coincides with a line on the main scale, an exact number of whole degrees is indicated. This is illustrated in Fig. 199A where the reading is precisely 22°.

The vernier on a bevel protractor enables readings to be taken to five minutes or $\frac{1}{12}$ of a degree. Each division on the vernier is this amount shorter than two divisions on the main scale.

If the zero line on the vernier does not coincide exactly with a line on the main scale it is necessary to find the vernier line which does coincide with a main scale line; and this indicates the number of five minutes or $\frac{1}{12}$ of a degree to be added to the number of whole degrees.

To take a reading, therefore, note the number of whole degrees, and then count in the same direction the number of divisions on the vernier scale from the zero line to the first line on the vernier scale that coincides with a line on the main scale. As each of these is five minutes, multiply by five and the number of minutes to be added to the whole number of degrees will be indicated.

As an example take a reading of 17°–25′ (Fig. 199B).

It will be noted that reading in a clockwise direction the vernier zero line has moved 17° and part of a degree, and continuing to read in the same direction the fifth line on the vernier is coincident with a line on the main scale.

Multiplying by five, this gives 25 minutes to be added to the 17° already obtained. This gives a reading of 17°–25'.

It will be noted that readings can be taken in either direction, clockwise or anti-clockwise, and it is important that the readings taken on the main scale and the vernier scale are in the direction in which the vernier line has moved.

Feeler gauges with blades ranging from ·03 mm to 1·0 mm in thickness are used to measure narrow gaps and to set up cutting tools a known distance away from the work, as in lathe-work, shaping and milling.

Fig. 200. Precision feeler gauge. (Courtesy: James Chesterman & Co. Ltd.)

The depth gauge, micrometer, vernier caliper gauge and feeler gauge are all measuring instruments whilst the radius gauge, gap, pin, plug and ring gauges, and dial test indicator do not measure but compare.

To check internal and external radii, *radius gauges* are used, see Fig. 201. By holding to a light source, inaccuracies can easily be seen.

To check contours other than regular radii, a template must be made; usually sheet steel is quite suitable, see Fig. 202.

Fig. 201. Radius gauges. (Courtesy: Moore and Wright (Sheffield) Ltd.)

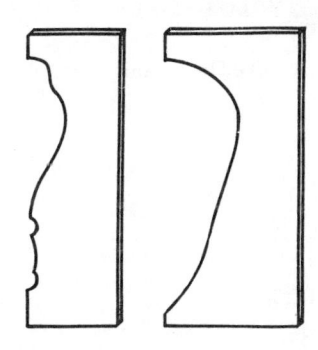

Fig. 202. Template

Gap gauges (or caliper gauges) are made for quick accurate checking of external diameters. The size may be the smallest permissible and called 'Not Go' or the largest, called 'Go'. If the 'Go' will fit over and the 'Not Go' will not, the cylinder is within the permissible limits of size (see Fig. 203). *NB*: For internal diameters the smallest permissible bore is the 'Go' and the largest is the 'Not Go'.

Fig. 203. Gap gauge (or caliper gauge)

Pin, Plug and Ring gauges, which are accurately lapped cylinders or rings, either plain or threaded, check not only the diameter but also whether the work is perfectly circular (see Fig. 204).

143

Fig. 204. Threaded plug and ring gauges. (Courtesy: The Horstmann Gear Co. Ltd.)

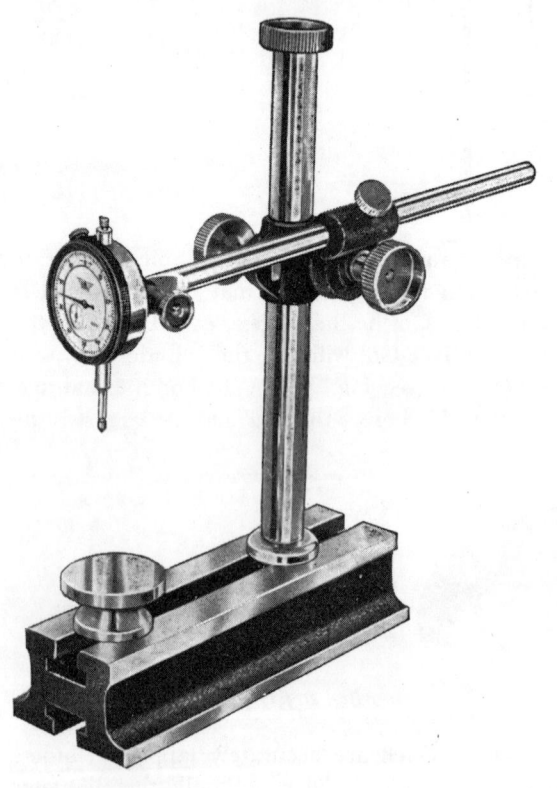

Fig. 205. Dial test indicator set up as a comparator. (Courtesy: J. E. Baty & Co. Ltd.)

BENCHWORK 145

Dial test indicators consist of a spring-loaded plunger operating a needle by a rack and pinion mechanism, and reading to ·002 mm. They are used to compare one overall size with another, test concentricity and parallelism, accurately align machine tools and many other applications, see Figs 205 and 243.

The sine bar is a bar with a straight upper surface and supported on two rollers at an exact and known distance apart. It is usually set up on a surface plate with one roller resting at a known height, on a combination of several slip gauges. Thus two sides of a right angle triangle are known and, using sine tables, the angle of the upper surface to the surface plate can be calculated (see Fig. 206).

Precision rollers and spheres can be used to facilitate the measurement of some curved and less accessible surfaces, such as measuring the width and angle of dovetail slides by using rollers (see Fig. 206).

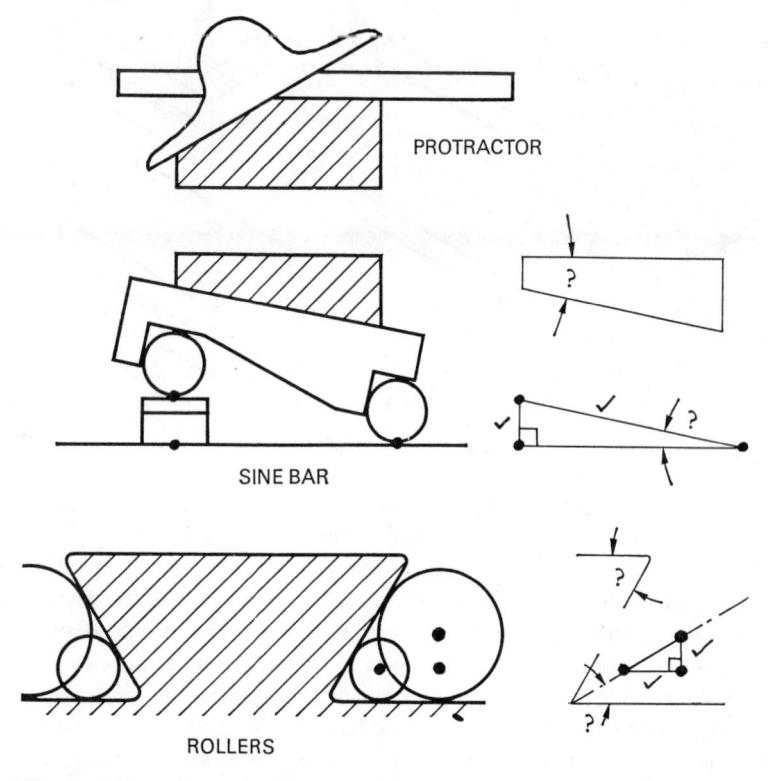

Fig. 206. Measurement of angles

All measuring instruments and gauges must be handled and stored carefully to preserve their accuracy.

8.7 Riveting

Unless the rivet size and shape are already specified in the working drawing, the necessary information is given in 4.8.

If more than one rivet is to be used, it is always sensible to mark out and drill for one rivet only. Then rivet up and drill the second hole; once two rivets have been riveted up, preferably at a distance apart, the remaining holes can be drilled. This procedure prevents the possibility of holes not being in alignment.

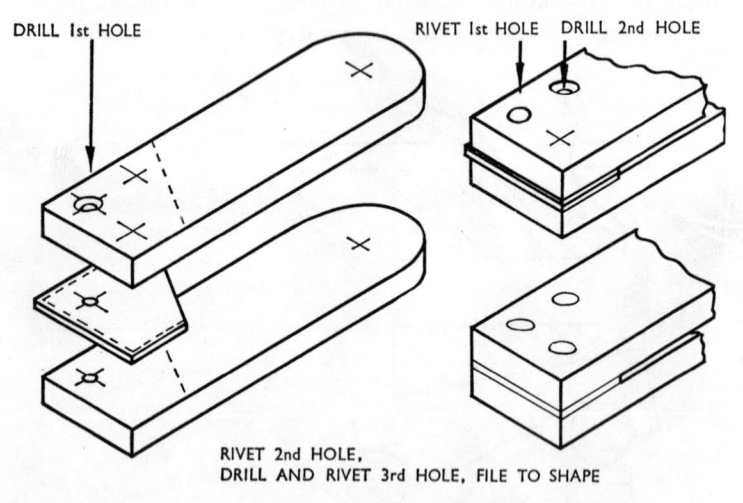

Fig. 207. *Procedure for riveting the stock of a sliding bevel*

The actual hand-riveting operation requires a dolly, set, snap and ball pein hammer. Rivets which are flat on the head, such as a full countersunk rivet can be supported by a firm flat surface, whilst a shaped head such as a round head rivet, requires a dolly, which, for the majority of cases can be an extra snap. If a standard snap cannot be used, one must be made to suit the job, using either a domed punch on red hot metal or a drill specially shaped on the end.

The pieces of metal, which should have all dirt and burrs removed are placed together and the rivet inserted. Should the plates be slightly out of alignment a very small bevel on the top of the rivet

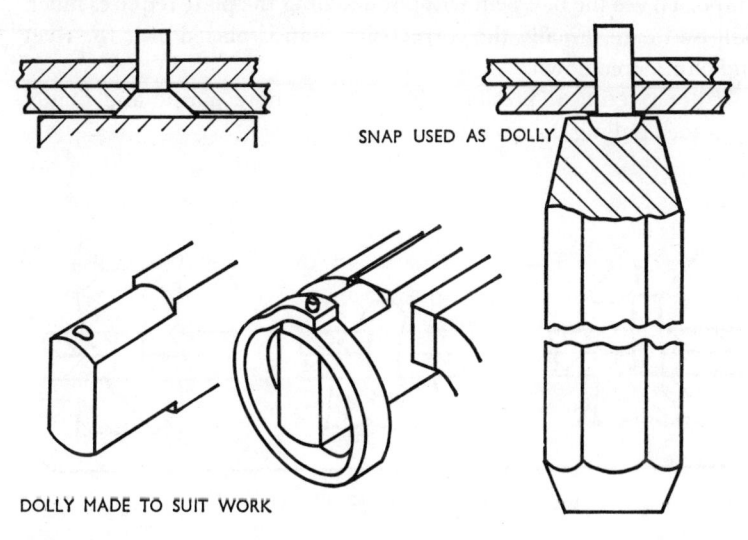

Fig. 208. Supporting the rivet

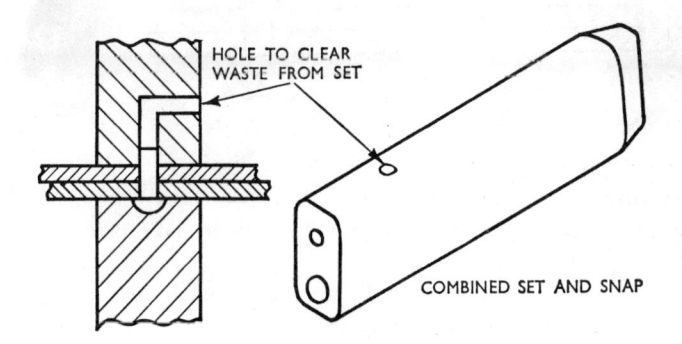

Fig. 209. Rivet set

will help to lead the rivet through. The parts with rivet inserted are placed over the snap or on large work it may be necessary for an assistant to hold the dolly against the rivet head. A set is next used to force the parts together, prior to riveting.

The ball pein hammer is next used, and an attempt should be made to work the rivet in as shown and not to produce a mushroom shape. To use the ball pein without touching the plate requires much skill and care. Finally the correct-size snap is placed over the rivet and hammered down.

If hot riveting is possible, the metal is more plastic and finally contracts, pulling the parts together.

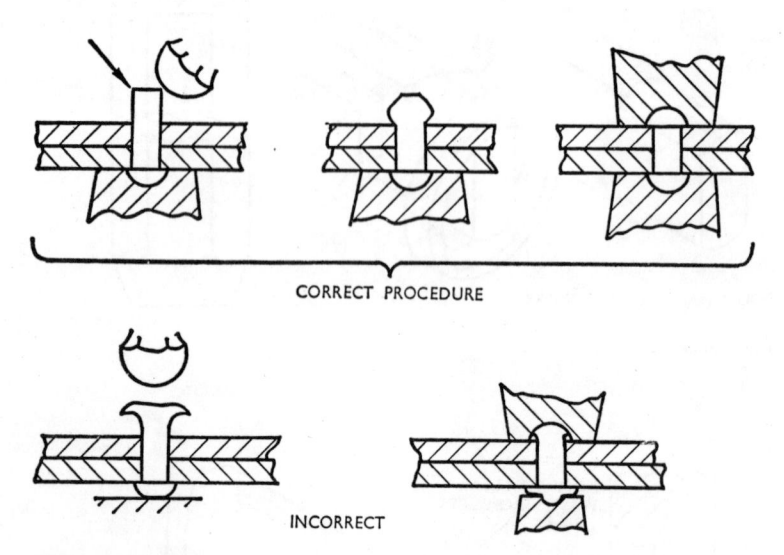

CORRECT PROCEDURE

INCORRECT

Fig. 210. Riveting

8.8 Threading

To thread an internal hole, the hole must first be drilled out to the correct 'tapping' size, see Appendix A.

Although internal threading can be accomplished by machine, most benchwork requires hand tapping only.

The first tap to be used is the taper tap, held in either a bar or chuck-type tap wrench.

The tap must be held in line with the hole and turned carefully. Once cutting has started it may be necessary to reverse occasionally to break off the metal chips, particularly if the hole is deep or the material tough. Tapping a hole open at both ends may require only the taper tap for a shallow hole, and a second and sometimes a bottoming tap for greater depths. A blind hole to be threaded to the bottom requires a bottoming tap to finish. Great care must be

TAPER TAP
4° PER SIDE

SECOND TAP
8° PER SIDE

BOTTOMING TAP
23° PER SIDE

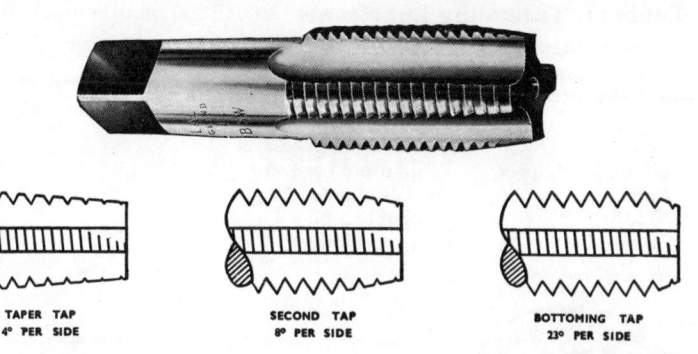

Fig. 211. Hand taps (taper, second and bottoming or plug). (Courtesy: Lehmann, Archer and Lane Ltd.)

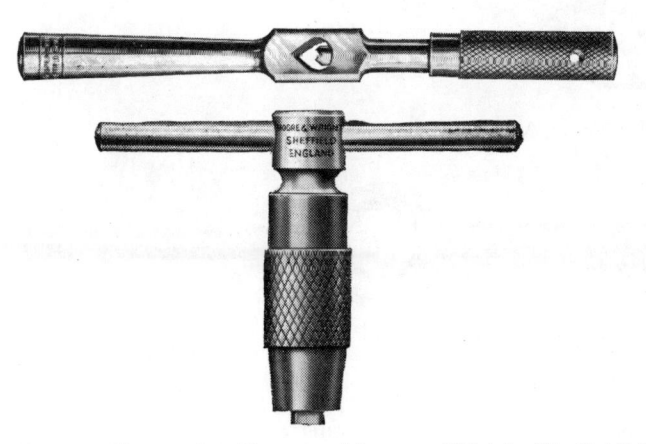

Fig. 212. Tap wrenches. (Courtesy: Moore and Wright (Sheffield) Ltd.)

taken not to overturn the tap and break it off. This can be avoided by measuring or marking the tap to the correct depth required. As the blind hole is tapped, occasionally withdraw the tap and shake out the cuttings from the hole.

To facilitate cutting, a lubricant should be used (see Table 11). To cut an external thread a die is used; this is commonly a circular split die, which can be closed or opened slightly. The die holder or stock has three screws; the centre one is pointed to locate in the split of the die and the two outer ones are blunt to locate in two depressions on either side of the split of the die.

Table 11. Threading Lubricants

Material to be tapped	Lubricant
Aluminium	Paraffin or Paraffin and Lard oil
Brass	Soluble or Light base oil
Bronze and Copper	Paraffin and Lard oil
Cast Iron	Dry or Light Soluble oil
Mild Steel	Sulphur base oil
Plastic	Dry, or cold water

(Courtesy: Lehmann, Archer and Lane Ltd.)

(Courtesy: Moore and Wright (Sheffield) Ltd.)

Fig. 213. Circular split die and die holder

The same principles that applied to the tap also apply to the die. Hold in line with the centre of the work (i.e. die holder square to work) and when cutting, only reverse in extreme circumstances, using a lubricant as suggested.

The difference lies in the fact that the die is very slightly adjustable. (*Note:* excessive adjustment will break the die.) For the first cut insert the die with the outer screws loose, and lightly tighten the centre pointed screw into the split, to open the die slightly. Then lock by tightening the outer screws.

After the first cut try the nut or work on the thread, and if too tight, take another cut, by loosening the centre screw slightly and tightening the outer screws. By this means of adjustment, the degree of tightness between threads can be regulated.

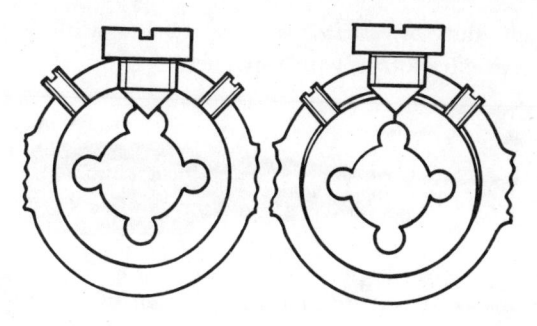

Fig. 214. Exaggerated principle of adjusting a die holder and split die

8.9 Bolting

To fasten or unfasten a nut or bolt (see 4.9), a *spanner* (or wrench) is normally used. The size is specified by 'size across flats' and increases from 7 mm to 20 mm in 1-mm increments.

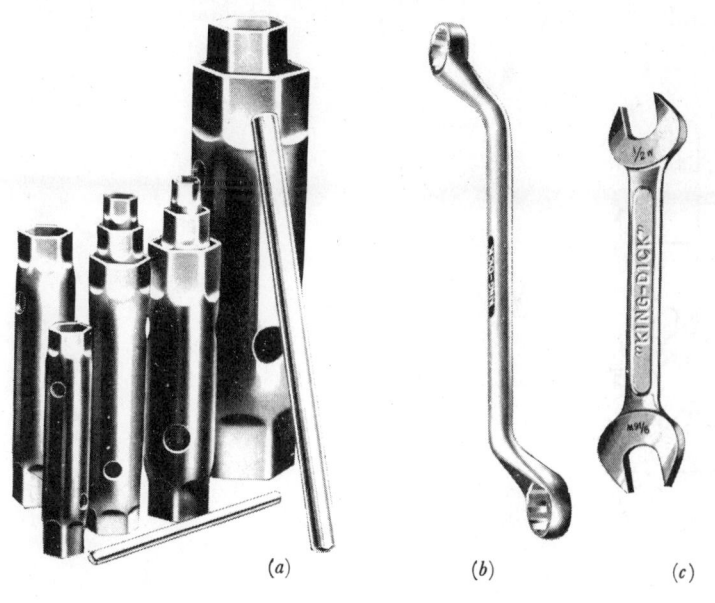

(a)   (b)   (c)

(a) *Tubular Box Spanners*
(b) *Double Offset Ring Spanner*
(c) *Double Open-ended Spanner*

Fig. 215. Spanners. (Courtesy: Abingdon King Dick Ltd.)

An engineers' heavy duty *screwdriver* is shown below with a hexagon provided to give extra torque with a spanner.

Fig. 216. Heavy duty screwdriver. (Courtesy: Moore and Wright (Sheffield) Ltd.)

To remove screws or bolts with the head broken off, use a *screw extractor*. Begin by drilling an appropriately sized hole down the centre of the bolt, insert the correct size screw extractor and with the aid of an ordinary tap wrench start a left-hand twist. The tapered spirals of the extractor grip the sides of the drilled hole and unscrew the broken part, leaving the threads of the work intact.

Fig. 217. Using a screw extractor

9

Drilling

9.1 Drilling Machines

Holes up to 8 mm diameter can be drilled using a *hand drill* as shown; for larger holes the handle is replaced by a breast plate at right angles to the drill; this is called a *breast drill* because extra pressure can be put on the drill by the weight of the operator's body.

Fig. 218. Hand drill. (Courtesy: C. & J. Hampton Ltd.)

For larger holes up to 25 mm diameter, the same mechanism can be used in a *hand-powered drilling machine*. The spindle holding the chuck can be screwed down into the work while it is still revolving, using the same principle as the modern power-driven machine described later.

Even larger holes up to 50 mm diameter can be drilled by hand, using a *drilling pillar* and *ratchet brace*.

Fig. 219. Ratchet brace and drilling pillar

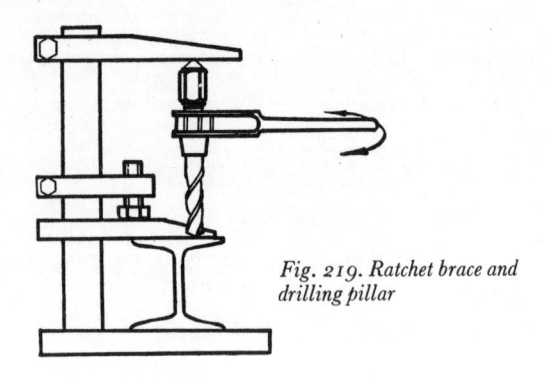

Power-driven sensitive drilling machines may be either floor (pedestal) or bench models, depending on the length of the column.

The construction and operation will be best understood by reference to Fig. 220, showing an exploded view, intended for spare parts identification.

In accordance with modern practice, the drive is from an individual electric motor (4). By changing the position of vee belt (3), the spindle pulley (12) can be driven at five different speeds. This is directly coupled to the driving sleeve (48) which rotates the spindle (58), incorporating at the lower end a taper socket. The upper half of the spindle (58) is splined, thus allowing movement up and down whilst still being rotated.

The up and down ('feed') movement is made by the sensitive star hand wheel (14, 15, 19) which rotates the quill activating gear (45). Using a 'rack and pinion' mechanism, the gear (45) moves the quill (54) up and down enabling the drill to be fed into the work. If the pressure is removed from the hand wheel, the return spring (59) will raise the quill (54) and spindle (58). A locking handle (31) allows the height and rotated position of the table to be adjusted. Locking bushes (66 and 67) can be loosened to allow the complete head to rotate on the column (44). Locknuts (17) and scale (18) act as a depth stop.

To increase the number of spindle speeds a gear box may be added, operated by a hand lever on the side of the machine.

Work which cannot be positioned under a drilling machine must be drilled using a portable drill. For speed and ease an electrically powered drill can be used, applying body pressure as for the breast drill.

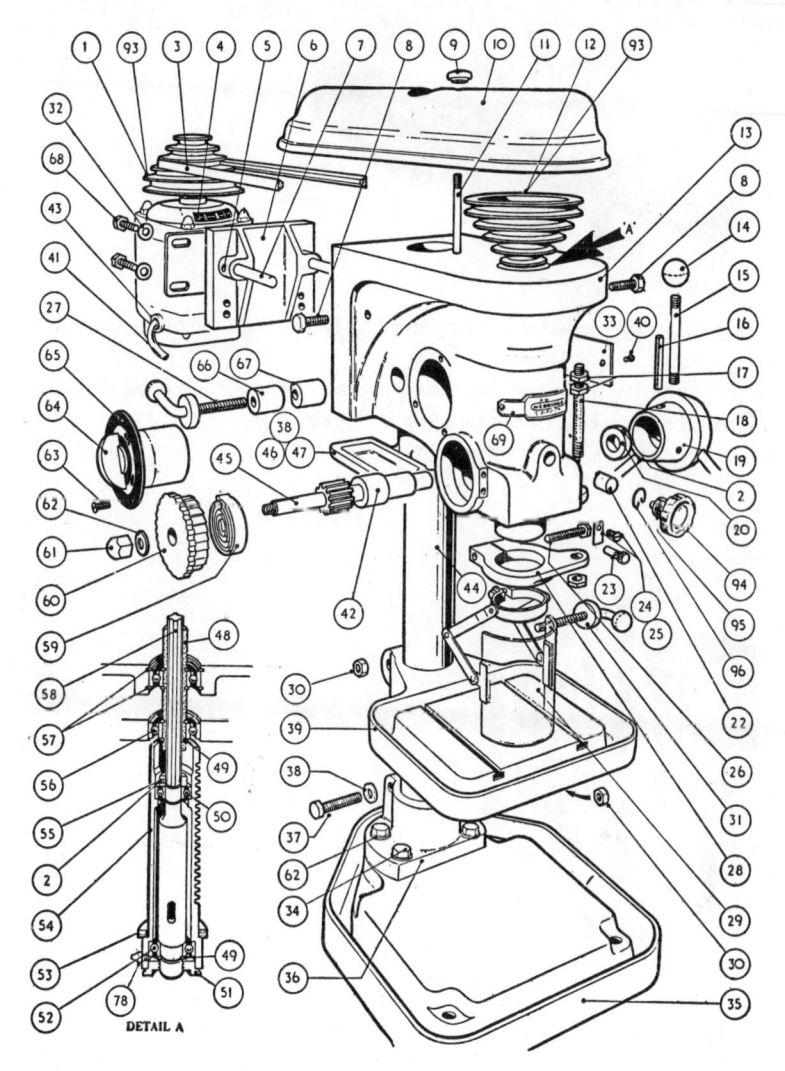

Fig. 220. *Exploded view of a power-driven sensitive drilling machine.* (Courtesy: W. J. Meddings Ltd.)

Drill chucks may either be threaded to thread directly on to the machine spindle or have a tapered hole. An *arbor* or adaptor is fitted into this tapered hole with an ISO Morse taper to fit the machine spindle (see Appendix A).

155

Fig. 221. Arbor for drill chuck. (Courtesy: The Jacobs Manufacturing Co. Ltd.)

The chuck itself may either have a plain bearing for light duty or be fitted with a ball thrust bearing for heavy duty.

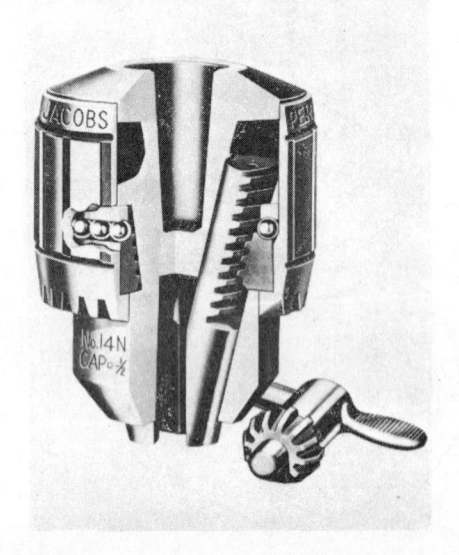

Fig. 222. Drill chuck fitted with ball thrust bearing. (Courtesy: The Jacobs Manufacturing Co. Ltd.)

9.2 Methods of Holding Work

The majority of work pieces to be drilled can be gripped in a machine vice. The particular feature of this vice is the provision of slots for holding down bolts and a strong and rigid construction.

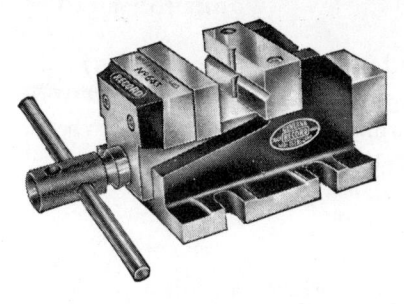

(Courtesy: C. & J. Hampton Ltd.)

(Courtesy: W. J. Meddings Ltd.)

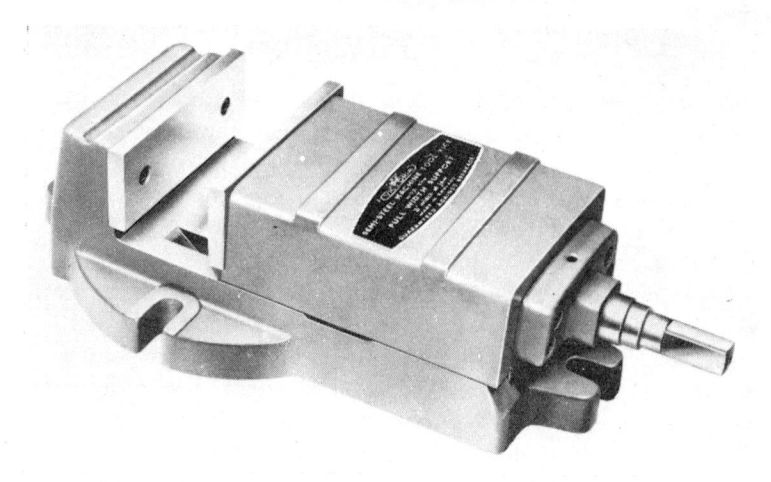

(Courtesy: B. Elliott (Machinery) Ltd.)

Fig. 223. Three types of machine vice

Sheetmetalwork might be gripped in hand vices, see Fig. 157, and supported on a wooden block. Castings or irregularly shaped work might be held directly on to the drilling table by holding down bolts, perhaps in conjunction with angle plates, vee blocks, jacks and miscellaneous packing, see Fig. 332.

9.3 Drills

A drill which can be made in the workshop to suit a particular purpose is the *flat drill*.

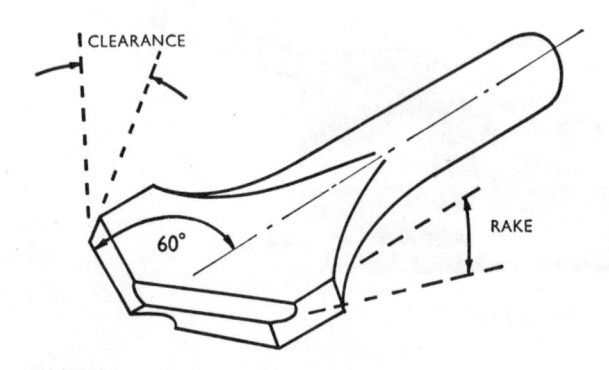

Fig. 224. Flat drill

The most commonly used drill is the *twist drill*, made of either carbon steel or high speed steel. The shank may have a morse taper shank as shown or a straight shank, in which case it is often called a 'jobber's drill'. The stock sizes increase from 0·32 mm to 1·00 mm by increments of either 0·02 or 0·03 mm, to 3·00 mm by 0·05 mm, to 14·00 mm by 0·10 mm, to 32·00 mm by 0·25 mm.

To produce the perfect drill point, the following must be correct: point and chisel angles, initial and total clearance and concentricity.

On a correctly ground drill the clearance angles increase gradually from the periphery to the chisel edge. On all sizes a chisel edge angle of 130° ensures correct clearance; the clearance at the periphery should decrease as the diameter of the drill increases.

A 3 mm diameter drill would require a periphery clearance angle of about 20° and a 12 mm diameter drill about 10°.

Grinding inaccuracies reduce cutting efficiency and produce oversize or irregularly shaped holes.

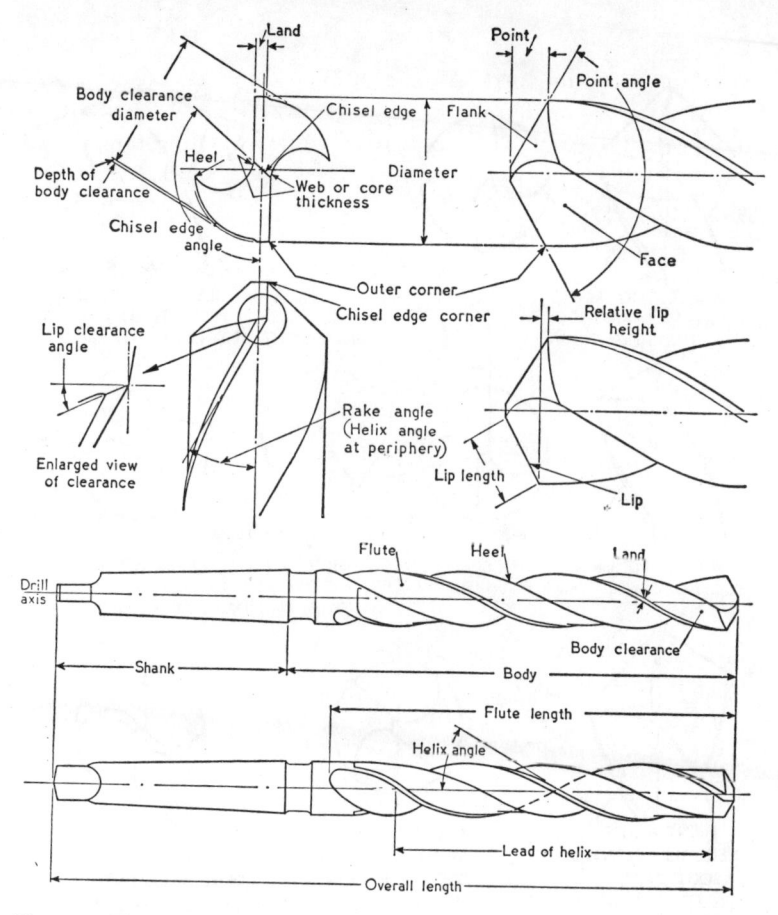

Fig. 225. Twist drill nomenclature in accordance with BS 328:1959. (Courtesy: British Standards Institution)

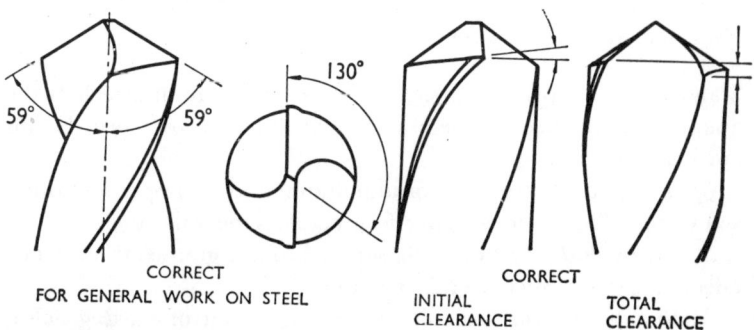

Fig. 226. Point grinding of drills

159

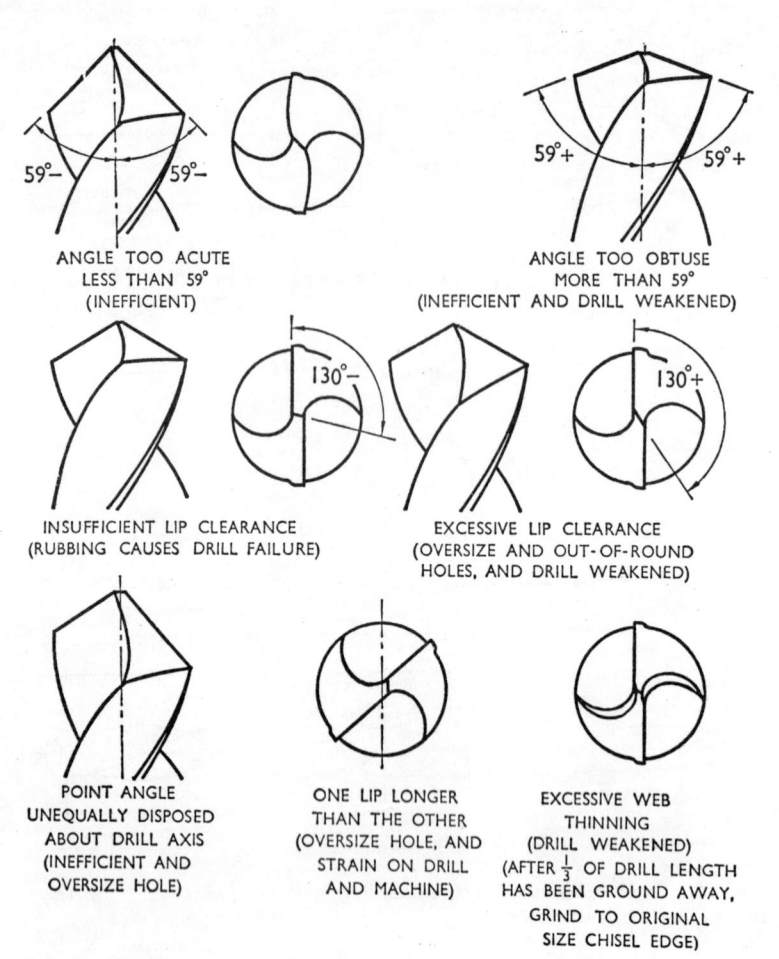

Fig. 227. Effects of incorrect grinding

Standard twist drills are designed for drilling iron and steel. If the quantity of one special type of work warrants the cost, special drills are available.

Quick helix drills are used for aluminium alloys, copper and other soft metals. The quick helix in effect increases the 'rake angle'.

Slow helix drills for brass, phosphor, bronze, gunmetal, etc. The effect here is to reduce the rake angle.

Multi-flute core drills for enlarging the diameter of existing holes; four-flute for drilled holes and three-flute for punched or cored holes.

QUICK HELIX DRILL

SLOW HELIX DRILL

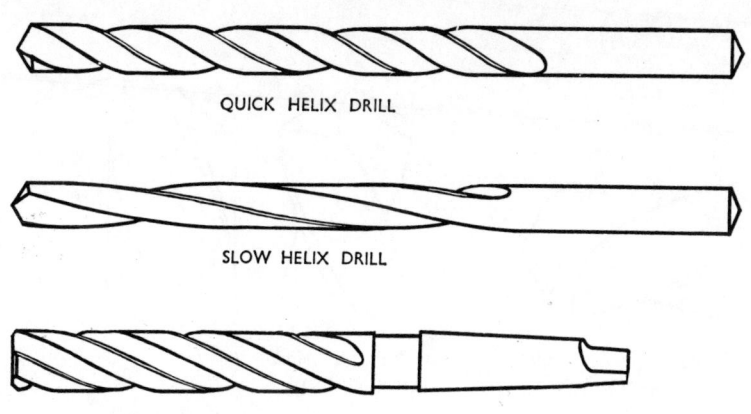

MULTI-FLUTE CORE DRILL

Fig. 228. Special drills

Where conditions demand a special drill and the amount of work does not warrant one, standard drills can be modified to improve their performance.

Hard metals A more obtuse (flatter) point will help.

Thin metal sections Drilling out-of-round can usually be prevented by thinning the chisel edge almost to a point. Heavily burred underside can be minimised by making the point angle more obtuse.

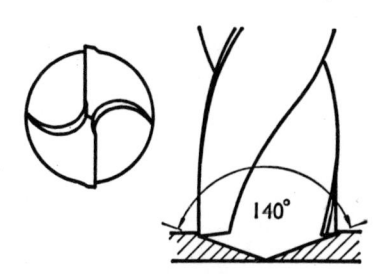

Fig. 229. Modifications to a standard drill for drilling thin metal

Soft or open grained cast iron can be drilled more efficiently if the cutting corner is ground to an inclusive angle of 90° for about a third of the lip length.

Brass requires a rake angle of about 15°, which aids chip breaking.

161

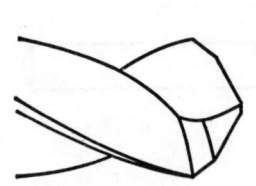

Fig. 230. Modification for drilling cast iron

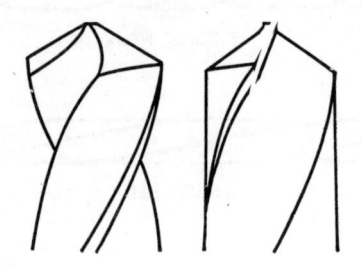

Fig. 231. Modification for drilling brass

The drill cutting speed should be calculated in exactly the same manner as for lathework, see 10.10. The speed may be reduced for deep holes, up to half normal. For cutting fluids and coolants, see 11.5.

If it is possible to regulate the feed of the drill into the work, calculate feed from the following table.

Table 12. Feeds for High-speed Steel Twist Drills

Drill diameter, mm	*Feed/Rev., mm*
1·6–3·0	0·04–0·06
3·0–4·0	0·05–0·10
4·0–5·5	0·075–0·15
5·5–8·0	0·10–0·20
8·0–11·0	0·15–0·25
11·0–14·5	0·20–0·30

As previously mentioned under marking out (see 8.1), holes which must be accurately located require, in addition to the centre punch mark, a circle with four dot punch marks. Centre the work under the drill and start drilling, but stop before the drill has reached say

DRILLING

one-third of its final cutting diameter. If the drilling is not equidistant from all four dot punch marks use a diamond pointed chisel to draw the drill over in the correct direction.

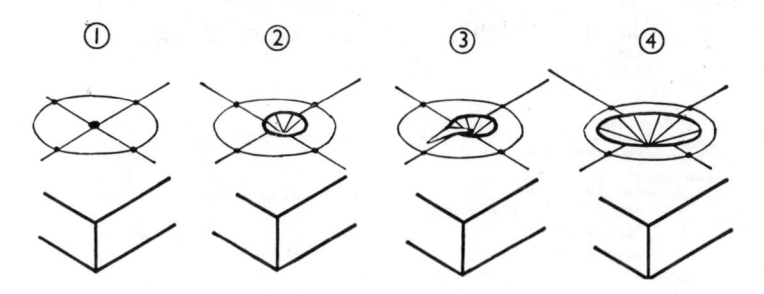

Fig. 232. Correcting an out-of-centre drill

9.4 Reaming

To finish a hole perfectly round, straight and to size, with a good surface, the hole is drilled undersize and then either a *machine* or *hand reamer* is used.

For steel, the drilled hole should have an allowance of approximately 0·3 mm up to 12 mm diameter, and approximately 0·4 mm to 0·8 mm for larger sizes.

The hand reamer is held in a tapwrench and rotated, allowing the reamer to cut and feed itself into the work, with the slightest of pressure. The flutes may be either straight or helical; and in both cases, care should be taken not to reverse the direction of rotation, as this will cause rapid wear to the cutting edges, whilst a helical reamer will screw itself into the hole. Continue to rotate in the same direction even when withdrawing the reamer from the hole.

9.5 Countersinking, Spotfacing and Counterboring

Cutters for *countersinking* may have either a straight or morse taper shank, and the cutting angle is normally either a 60° or 90° included angle. If this is unobtainable, a standard twist drill can be ground to the required angle and the rake reduced to zero, see Fig. 234.

Spotfacing cutters are used to provide flat circular seatings on rough or uneven surfaces at right angles to existing holes.

Counterboring cutters increase the diameter of existing holes.

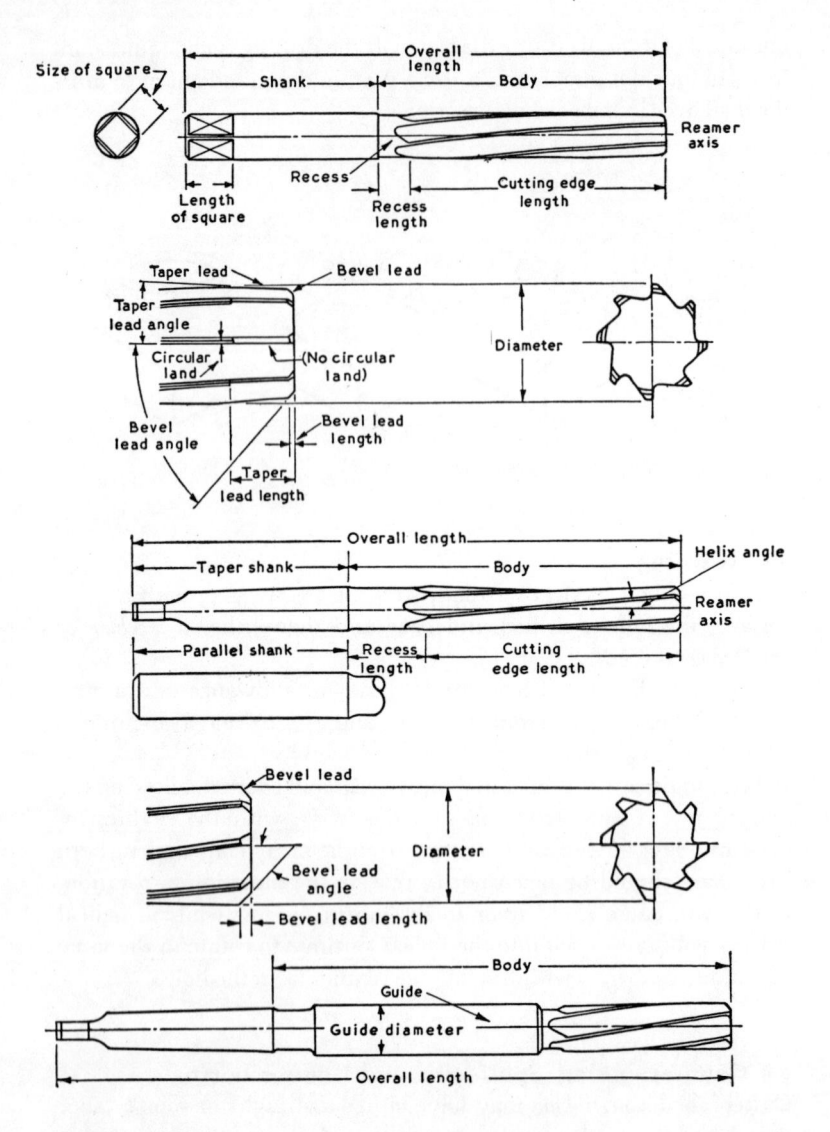

Fig. 233. Reamer nomenclature in accordance with BS 122, Part 1 : 1953. (Courtesy: British Standards Institution)

Fig. 234. *Countersinking cutter*

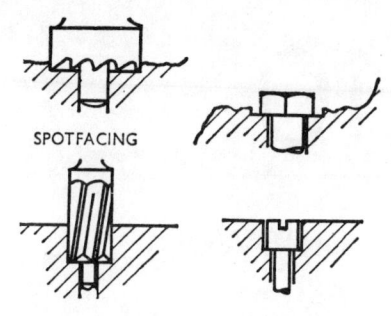

Fig. 235. *Spotfacing and counterboring*

10

Lathework

10.1 Lathes

Lathes rotate material against a cutting tool. The earliest were motivated by a thong wrapped around the article, later models by a treadle wheel, later still by overhead shafting from a single power source and belts to each machine, and today the vast majority of lathes are driven by individual electric motors. The size and types of lathe vary considerably from watchmakers' lathes turning shafts smaller than a pin, to huge lathes turning work one or more metres in diameter.

In Europe the size of a lathe is described by the height of its centre (H) or radius. In the USA the size is described by swing (S) or diameter and bed length (B).

A popular size of lathe, with a centre height of 115 mm and distance between centres (D) of 600 mm, would have a swing of 230 mm and the bed length would be about 1200 mm.

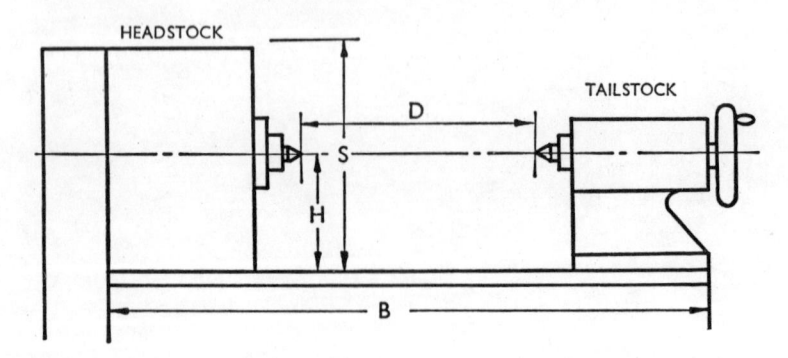

Fig. 236. *Lathe size and capacity*

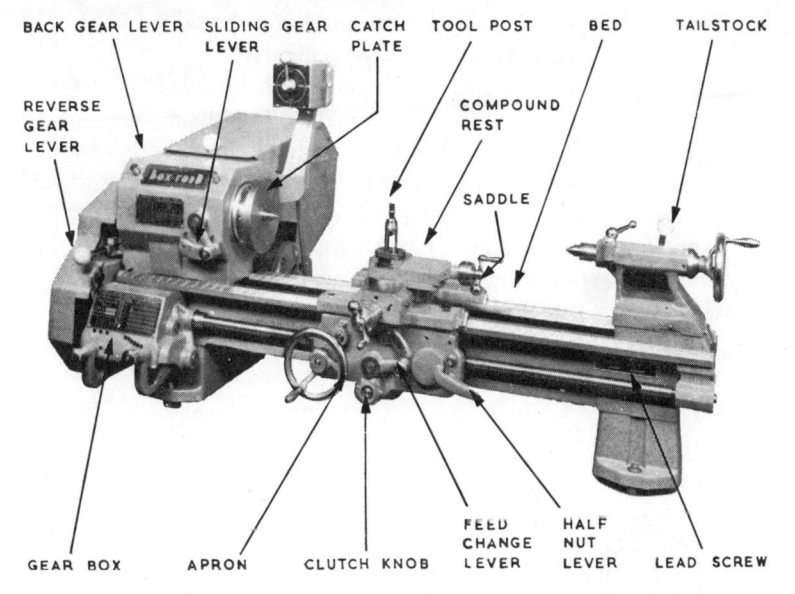

Fig. 237. The main parts of a lathe. (Courtesy: T. S. Harrison & Sons Ltd.)

Fig. 238. Inside of apron. (Courtesy: T. S. Harrison & Sons Ltd.)

For accurate and sustained work the lathe should be level on a solid floor, and cleaned and lubricated regularly.

The *bed* of a lathe is a heavy casting, with inverted 'V' ways to locate accurately the headstock, carriage and tailstock.

By turning the apron hand wheel, a pinion in mesh with a rack on the bed, moves the carriage. The more expensive lathes are fitted with a *leadscrew* for screw cutting and a *feedshaft* (a plain shaft with a keyway) for imparting feed motion to the carriage. This is often modified by having a keyway in the leadscrew, as shown in Fig. 238, driving a worm which powers longitudinal and cross-feeds. The half nut lever for screwcutting can only be used when the feed mechanism is in neutral.

The feed motion can be reversed as shown in Fig. 239 and Fig. 315.

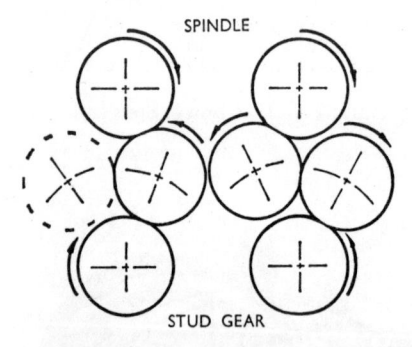

Fig. 239. Tumbler gear reversing mechanism

The *headstock* houses the *spindle* which is hollow with a morse taper hole and external screw thread on one end, and a pinion for driving the leadscrew and feedshaft on the other, see 10.13. The spindle speed may be varied either by an all gear mechanism or by a stepped pulley and back gear.

For the highest revolutions per minute of the spindle and work, the back gear is moved out of mesh, the belt moved to drive from large to small pulley and the pin on the large gear wheel engaged with the pulley. For the lowest r.p.m., the pin is withdrawn, the drive from small to large pulley and the back gear is engaged. Never attempt to engage the back gear whilst the spindle is revolving.

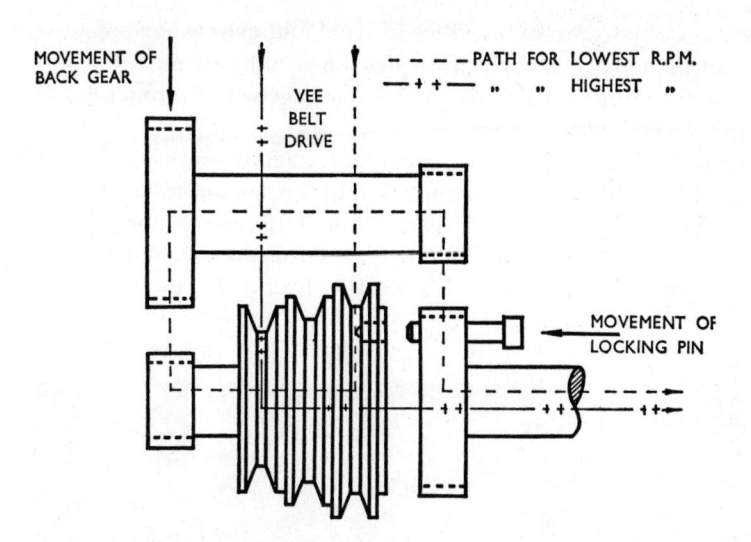

Fig. 240. Principle of pulley and back-gear drive

10.2 Self-centring Chuck

This chuck has 3 jaws located on a scroll, so that as the scroll is rotated, the jaws move equal amounts in or out.

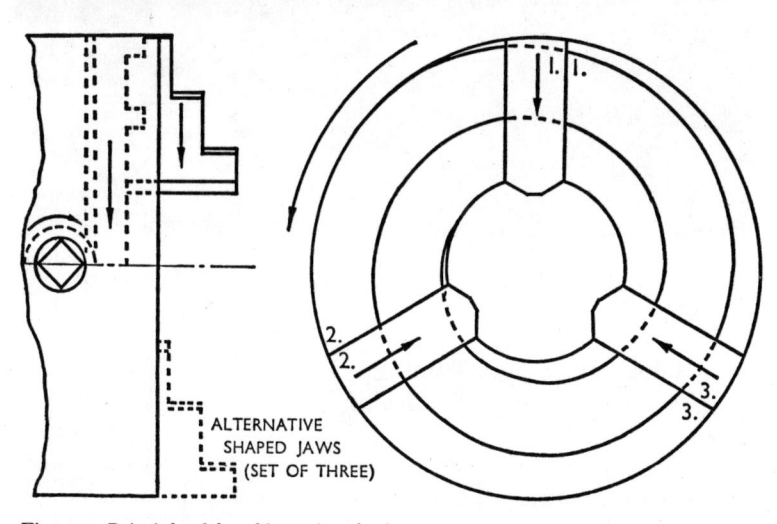

Fig. 241. Principle of the self-centring chuck

Two sets of jaws are required for internal and external gripping. It should be noted that each jaw is machined to locate on a different part of the scroll; when replacing jaws, engage with the outer scroll, in the correct order.

This chuck will quickly grip round or hexagonal work in a central position, but once work has been taken out, it can never be replaced with accuracy of more than say 0·1 mm. Therefore the major uses of this chuck are for work which may be finished at one setting, and for preliminary work, such as centre drilling before mounting between centres, see 10.4.

Fig. 242. Round work held in a self-centring chuck. (Courtesy: T. S. Harrison & Sons Ltd.)

10.3 Independent Jaw Chuck

This chuck has four jaws, each independent of the other and reversible.

It is capable of firmly holding square, round or irregular shapes in either a concentric or an eccentric position, and the work may be set up as accurately as required.

LATHEWORK

To centre round work, first position using the concentric rings on the chuck as a guide; then revolve against a piece of chalk to mark the side furthest off centre.

For accurate centring of clean round work use a sensitive dial indicator which will show eccentricity to 0·002 mm as the work is revolved slowly by hand.

Before machining, securely tighten all jaws.

Fig. 243. Dial test indicator. (Courtesy: J. E. Baty & Co. Ltd.)

Fig. 244. Centring work in chuck, with dial indicator. (Courtesy: T. S. Harrison & Sons Ltd.)

Eccentric work should be marked out and a centre punch mark made for the centre of the turning, drilling, etc. The work may be set approximately to centre, by using the tailstock centre as a guide. For more accurate work a centre finder may be used, which magnifies the error several times.

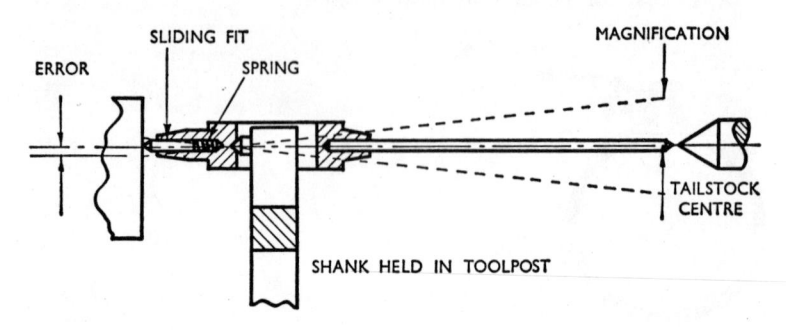

Fig. 245. Centre finder

Before mounting a chuck on the lathe spindle, clean and oil the threads and mating surfaces. Screw the chuck on by hand, without over-tightening.

To remove a chuck, engage the back gear and place a wooden block between the chuck jaw and the rear of the bed. Turn the pulley by hand, and when loosened remove the chuck carefully with both hands. A piece of wood may be placed over the bedway as a safeguard against dropping the chuck.

To hold drills, reamers and taps, etc., in both the headstock and tailstock spindles a *drill chuck* is used, see Figs 221, 222 and 246.

10.4 Centres
Work turned between centres may be taken out and either the ends reversed or replaced as before, with reasonable accuracy.

Figure 247 shows how the headstock centre is held in a taper-reducing sleeve, both of which may have a 'witness' mark to line up with a similar mark on the spindle nose. As this centre revolves with the work it is called the 'live' centre and is often unhardened in order that it may be lightly turned to ensure absolute concentricity. The tailstock centre is called the 'dead' centre because it is stationary. It is always hardened and should be kept lubricated to prevent

Fig. 246. Drill chuck located in tailstock. (Courtesy: T. S. Harrison & Sons Ltd.)

overheating. An alternative to the tailstock centre is the half-centre which is used to allow the tool to cut up to the centre of the work.

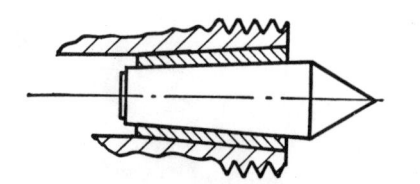

Fig. 247. Headstock centre and sleeve 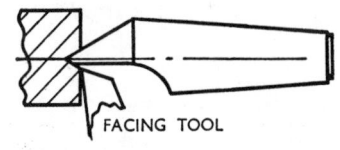   *Fig. 248. Half-centre*

Worn or damaged hardened centres must be reground. This may be done using an electric grinding attachment in place of the tool post.

To prepare the work either find the centre, see 8.1, or if suitable, grip in the self-centring chuck and face; then drill using a combination centre drill. Work between 10 mm and 25 mm diameter requires

173

Fig. 249. Grinding a 60° centre in the lathe. (Courtesy: T. S. Harrison & Sons Ltd.)

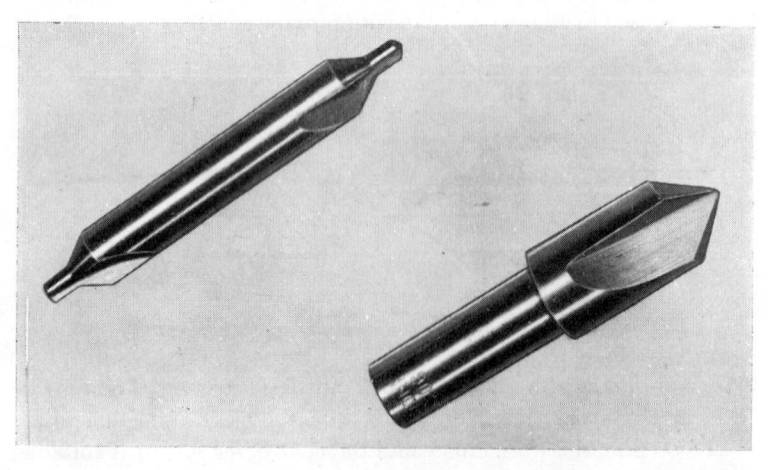

Fig. 250. Combination centre drill and 90° centre reamer. (Courtesy: T. S. Harrison & Sons Ltd.)

a drill of 6 mm diameter body, to leave a tapering shoulder 2 mm wide. Set the spindle speed to a high rev. per min. and take great care, withdrawing the tool frequently, to clear chips of metal.

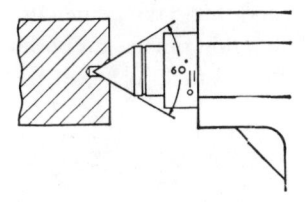

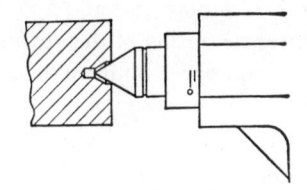

Fig. 251. Correctly drilled centre hole. (Courtesy: T. S. Harrison & Sons Ltd.)

Fig. 252. Centre hole drilled too deep. (Courtesy: T. S. Harrison & Sons Ltd.)

Before inserting the centres, thoroughly clean the centres, holes and sleeve. Unless the centres are known to be in alignment, they must be checked. Either bring the two centres together or examine marks on the end of the tailstock, see Fig. 253. Loosen the tailstock clamp lever, and by adjusting two side screws the tailstock centre may be set roughly in alignment. When making the rough adjustment, note which screws move the tailstock to left or right; this varies with different makes of lathe.

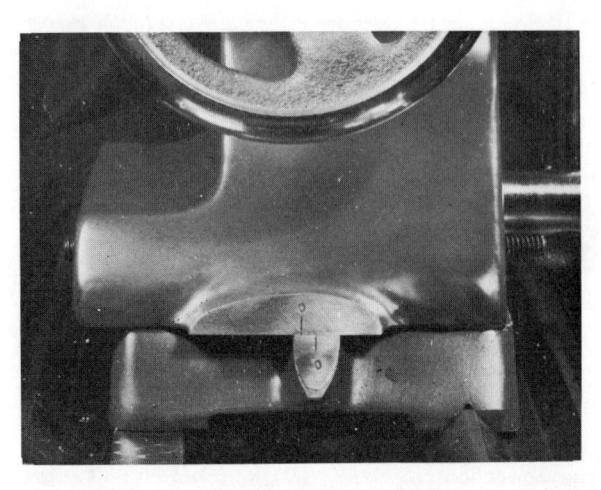

Fig. 253. Tailstock body offset. (Courtesy: Boxford Machine Tools Ltd.)

One method of aligning the centres accurately is to hold a parallel mandrel (about 25 mm diameter) between centres, mount a dial indicator in the toolpost and check for no variation over the length of the mandrel. Another method is to turn two collars on a shaft (about 40 mm diameter and 250 mm long) and then take a fine cut with the same setting of the cutting tool. Use a micrometer on both ends and compare. Both methods enable the tailstock to be set to within 0·025 mm.

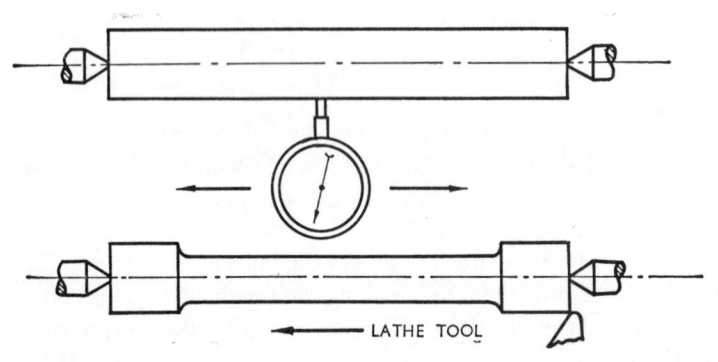

Fig. 254. Accurate methods of aligning centres

Before mounting between centres, secure either a *cranked lathe carrier* or *dog* to the work, driven by the *catch* or *driving plate*, as shown in Fig. 265, or a *straight lathe carrier* driven by a *pin*, see Fig. 257.

Fig. 255. Cranked lathe carrier (Dog) (Courtesy: T. S. Harrison & Sons Ltd.)

Fig. 256. Straight lathe carrier (Dog). (Courtesy: T. S. Harrison & Sons Ltd.)

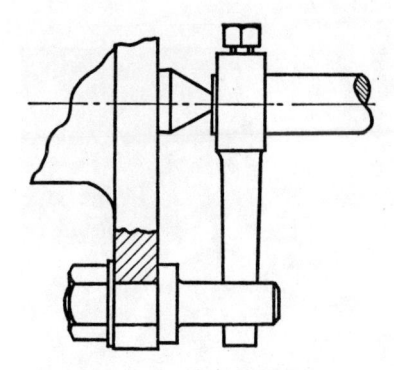

Fig. 257. Driving pin

When mounting the work, be sure to lubricate the centre hole running on the tailstock centre. Adjust the centre to have the minimum of overhang from the tailstock body before locking the body to the bed. The tailstock centre should be firm against the work; if the work is held too tightly it overheats and quickly volatilises the lubricant, probably damaging the centre; if held too loosely it cuts unevenly and may fly out. As the work becomes hot when turning and consequently expands, stop and adjust the tailstock.

10.5 Face Plate

This is a plate screwed on to the spindle nose with radial slots or various holes on its machined face (Fig. 258). Work which is difficult or impossible to hold by any other means can be securely bolted directly or indirectly to the face plate. If the work is to be set to run true to a machined surface use a dial indicator, or for a centre punch mark use a centre finder.

When starting to mount the work it may be found to be easier to work on the bench. A piece of paper between the face plate and the work will help minimise slipping. Care should be taken to support the work with packing if distortion is likely when clamping. If the work is off centre, balance weights should be securely bolted opposite the mass of metal.

10.6 Mandrels

Work which has previously been bored can often only be finished by using a mandrel. A mandrel will hold a bored hole true to the axis of the lathe.

Fig. 258. Offset hole being bored on the face plate. (Courtesy: T. S. Harrison & Sons Ltd.)

Work with a finished hole can be held on a *standard lathe mandrel*, which has a slight taper of 1 in 2000, and which can be bought hardened and tempered in various sizes from 5 mm to 32 mm diameter.

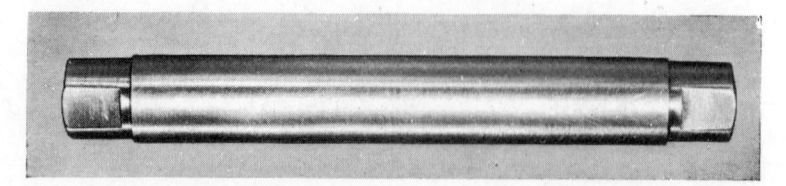

Fig. 259. A lathe mandrel. (Courtesy: T. S. Harrison & Sons Ltd.)

The mandrel and hole must be clean and oiled before pressing together. If possible, arrange for the work to be driven by a face plate or other means, rather than rely entirely on the friction

LATHEWORK 179

between work and mandrel; this is especially true for large-diameter work.

For many jobs in the workshop, *special mandrels* must be made. Some may be plain with a slight taper, as in Fig. 259, or may be shouldered and held by a nut and washer.

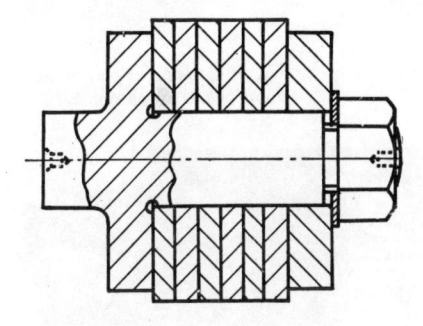

Fig. 260. Nut mandrel

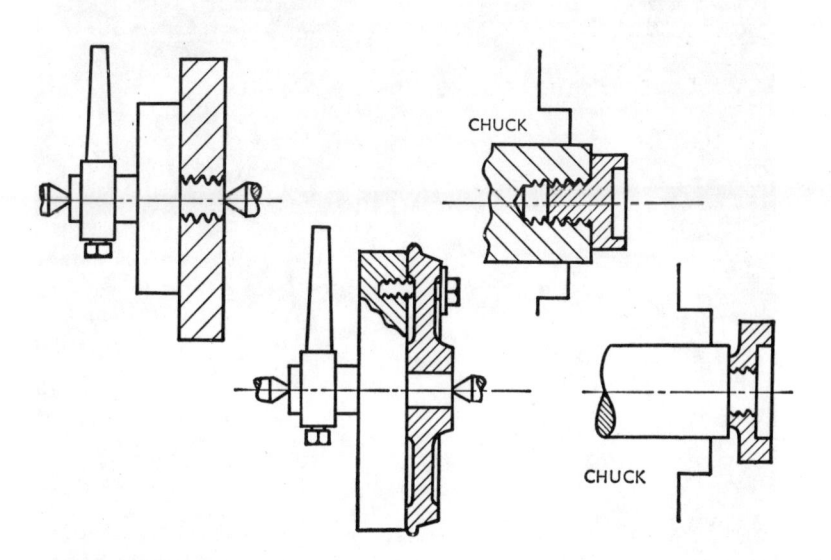

Fig. 261. Special mandrels

Stub mandrels are held in the chuck of a lathe, and once removed cannot be replaced accurately. Some articles can be made more quickly and economically by utilising part of the work as a stub mandrel. A typical example is the plumb bob.

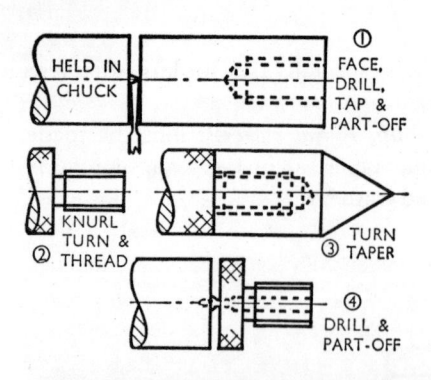

Fig. 262. Utilising part of the plumb bob as a stub mandrel

Fig. 263. Fixed steady attached to lathe bed. (Courtesy: T. S. Harrison & Sons Ltd.)

10.7 Steadies

To support either long slender work or work which cannot be supported by the tailstock centre, two types of steady are used.

The *fixed steady* is bolted to the lathe bed in a suitable position, and the top half is hinged to swing up and back to allow the work to be set up. The top is clamped down and the three jaws pushed in by screws to just support the work, but not deflect it; the jaws are then locked in position. The point of contact between jaws and work is then well lubricated and the work turned by hand to be sure it revolves freely, see Fig. 263.

The *travelling steady* is fixed to the carriage and travels along

Fig. 264. Travelling steady attached to lathe saddle. (Courtesy: T. S. Harrison & Sons Ltd.)

preventing slender work from springing away from the tool. The two jaws bear on the finished diameter and must therefore be reset just after each cut has started. The travelling steady allows work to be machined over the full length in one cut, whereas with the fixed steady only part can be machined, see Fig. 264.

Sometimes a combination of one or more holding methods is required, such as holding one end in a chuck or on the face plate, and the other end in the tailstock centre, and/or given support with a steady, see Fig. 265.

Fig. 265. Both fixed and travelling steadies in use. (Courtesy: T. S. Harrison & Sons Ltd.)

10.8 Lathe Tools

Lathe tools are available as:

Carbon steel which is cheap and can be forged to shape. When standard tools cannot be used, a piece of carbon steel can often be

LATHEWORK

forged, ground, hardened and tempered to suit the particular purpose, see Fig. 266. The main disadvantage is that once overheated, the tool will 'blue' and become soft, see 1.16.

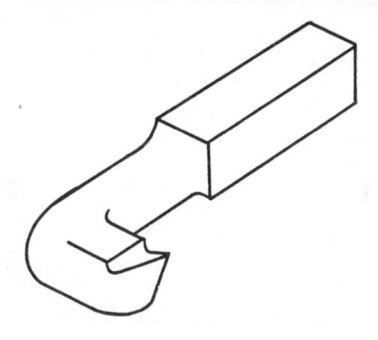

Fig. 266. Special purpose carbon steel tool

Although infrequently used, it is possible to turn materials using a hand rest and hand tools made of carbon steel. With the lathe set at higher spindle speeds, it is quite easy to turn wood and plastic, and with care, brass. The main advantage is that free flowing contours are possible; for this reason brass candlesticks are finished by hand turning, see Fig. 267.

Fig. 267. Wood turning in the lathe (similar to hand-turning brass). (Courtesy: T. S. Harrison & Sons Ltd.)

Tungsten carbide tipped tools are expensive and brittle, and are only suitable on modern lathes with the necessary high spindle speeds and power. The tip of tungsten carbide is brazed on to a shank of relatively inexpensive carbon steel, see Fig. 268.

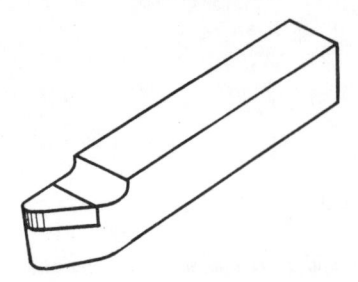

Fig. 268. Tungsten carbide tipped tools

High-speed steel retains hardness up to 600°C and is available as a *solid end* butt welded to a carbon steel shank, as a *tip* brazed to a carbon steel shank, or as a *bit* mounted in a holder, see Fig. 269.

The choice between solid tools or replaceable bits mounted in a holder is one of personal preference.

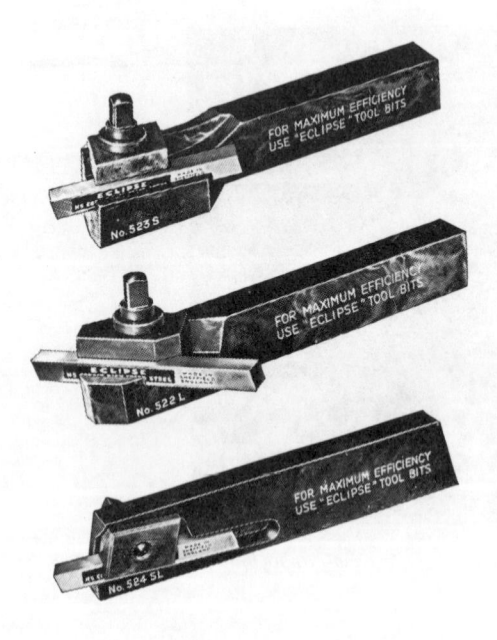

Fig. 269. Tool bit holders. (Courtesy: James Neill and Company (Sheffield) Limited)

LATHEWORK

Figs 244 and 264 clearly show the *American type toolpost*, which allows the toolholder to rock and therefore vary the height of the tool quickly and easily. A disadvantage is that, as it rocks, the angle of the tool to the work varies.

Fig. 270 shows a heavier type of lathe fitted with an *English type* toolpost. The tool is adjusted to height by parallel packing under the shank. (*Note*, on this lathe, the separate leadscrew and feedshaft; and that the feed change is by a push and pull knob.)

Fig. 270. Lathe carriage. (Courtesy: T. S. Harrison & Sons Ltd.)

A *four-way toolpost* saves tool changing and also requires packing under the tools. Four tools can be set up, and by revolving about a central cone seating, a spring-loaded plunger locates in four stations, before clamping down.

Fig. 271. A four-way toolpost in use on the lathe. (Courtesy: T. S. Harrison & Sons Ltd.)

The cutting action of the lathe tool and the need for clearance and rake angles should be understood.

Table 13. Lathe Tool Angles
(For more detailed table see Appendix A)

Metal	Approximate true rake	Clearance
Aluminium and light alloys	40°	
Steel	20°–30°	6°–10°
Cast Iron	10°–20°	
Brass	0°	

The angles given in the table are for guidance only; for example, a high carbon steel would require less rake than a low carbon steel, and a chilled cast iron less than a soft cast iron. Discretion would also be required when giving clearance: a boring tool may require extra grinding to clear the work.

When setting the tool in the toolpost it is helpful for a student to make the practice of always setting the cutting edge to the centre

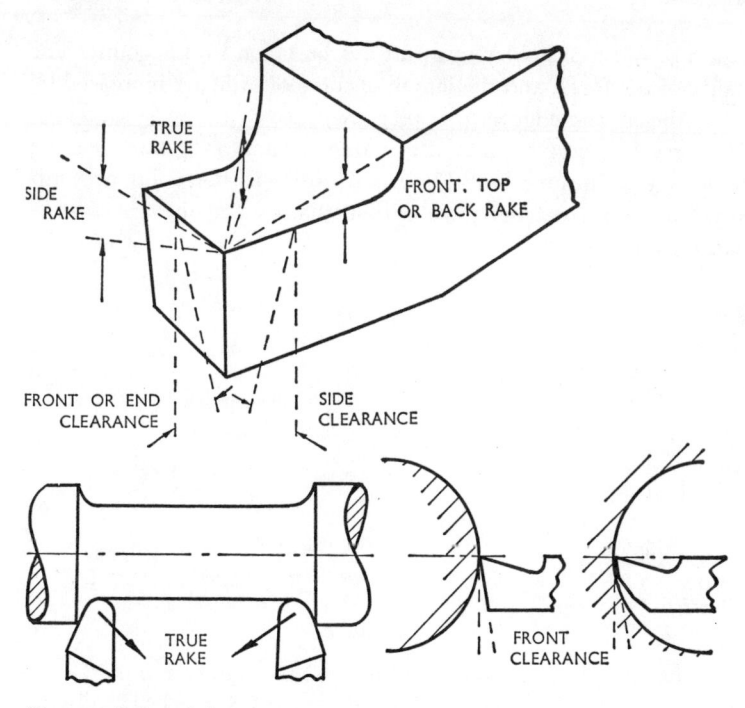

Fig. 272. Rake and clearance

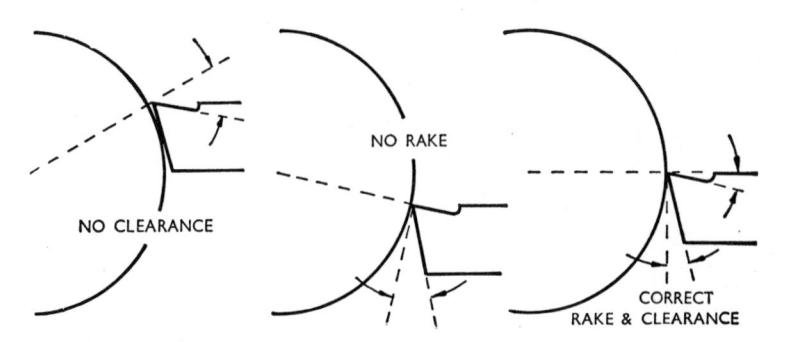

Fig. 273. Setting above, below and at centre height

height of the work using the tailstock centre as a guide. If the height of the cutting edge is varied the effective rake and clearance angles are also varied.

When grinding tool bits, the angle made by the tool bit with the

187

bottom of the tool holder must always be taken into account. The quality of the finish and the length of the tool's life are increased by honing the cutting edge with an oil stone.

The *roughing tool* reduces the diameter almost to size, leaving enough for a finishing cut. The small radius at the point prevents the point from breaking down without hampering the free-cutting qualities of the tool.

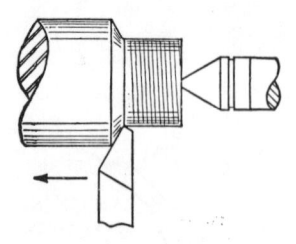

Fig. 274. A roughing tool. (Courtesy: T. S. Harrison & Sons Ltd.)

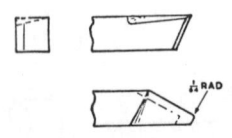

Fig. 275. Detail of roughing tool bit. (Courtesy: T. S. Harrison & Sons Ltd.)

The *finishing tool* has a bigger radius, approximately 1 mm. If the cutting edge is well honed and a fine power transverse employed, a very smooth finish can be obtained. The tool is also referred to as a general turning tool; it is similar to a side tool which is used for surfacing and facing. If the tool cuts from right to left it is called a right-hand tool.

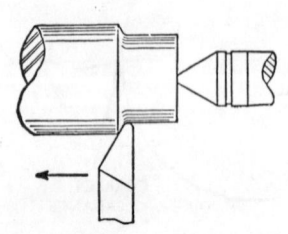

Fig. 276. A finishing tool. (Courtesy: T. S. Harrison & Sons Ltd.)

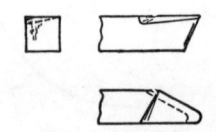

Fig. 277. Detail of finishing tool bit. (Courtesy: T. S. Harrison & Sons Ltd.)

The *round-nosed tool* is flat on top to allow it to be fed in either direction, and is useful for reducing the centre of a shaft.

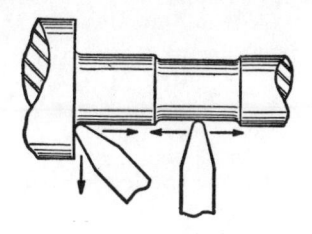

Fig. 278. Round-nosed tool. (Courtesy: T. S. Harrison & Sons Ltd.)

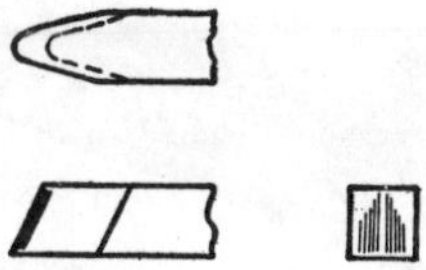

Fig. 279. Detail of round-nosed tool. (Courtesy: T. S. Harrison & Sons Ltd.)

The *facing* or *knife tool* is used for facing the ends of shafts and machining a square corner. The tool may be a right- or left-hand. Care should be taken not to bump against the tailstock centre, damaging the tool and work; the tailstock half-centre may help. Note in Fig. 280 how the tool cuts only at the tip and the remainder just clears the work.

Fig. 280. Right-hand facing tool. (Courtesy: T. S. Harrison & Sons Ltd.)

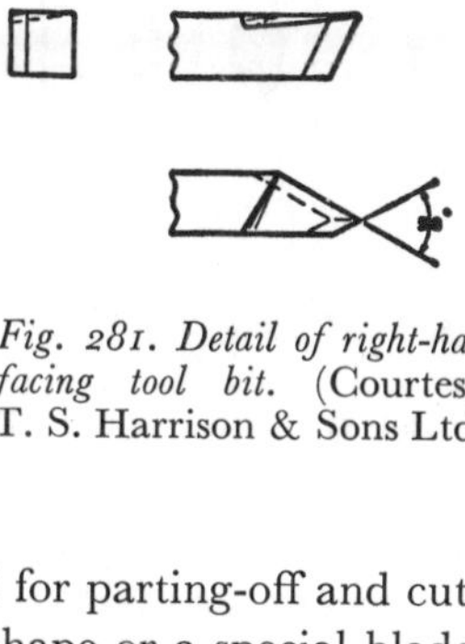

Fig. 281. Detail of right-hand facing tool bit. (Courtesy: T. S. Harrison & Sons Ltd.)

The *parting-off tool* which is used for parting-off and cutting grooves may be a solid tool ground to shape or a special blade and holder as shown in Figs 282 and 283.

The blade should be ground to give clearance on both sides and front, and a slight top rake. If the front edge of the tool is at a slight angle as shown, both faces can be finished cleanly.

Before parting-off, lock the carriage and halve the spindle speed for that size work and feed in carefully. If the chips have difficulty in clearing, take another light cut down one or both faces.

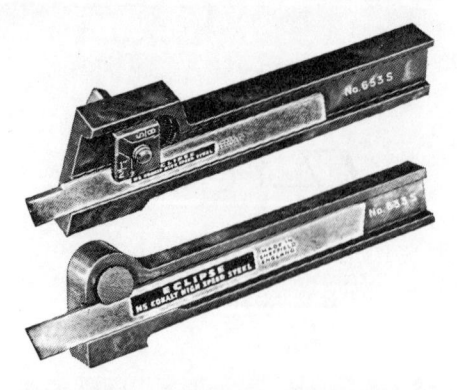

Fig. 282. Parting-off (cutting-off) tool holders.
(Courtesy: James Neill and Company (Sheffield) Limited)

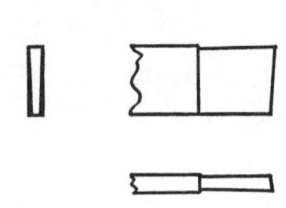

Fig. 283. Detail of parting-off tool

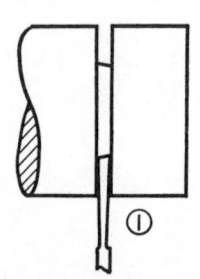

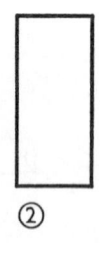

Fig. 284. Parting-off in the lathe

For *boring tools* see 10.12 and for *screw-cutting tools* see 10.13.

Form tools are specially ground for the form or profile required on the work. This may be a radius or dome as shown in Fig. 285; if the working drawing states a certain radius, then the form tool is ground to fit the appropriate radius on a radius gauge, see Fig. 201.

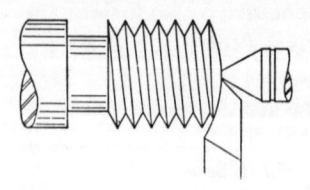

Fig. 285. Finishing end with form tool.
(Courtesy: T. S. Harrison & Sons Ltd.)

LATHEWORK

To turn or bore a spherical surface a *spherical turning attachment* can be made to fit in place of the compound rest (compound or top slide). The tool must be reset for every cut and the handle pulled round slowly and evenly.

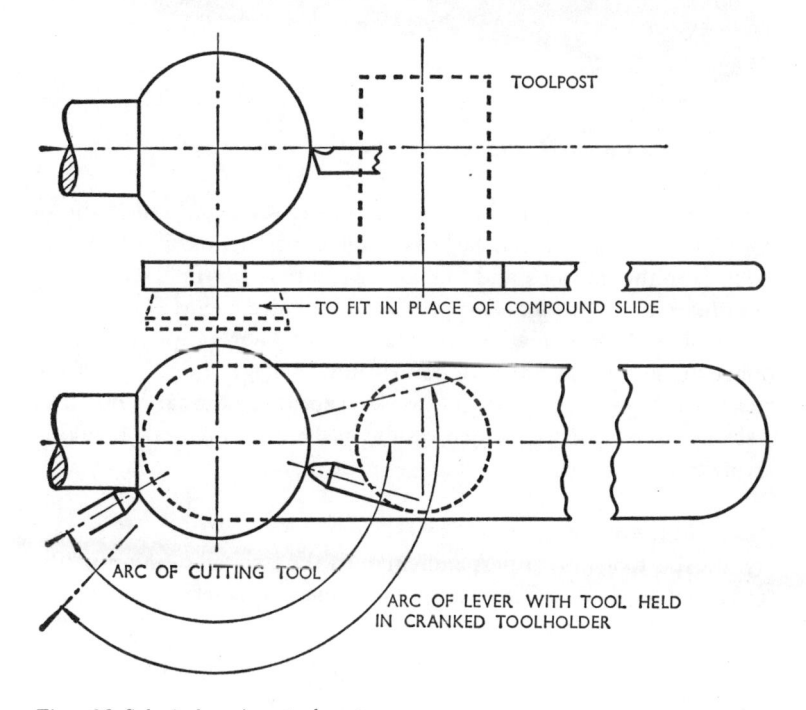

Fig. 286. Spherical turning attachment

The *knurling tool* is used to press a pattern on to the cylindrical surface of lathe work.

Fig. 287. Knurling. (Courtesy: T. S. Harrison & Sons Ltd.)

Fig. 288. Knurling tool. (Courtesy: T. S. Harrison & Sons Ltd.)

The process puts considerable strain on the work and lathe; therefore it is better to knurl as early as possible, before finishing cuts, and to be sure the tailstock and tool are as secure as possible. The tool is set square to the work and approximately centre height. The spindle speed should be as low as possible and the knurls kept well oiled. Start the lathe and force the knurls into the right-hand end of the work and then feed down the work. Repeat if necessary, but take care not to over-knurl, which results in the raised pattern breaking away from the work.

10.9 Surfacing

When the tool moves perpendicular to the axis of rotation of the work and produces a flat surface, it is termed surfacing (or facing).

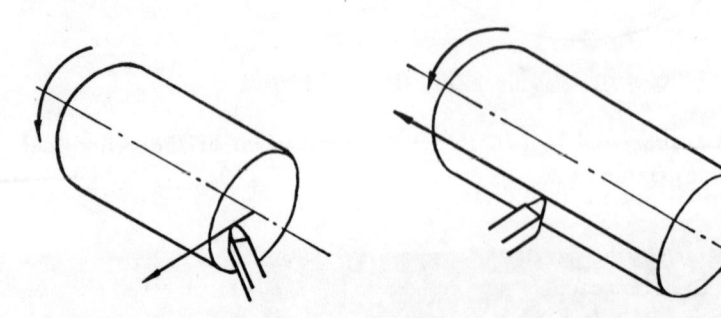

Fig. 289. Production of a flat surface

Fig. 290. Production of a cylindrical surface

The work is set up in the lathe and a suitable surfacing tool selected, see Fig. 280. It is most important with all machine work to have the least amount of tool and work overhang, combined with safe clear-

LATHEWORK 193

ance between the moving parts. Before starting, turn the work over by hand, to check that all parts are clear.

When surfacing to the very centre of work, it is important to set the tool exactly to centre height.

10.10 Sliding (Parallel Turning)

When the tool moves parallel to the axis of rotation of the work a cylindrical surface is produced.

Set up the work and tool as before, and calculate the correct spindle speed.

Table 14. Cutting Speeds
(Approximate surface speeds under average conditions, using high-speed tools; for a more detailed table see Appendix A)

	Speed (m/min)	
	Screw-cutting	Roughing–Finishing
Aluminium	20	90–150
Brass	20	50–120
Mild Steel	10	30–45
Cast Iron	10	20–30

The speeds given should only be taken as a guide. Carbon steel tools will require lower speeds (approximately half the values given), and tungsten carbide tipped tools higher (approximately three times the values given).

To calculate the required spindle speed, use the following formula:

$$\textbf{Spindle Speed (revolutions per minute)} = \frac{\textbf{Cutting Speed}}{\textbf{Work Circumference}}$$

Multiply the cutting speed by 1000, to bring to millimetres per minute. For practical purposes, it is sufficient to take the circumference, πD, as $3 \times D$.

Example 1 *Find the spindle speed for a 10 mm diameter mild steel bar.*

$$\textbf{Spindle Speed} = \frac{30 \times 1000}{3 \times 10} = 1000 \text{ rev/min.}$$

Example 2 *Find the spindle speed for a 50 mm diameter aluminium casting.*

$$\text{Spindle Speed} = \frac{90 \times 1000}{3 \times 50} = 600 \text{ rev/min.}$$

If working to a shoulder, chalk the work and mark with jenny calipers, see Figs 135 and 136. To produce a cylindrical surface, first rough down, measuring with outside calipers and rule, see Fig. 192. Then change to a finishing tool and take another cut, but at the end of the cut either do not withdraw the tool, note the reading on the cross-slide collar, or set the collar to zero. It is then possible to re-position the tool as before the last cut.

Measure the diameter using a micrometer, see Fig. 194. From this measurement subtract the required diameter, and this gives the amount to be removed. The tool must be moved in half this amount since it moves a radius but generates the diameter.

Example *30 mm diameter bar to be reduced to 20 mm diameter.*
1. Use roughing tool to approximately 21 mm diameter.
2. Use finishing tool and measure, say 20·2 mm diameter.
3. Move tool in 0·1 mm for final cut.

Fig. 291. A micrometer collar. (Courtesy: T. S. Harrison & Sons Ltd.)

LATHEWORK 195

A good surface finish can be achieved by using a sharp, well-supported finishing tool, a cutting lubricant, a higher spindle speed and a fine power feed.

10.11 Taper Turning

When the tool moves at an angle to the axis of rotation of the work, and produces a conical surface, it is termed taper turning.

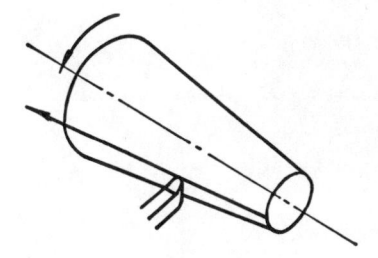

Fig. 292. Production of a conical surface

The working drawing may specify the taper either in degrees or in millimetres per centimetre, or as diameters a certain distance apart. Quite often the student must make simple calculations. Natural tangent tables (in half degrees) are included in Appendix B.

The *compound rest* (compound or top slide) is used for turning and boring short tapers, as Example 1. The taper must first be calculated in degrees and the rest may be rotated to any angle, but the length of cut is limited to about 50 mm and must be fed by hand. A grinding attachment may replace the toolpost, see Fig. 249.

Example 1

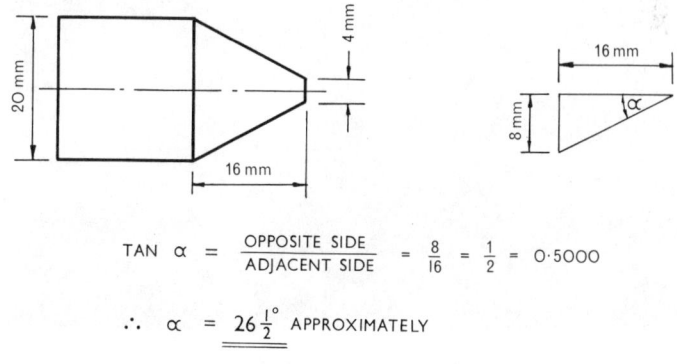

$$\tan \alpha = \frac{\text{OPPOSITE SIDE}}{\text{ADJACENT SIDE}} = \frac{8}{16} = \frac{1}{2} = 0.5000$$

$$\therefore \alpha = \underline{\underline{26\tfrac{1}{2}^\circ}} \text{ APPROXIMATELY}$$

Fig. 293. Example 1

Note in Fig. 294 the previously taper turned work resting on the headstock casing.

Fig. 294. Boring a taper with compound rest. (Courtesy: T. S. Harrison & Sons Ltd.)

LATHEWORK

For turning long tapers, as Example 2 and Example 3, *set over (offset) the tailstock*. The tool continues to feed parallel to the bed but the tailstock is set over, thus changing the axis of rotation of the work. If the set over is excessive, considerable strain is put on the centres and centre holes, see Fig. 297.

Example 2

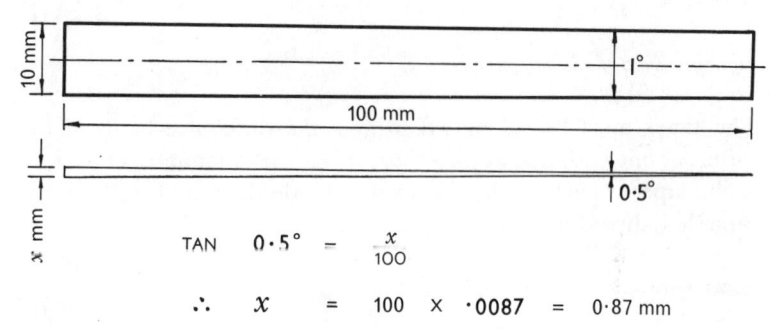

$$\text{TAN } 0.5° = \frac{x}{100}$$

$$\therefore x = 100 \times 0.0087 = 0.87 \text{ mm}$$

Fig. 295. Example 2

Example 3

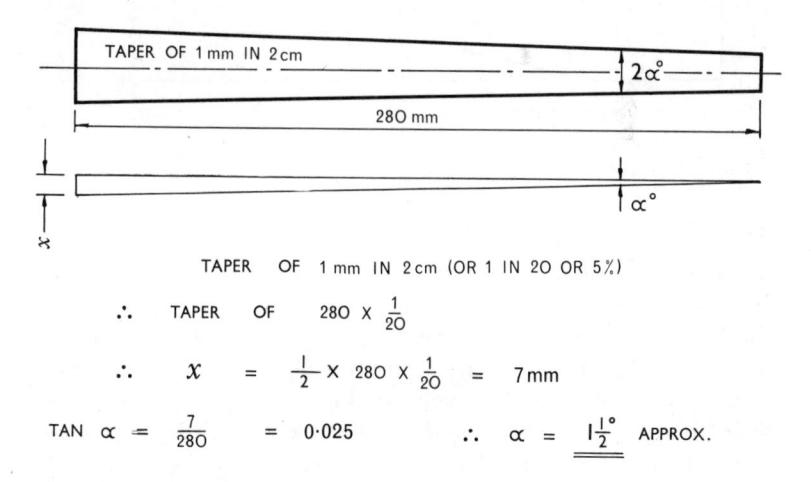

TAPER OF 1 mm IN 2 cm (OR 1 IN 20 OR 5%)

$$\therefore \text{ TAPER OF } 280 \times \frac{1}{20}$$

$$\therefore x = \frac{1}{2} \times 280 \times \frac{1}{20} = 7 \text{ mm}$$

$$\text{TAN } \alpha = \frac{7}{280} = 0.025 \quad \therefore \alpha = 1\frac{1}{2}° \text{ APPROX.}$$

Fig. 296. Example 3

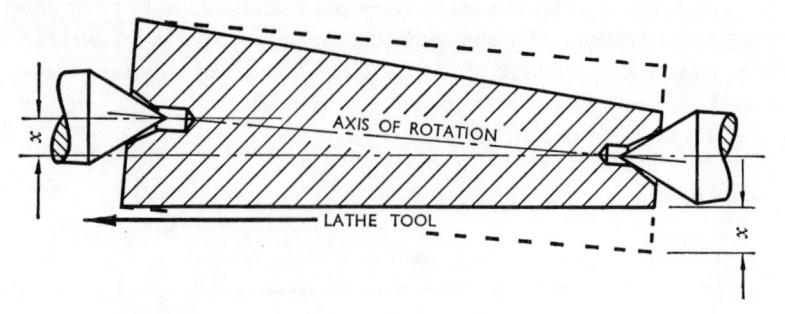

Fig. 297. Effect of tailstock set over

The taper must be calculated to give the difference between the radius at one end, and at the other; this is the amount of set over, x. If the taper is part of a longer length, divide the total length by the taper length and multiply by x, see Fig. 298.

Example 4

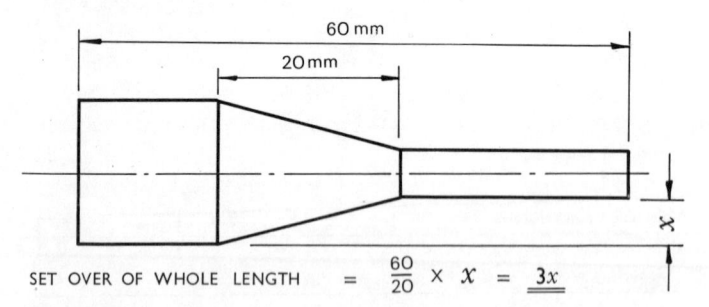

SET OVER OF WHOLE LENGTH $= \frac{60}{20} \times x = \underline{\underline{3x}}$

Fig. 298. Example 4

An approximate method of measuring the set over is to move the tailstock centre up to the headstock centre and measure with a rule.

An accurate method is to use the micrometer collar on the cross-slide. First a bar of metal with a smooth rounded end is held in the toolpost at right angles to the centre line of the lathe and at centre height. By using a feeler gauge, see Fig. 200, and say a 0·2 mm feeler, it is possible to position the end at a known distance from the centre line of the lathe. This may be done by setting to part of the spindle or to parallel work held centrally. The tailstock may

LATHEWORK   199

then be set over, by moving the cross-slide, as in the example, and setting the tailstock spindle to the end of the bar of metal using the same feeler (see Fig. 299).

```
SPINDLE
OR                          3 mm        TAILSTOCK
PARALLEL      40mm DIA.                 SPINDLE
WORK
                                                              30mm DIA.
                  ─── FEELER GAUGE
                  ─── BAR OF METAL ───

END OF METAL PLUS FEELER FROM CENTRE    =  20 mm
SET OVER PLUS RADIUS OF TAILSTOCK SPINDLE  =  3 mm + 15 mm = 18 mm
                THE CROSS SLIDE MOVEMENT  =  20 mm − 18 mm = 2 mm
```

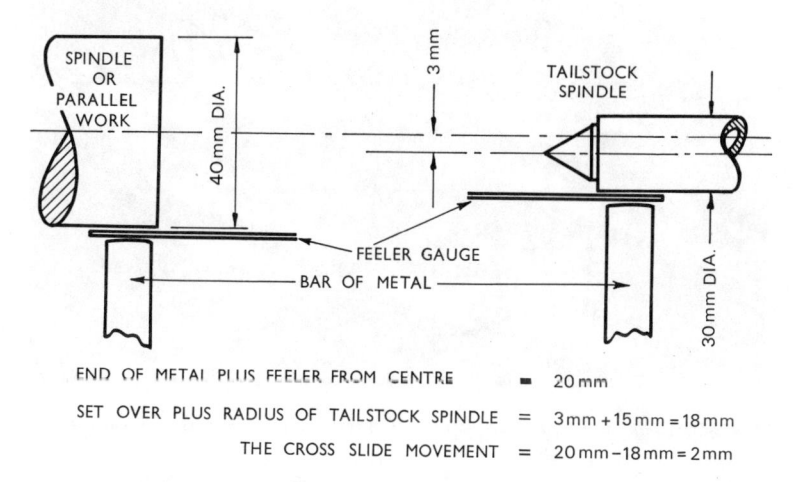

Fig. 299. Example of calculations, to set over tailstock 3 mm

It should be noted that the thickness of the feeler is immaterial.

In the example of tailstock set over, the bar end is moved *in* 2 mm divisions on the micrometer collar. If the bar end requires moving *out* an accurate amount, note the reading on the dial, calculate the reading required, and then take the cross-slide out and move in again to the correct position. This is necessary, otherwise part of the dial movement will be used taking up slackness and not actually moving the cross-slide.

When turning tapers by offsetting the tailstock, there is always the inconvenience of resetting the tailstock accurately, see p. 176. If available, a much better method is to use the *taper turning attachment*. This may be used for turning and boring, and to bigger angles than would be possible between centres.

The carriage continues to follow the bedways, but the cross-slide is disconnected by removing the cross-feed leadscrew nut, and made to follow a slide set at an angle to the bedways. Thus the tool follows the swivel slide and the cross-feed is out of action, which necessitates the compound rest, as in Fig. 300, to be moved through 90° to be used to feed the tool in for successive cuts (not all lathes).

Fig. 300. Plain taper turning attachment. (Courtesy: T. S. Harrison & Sons Ltd.)

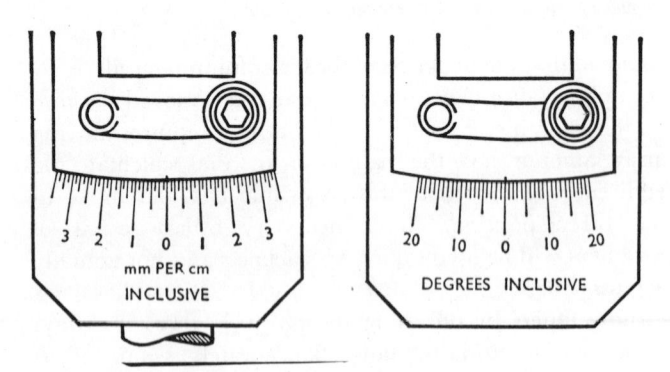

Fig. 301. Graduations on taper swivel slide

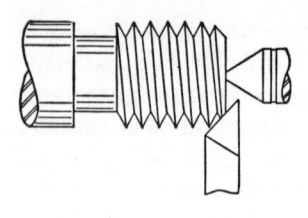

Fig. 302. 45° chamfer at end of thread. (Courtesy: T. S. Harrison & Sons Ltd.)

LATHEWORK

The taper may be tested with a taper plug or ring gauge, or with a micrometer in conjunction with balls and/or rollers, on a surface plate. Standard tapered holes can be reamed by hand, after taper boring. A table of ISO Morse Taper Shanks is included in Appendix A.

To bevel work, a *form-tool* is used; only very short tapers may be formed to a good finish without chatter marks. It is usual to set the angle by eye or more accurately using a protractor.

10.12 Boring

When a single point tool cuts in a hole, enlarging the internal diameter, it is called boring. There are basically two methods; in one the work rotates and in the other the tool rotates.

The most common method is to use a *boring tool* which is very much like a left-hand turning tool, but with a bigger front clearance. The shank is held in the toolpost.

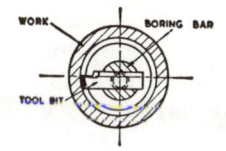

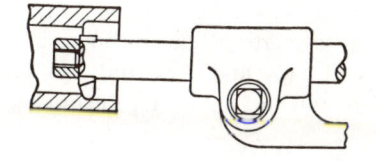

Fig. 303. Boring tool. (Courtesy: T. S. Harrison & Sons Ltd.)

Fig. 304. Boring tool bit and boring bar. (Courtesy: T. S. Harrison & Sons Ltd.)

The spindle speed is calculated in exactly the same way as for external turning. A 50 mm outside diameter and a 50 mm diameter bored hole in an aluminium casting would both require 600 rev/min, see 10.10.

For boring large work, a *lathe boring table* is used. The boring bar is held in the chuck as Fig. 305 or held between centres, and the work fed on to the revolving tool.

10.13 Screwcutting

A screw is a cylinder with a helical ridge called the thread, running round it. The thread may be produced by several methods, depending upon the quality and quantity required. One method has already been discussed, see 8.8, but the most versatile method is to use a

Fig. 305. Boring a component mounted on the boring table. (Courtesy: T. S. Harrison & Sons Ltd.)

screwcutting lathe. The craftsman is not dependent upon expensive ranges of taps and dies, but can cut various thread forms and diameters; he may also vary the pitch and lead if required.

Definitions
Minor, root or core diameter The minor or root diameter of a screw is the full diameter less twice the depth of thread and is measured at right angles to the axis.
Full, outside or major diameter The full or major diameter of a screw is the diameter by which most screws, bolts, etc., are recognized and is usually a nominal size such as 10 mm ISO Metric Thread—Coarse Series, which indicates that the outside diameter of the thread is 10 mm diameter nominally, but in normal commercial practice may be say 0·1 mm smaller than 10 mm.
Pitch The pitch of a screw thread is the distance from the centre of one thread to the centre of the next thread and is measured parallel to the axis.
Lead The lead of a screw is the distance the screw advances along its axis in one complete turn. If the screw is a single start then the lead and the pitch are equal. With a two-start or double thread screw the lead is twice the pitch.

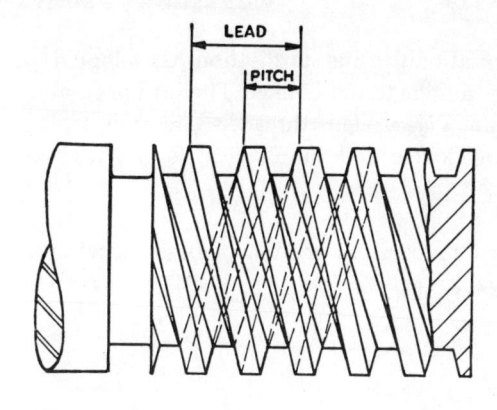

Fig. 306. A double (or two-start) thread. (Courtesy: T. S. Harrison & Sons Ltd.)

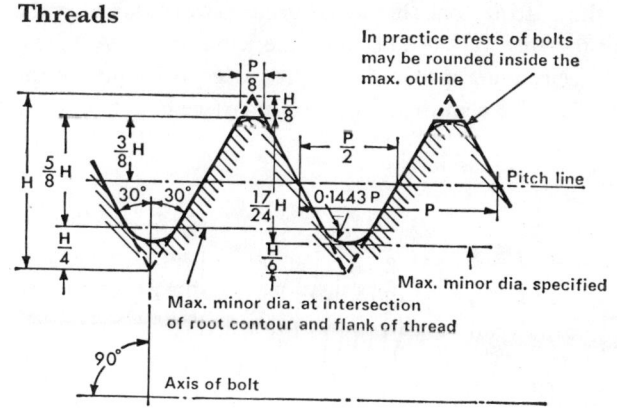

Threads

Fig. 307. ISO Metric thread form (bolt)

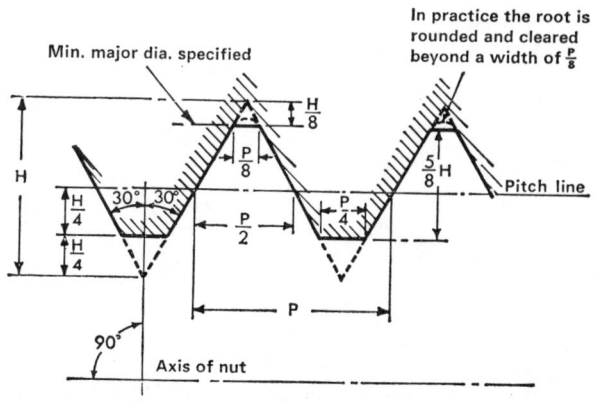

Fig. 308. ISO Metric thread form (nut)

203

The International Organisation for Standardisation has adopted a thread form which is very similar to the Unified Thread Form, and is known as the *ISO Metric Thread*. This thread is now universally accepted and has both a Coarse and Fine series; for details see Appendix A.

The square thread is used to transmit motion in both directions, such as in a vice or screw jack.

$$D = \frac{P}{2}; \quad F = \frac{P}{2}$$

The sides of the cutting tool should be ground to conform to the helix angle of the thread. To determine the helix angle, 'A', draw AB equal to the circumference and at right angles, BB, equal to the lead. The sides C and D require a little clearance (see Fig. 310).

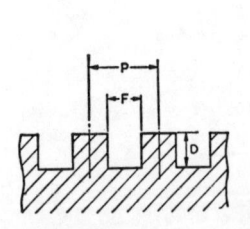

Fig. 309. *Square thread form.* (Courtesy: T. S. Harrison & Sons Ltd.)

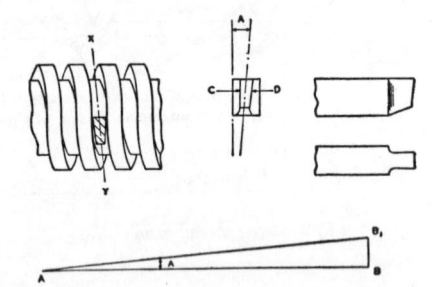

Fig. 310. *Tool for square thread.* (Courtesy: T. S. Harrison & Sons Ltd.)

The Acme thread is easier to cut than the square thread and allows easier engagement of half nuts, as in Fig. 238

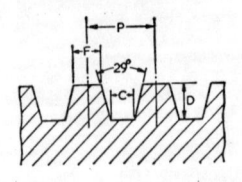

$$D = 0.500\ P + 0.25\ \text{mm} \quad F = 0.3707\ P \quad C = 0.3707\ P - 0.13\ \text{mm}$$

Fig. 311. *Acme thread.* (Courtesy: T. S. Harrison & Sons Ltd.)

LATHEWORK

The Metric Trapezoidal thread form is very similar to the Acme, except that the thread angle is 30°, and it is also used for leadscrews.

Before cutting a screw thread in the lathe, the pitch in mm must be known. If the work is to have exactly the same pitch as the leadscrew, then for every revolution of the work the leadscrew must turn once, e.g. if the leadscrew has a pitch of 3 mm, the tool will move 3 mm for each revolution of the leadscrew, cutting a thread of 3 mm pitch as the work revolves once.

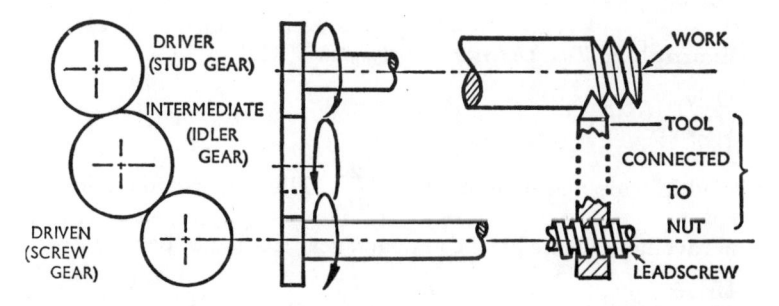

Fig. 312. Principle of a simple gear train

If the revolutions of work and leadscrew are to be equal, then the number of teeth on the driver and driven gears must be equal. The intermediate gear merely transmits the motion and keeps both turning in the same direction. If the work is to have half the pitch of the leadscrew, the driver must revolve at twice the speed and hence be half the size of the driven.

This may be summarised as:

$$\frac{\text{Pitch of work}}{\text{Pitch of leadscrews}} = \frac{\text{Leadscrew r.p.m.}}{\text{Work r.p.m.}} = \frac{\text{Driver teeth}}{\text{Driven teeth}}$$

On many lathes the gears required for a range of pitches have been previously worked out, and are tabulated on the lathe. Other lathes have no such chart, and the operator must make his own calculations.

Let us assume that the lathe has a leadscrew of 3 mm and has a range of gears from 20 t. to 120 t. in steps of 5 teeth (for imperial lathes with leadscrews in threads per inch a 127 t. gear is used, since $1 : 25 \cdot 4 = 5 : 127$).

Example 1 *To cut a screw of 1·0 mm pitch (M6)*

$$\frac{\text{Driver}}{\text{Driven}} = \frac{1\cdot0}{3\cdot0}$$

Multiply top and bottom by $30 = \frac{30}{90}$. Use a simple gear train with a driver gear of 30 t. and a driven gear of 90 t. with any suitable size intermediate gear between. (N.B. Equally suitable would be 20/60, 25/75, 35/105 and 40/120.)

Example 2 *To cut a screw of 0·4 mm pitch (M2)*

$$\frac{\text{Driver}}{\text{Driven}} = \frac{0\cdot4}{3\cdot0}$$

Multiply top and bottom by $50 = \frac{20}{150}$. This ratio is too big for the gears available; therefore a compound gear train must be used.

$$\frac{\text{Driver}}{\text{Driven}} = \frac{0\cdot4}{3\cdot0} = \frac{2 \times 2}{5 \times 6} = \frac{40 \times 20}{100 \times 60}$$

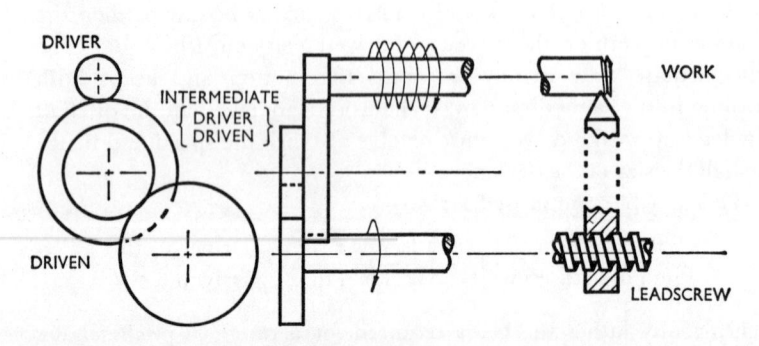

Fig. 313. Principle of a compound gear train

A 40 t. could drive a 100 t. on the intermediate stud which is coupled to a 20 t. driving a 60 t. on the leadscrew.

Equal size gear wheels revolve the stud and spindle at the same speed, but the direction may be reversed (for left-hand threads) by the tumbler gear mechanism, see Fig. 239 and Fig. 314.

Fig. 314. Set up of standard change gear lathe for cutting screw threads. (Courtesy: T. S. Harrison & Sons Ltd.)

The more expensive lathes dispense with loose change gears, and use a gear box, see Fig. 315.

There are several techniques for screwcutting, depending upon the tool approach for successive cuts.

(*a*) *Straight* (by the cross slide).
(*b*) *Sidestep* (taking a little from alternate flanks).
(*c*) *Angular* (considered the best and described below).

The following technique of screwcutting refers to a single vee thread; similar principles apply to others.

The tool is ground to the correct angle using a screwcutting (threading tool) gauge and for the end radius a screw pitch (screw thread) gauge, which is primarily for checking the pitch of the thread, see Figs. 316, 317 and 318.

Clearance is required and little or no rake for cast iron or brass and only 10°–20° for steel (*Note:* rake alters the thread flank angles).

Fig. 315. Quick change lathe with Norton type gear box. (Courtesy: T. S. Harrison & Sons Ltd.)

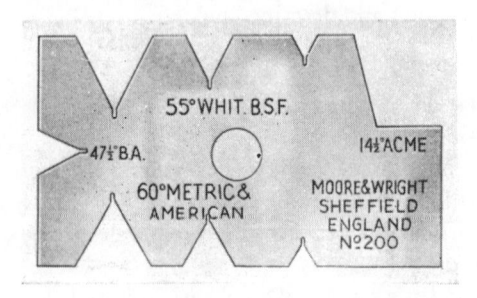

Fig. 316. Screwcutting gauge. (Courtesy: Moore and Wright (Sheffield) Ltd.)

Fig. 317. Screw pitch (screw thread) gauge. (Courtesy: Moore and Wright (Sheffield) Ltd.)

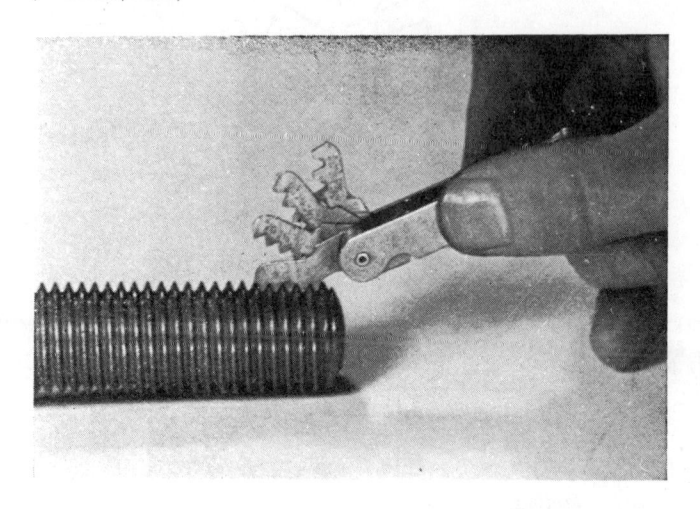

Fig. 318. Using a screw pitch gauge. (Courtesy: T. S. Harrison & Sons Ltd.)

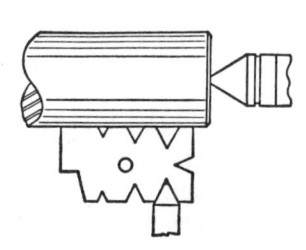

Fig. 319. Tool bit set-square for external screw threads. (Courtesy: T. S. Harrison & Sons Ltd.)

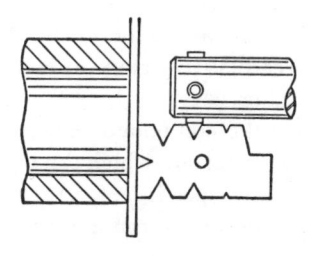

Fig. 320. Tool bit set-square for internal screw threads. (Courtesy: T. S. Harrison & Sons Ltd.)

The compound rest is set over to half the thread angle or for a smoother finish very slightly less (i.e. 29° for an ISO Metric thread), see Fig. 321, and the tool set at centre height and square to the work.

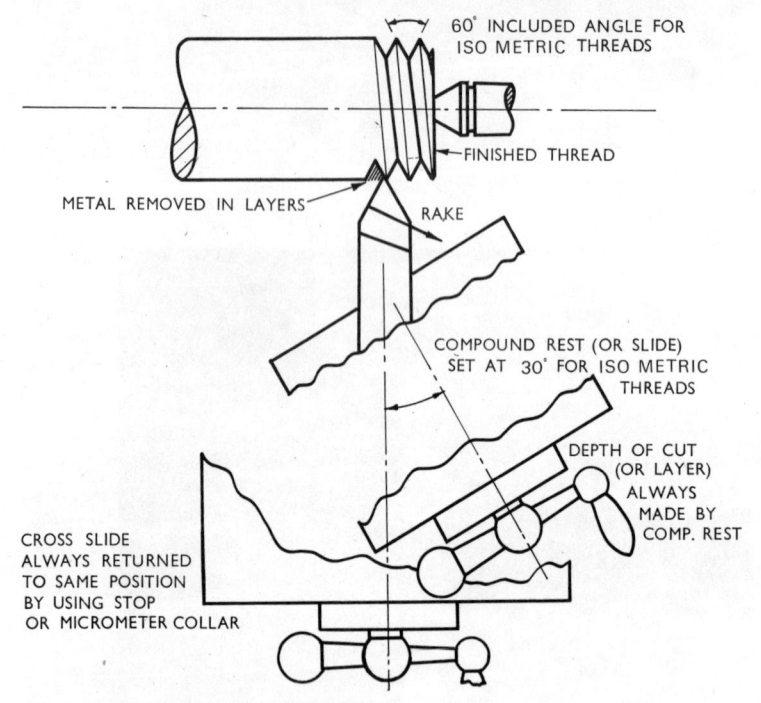

Fig. 321. Principle of cutting vee threads

Move the carriage and cross-slide so that the point of the tool is level at the start of the thread. Set the cross-slide dial to 'o', or use the thread-cutting stop, to enable the tool to be reset before each cut, see Fig. 322.

Move the compound rest in so that the tool point may make a very light trial cut, which can be checked for the correct pitch.

The lathe speed, see 10.10, should be slow enough to enable the operator either to stop in a groove or in a hole drilled at the end of the thread.

Before making a trial cut the method of locating the tool in the thread must be decided upon. This requires the leadscrew, spindle and carriage always to be in the same relative positions. If the lathe

Fig. 322. Thread cutting stop in use. (Courtesy: T. S. Harrison & Sons Ltd.)

can be reversed, the half-nuts, see Fig. 238, which engage the carriage to the leadscrew need not be disengaged and relative positions are always maintained. In this case the tool is withdrawn from the work and reversed just beyond the starting position, to take up the slackness (backlash) before bringing back ready for another cut.

A more convenient method is to use the dial indicator (Chasing dial) which indicates the relative positions of the leadscrew, spindle and carriage. The position on the dial when the half-nuts should be engaged will vary between lathes and threads to be cut (see Fig. 323), and this information is normally supplied with the lathe.

If the lathe is equipped with neither reverse nor a dial indicator, the catch plate, leadscrew and carriage must be chalk-marked to a fixed

Fig. 323. Thread dial indicator. (Courtesy: Boxford Machine Tools Ltd.)

part of the lathe, and the marks lined up before engaging the half-nuts.

At the end of the trial cut, the tool is withdrawn and moved back to the starting position, either using the 'o' mark on the dial, or the thread-cutting stop. The compound rest is moved in about 1 mm for

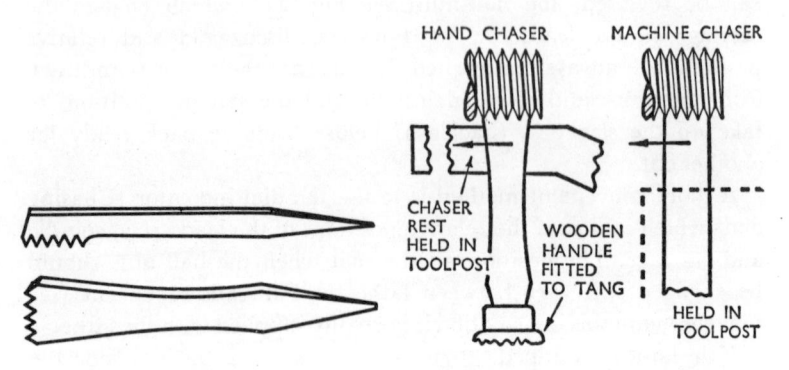

Fig. 324. Inside and outside hand chasers   *Fig. 325. Chasing a thread in the lathe*

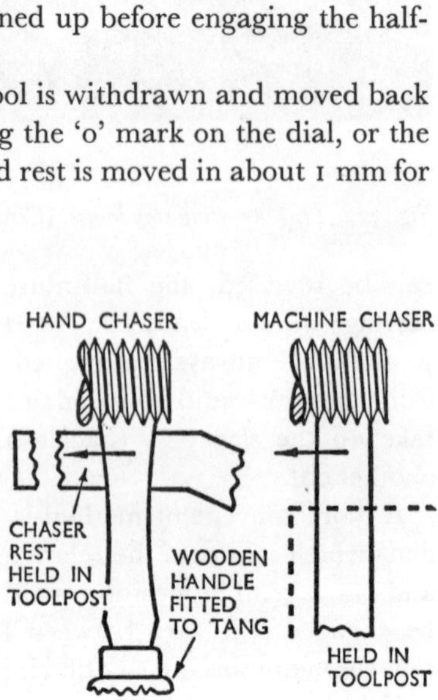

212

the first real cut, and if cutting a thread in steel, oil should be applied. The total distance the compound slide moves in at an angle will be greater than the normal thread depth, and can be calculated trigonometrically.

When the thread has been cut to depth, a chaser is used to finish the thread to the correct profile. The work may then either be offered to its mating part, or to a good nut or bolt (as substitutes for ring and plug screw gauges). If necessary the chasing may be repeated.

A thread can be cut, or cleaned up as in chasing by using taps and dies. The lathe is stopped and the work pulled over by hand, whilst the tailstock guides the tap or die.

Fig. 326. Tapping in the lathe. (Courtesy: T. S. Harrison & Sons Ltd.)

Fig. 327. Cutting thread with die head in tailstock. (Courtesy: T. S. Harrison & Sons Ltd.)

11

Machinework

11.1 Shaping and Planing Machines

These machines both produce flat surfaces using a single point tool. The shaper is used for all but the largest work and is advantageous for quick setting-up of work and tool.

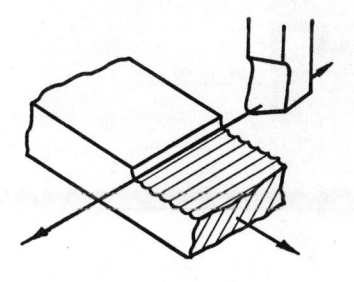

Fig. 328. Principle of shaping

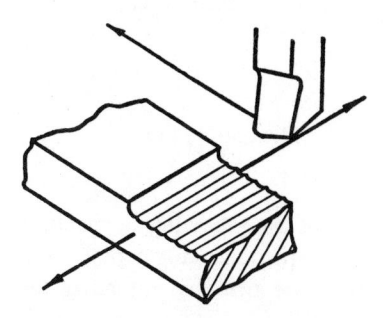

Fig. 329. Principle of planing

The crank drive of the shaping machine gives a slow forward cutting stroke and a quick return as illustrated in Fig. 331. To reduce the length of the ram stroke, the sliding block must be moved nearer to the centre of the wheel.

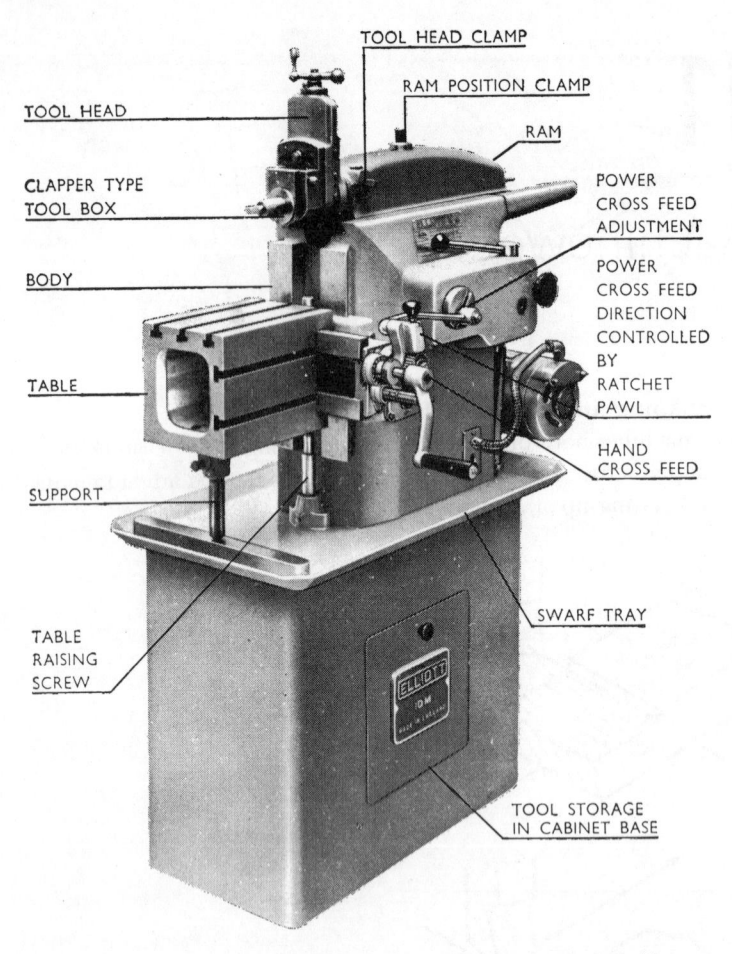

Fig. 330. Shaping machine. (Courtesy: B. Elliott (Machinery) Ltd.)

The work can be held by one or more of the following: a machine vice (see Fig. 223), parallel strips, clamps, jack, angle plate and vee blocks. The table must also be made firm by adjusting the support, once the height has been set.

The cutting tools are similar to turning tools but with slightly more front clearance. The ram stroke and position are adjusted to approximately 20 mm overrun on either side of the work. As the return stroke is made, the tool held in the clapper box lifts and avoids

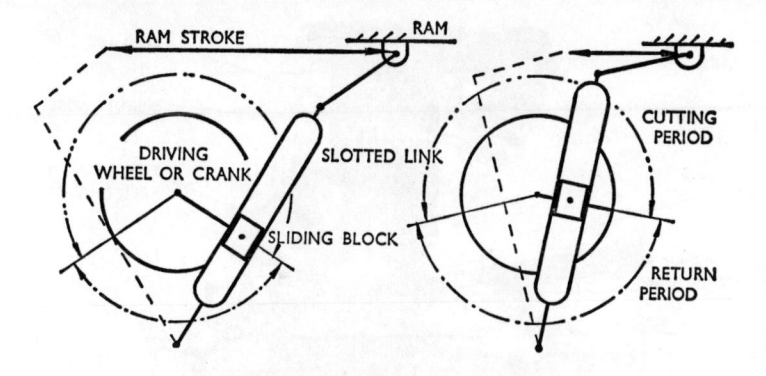

Fig. 331. Slotted link quick-return mechanism

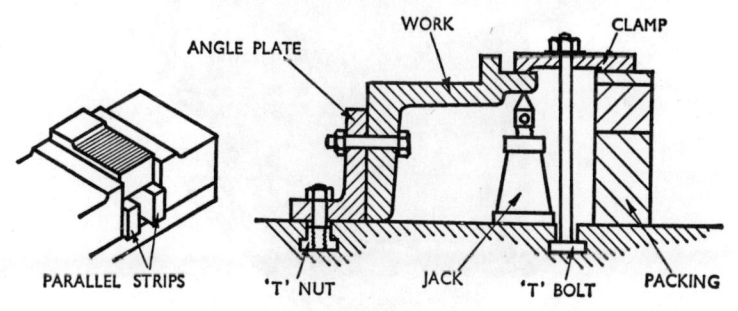

Fig. 332. Methods of securing work

rubbing the surface; once clear, it drops back with a characteristic 'clapping' sound.

11.2 Milling

Milling machines are particularly suitable for quantity production. The machine uses circular multi-cutting edge cutters which can be obtained in a variety of shapes and sizes, and require a tool and cutter grinding machine for resharpening. Although setting-up takes longer, the actual machine time per article is less than for the shaping machine particularly if several cutters are used at once, 'gang milling'.

For maximum rigidity the cutter and support must be positioned as near to the body of the machine as is practicable. Additional support

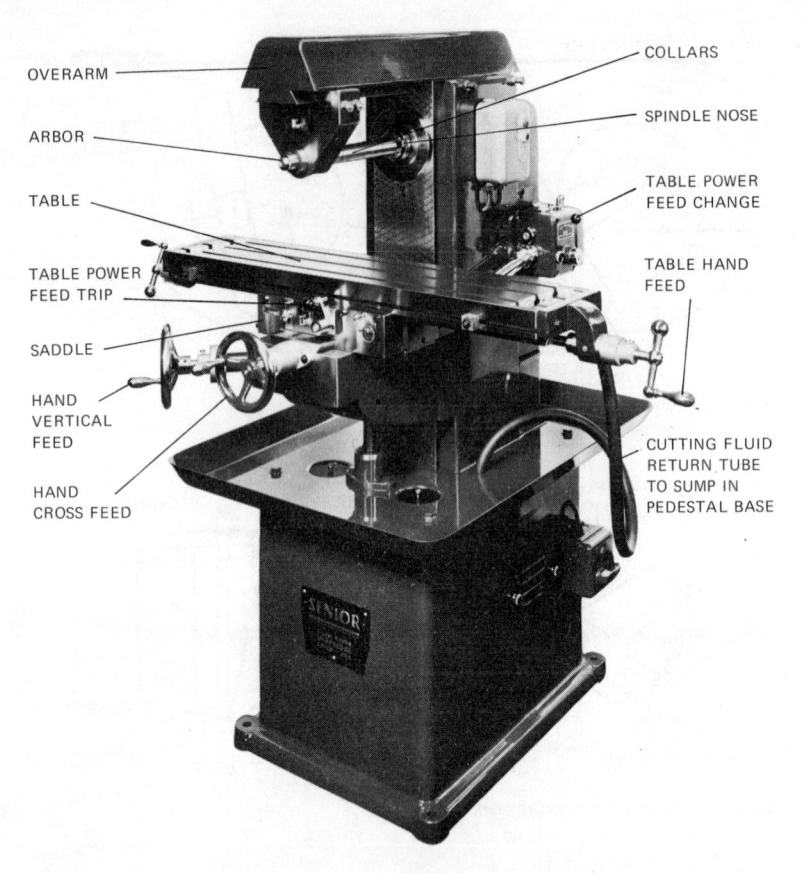

Fig. 333. Plain horizontal milling machine. (Courtesy: Tom Senior (Liversedge) Ltd.)

for the end of the arbor is sometimes provided. such as a second bracket and braces extending up from the body of the machine, When milling a keyway or flats on the end of a shaft, it is sometimes possible to use vee blocks as shown in Fig. 334.

The spindle revolutions per minute are varied either by gears or by a cone and back gear arrangement as on lathes. The cutting speed is calculated as for lathework, substituting the diameter of the cutter for the diameter of work. When setting up the cutter, it is better to arrange for 'up-cut' milling rather than 'down-cut' milling which can lead to the cutter climbing the work.

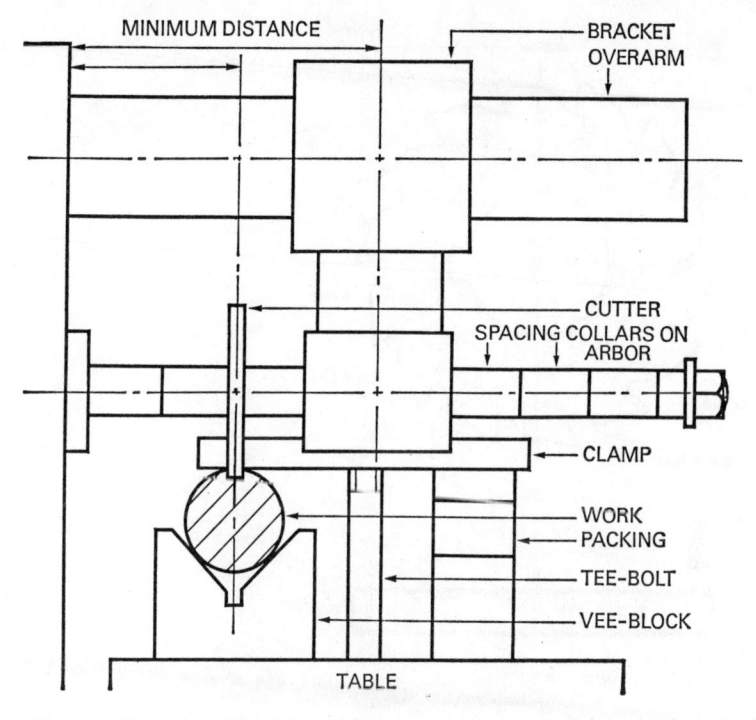

Fig. 334. Set-up for milling a keyway in a shaft

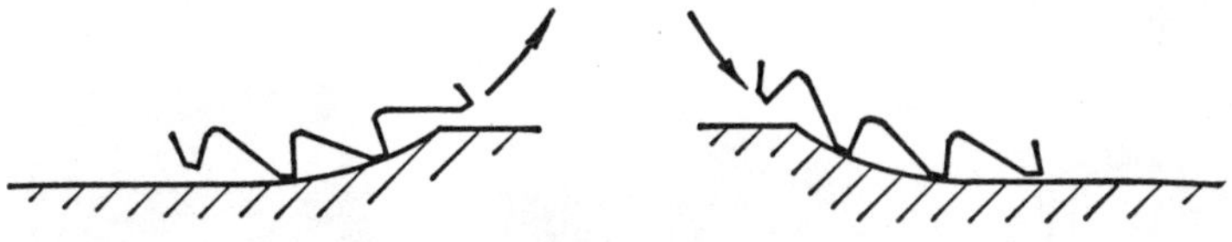

Fig. 335. (a) 'Up-cut' milling (b) 'Down-cut' milling

The majority of cutters are held on the arbor between collars clamped tightly by a nut. Small cutters can be driven by friction whilst large ones require a key.

End mills and face cutters either fit directly into a taper in the spindle nose, on to a stub arbor or into a special chuck.

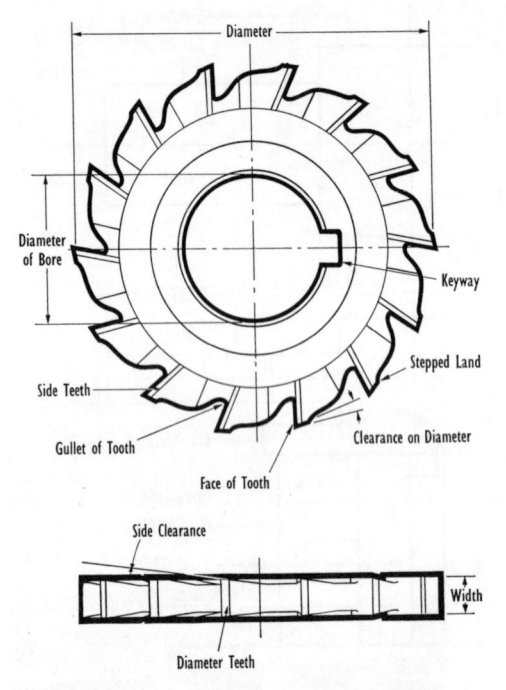

Fig. 336. Side and face milling cutter nomenclature. (Courtesy: The Sheffield Twist Drill and Steel Company Ltd.)

Fig. 337. Milling cutters held on arbor. (Courtesy: The Sheffield Twist Drill and Steel Company Ltd.)

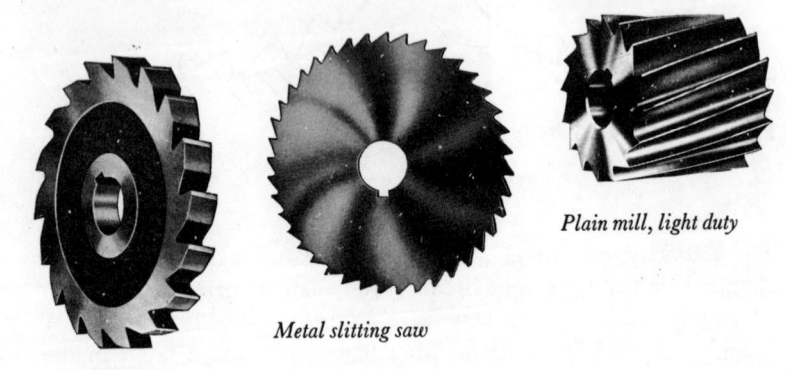

Plain mill, light duty

Metal slitting saw

Slotting cutter

220

*Fig. 337
(continued)*

Concave cutter

Side and face cutter, light duty

*Fig. 338. End mill in chuck.
(Courtesy: Clarkson
(Engineers) Ltd.)*

Fig. 339. Throw away cutter (up to 6 mm dia.) in special chuck. (Courtesy: Clarkson (Engineers) Ltd.)

221

Fig. 340. Face mill. (Courtesy: The Sheffield Twist Drill and Steel Company Ltd.)

Fig. 341. Vertical attachment. (Courtesy: Tom Senior (Liversedge) Ltd.)

It is often more convenient for setting up and view of the work if the end or face mill can work from above; for this reason a vertical attachment or vertical milling machine is used.

11.3 Grinding

Lathe and shaper tools can be ground off-hand on abrasive wheels on either bench or floor (pedestal) grinders, and also with abrasive blocks.

The dimensions of wheels are given in the order: outside diameter × thickness × hole diameter, and for blocks: height × width × length. The characteristics of the wheel which must be designated are: nature of abrasive, grain size, grade, and nature of bond.

Grinding wheels are made with aluminium oxide (fused alumina), silicon carbide, diamond abrasive and less commonly boron carbide. For off-hand grinding fused alumina marked 'A' is used, see 11.4. The grain size ranges from 8 (coarsest) to 600 (finest).

Grade in grinding wheels is a measure of the tenacity with which the bonding agent holds the abrasive particles into a solid form. If the bond is strong, the wheel is considered to be hard and similarly a soft wheel has a weaker bond. The range is from 'A' (very soft) to 'Z' (very hard).

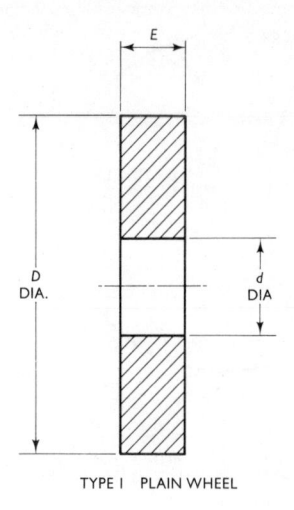

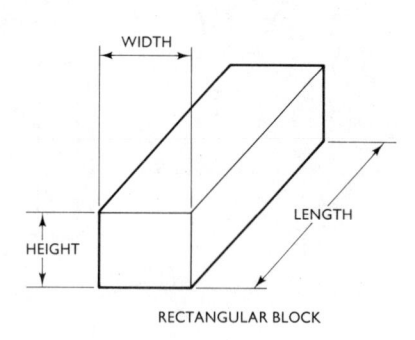

Fig. 342. Shapes of bonded abrasive products BS 4481: Part I: 1969. (Courtesy: British Standards Institution)

The bond may be one of several types with a vitrified bond 'V' used for off-hand grinding wheels.

Grinding wheels suitable for off-hand grinding, and marked in accordance with BS 4481 : Part 1 : 1969 could read:

Shape	Dimensions	Characteristics
Type 1	150 × 16 × 13	A 30—Q—V
Type 1	200 × 20 × 16	A 60—O—V

Before grinding, ensure that the driving spindles are free from vibration and end-play, and the wheel secure (blotting paper washers on either side of the wheel help to spread the pressure). The tool rest should be close to but not touching the wheel.

The grinding wheel rotation should always be such that the pressure is against or into the top of the tool, never away from the cutting edge.

The tool must be kept moving across the wheel face to avoid heavy wear in one spot. Regularly true the wheel with a Huntington or star-type dresser, see Fig. 343.

If the tool overheats do not immerse in water. Either allow it to cool naturally or immerse the shank only.

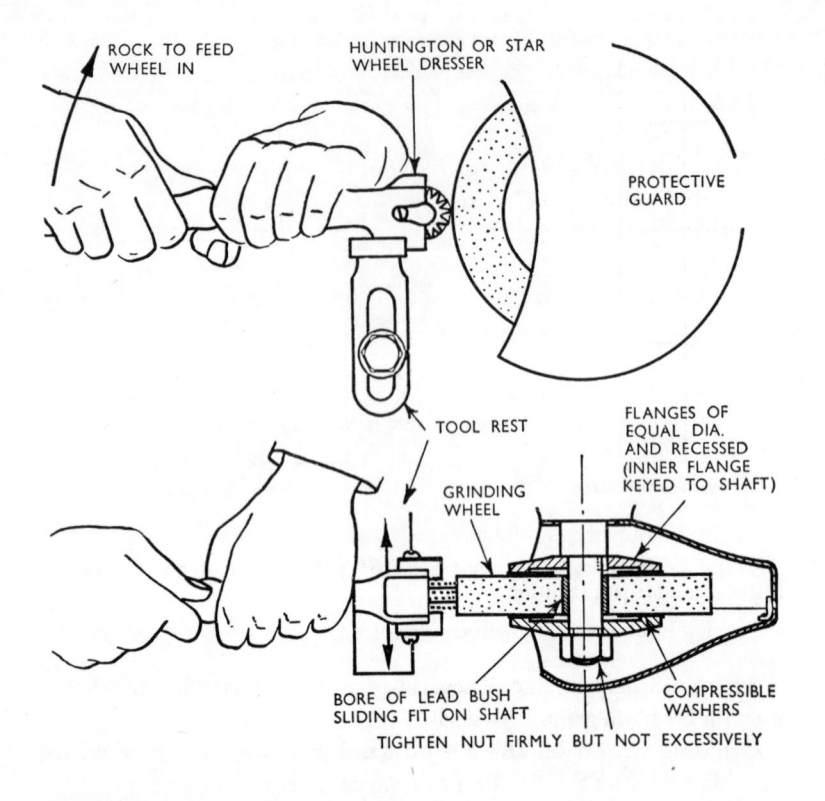

Fig. 343. Truing and dressing a grinding wheel

11.4 Abrasives

The two main abrasive materials used in metalworking are aluminium oxide and silicon carbide.

Aluminium Oxide (or *fused alumina*) is a manufactured material produced by the fusion of bauxite. It is a tough, sharp abrasive, suitable for the grinding of metals of high tensile strength, such as steel.

Emery is an impure corundum, which is the naturally occurring crystalline form of aluminium oxide, and has varying properties.

Silicon Carbide is a man-made mineral of extreme hardness and sharpness, suitable for the grinding of materials of low tensile strength, such as cast iron, brass, bronze, aluminium and cemented carbides.

MACHINEWORK 225

Abrasives are available as powder, grinding paste, lapping compound, and variously-shaped stones and wheels, and on cloth in grades 0, FF, F, 1, 1½, 2, 2½, 3 to 4 which is the coarsest, and on buffing sticks, size 300 × 22 × 6 mm in grit numbers 00, 0, 1, 2, 3.

To finish silversmith's work (copper, silver, brass, etc.) two natural stones may be used, Tam-o'-Shanter stones (measuring 150 × 38 × 13 mm approximately) and Water of Ayr stones (measuring 100 × (6 or 13) mm square).

Pumice powder, tripoli and rouge compositions have been mentioned in 6.14.

11.5 Cutting Fluids. Sometimes referred to as Coolants or Cutting Lubricants

Their functions are:

(1) To cool work and tool, lessening distortion.
(2) To lubricate, reducing power consumption.
(3) To prevent welding of chip to tool.
(4) To wash away chips and swarf.
(5) To improve surface finish.
(6) To protect against corrosion.

They may be divided into three main classes:
Soluble oils are mineral oils treated to yield an emulsion ('slurries' or 'suds') when added to water. They may be used neat for maximum lubrication or diluted to increase the cooling power. To dilute, follow the supplier's instructions, in which the ratio of oil to water may be 1 : 30. A protective film is left which is rust-resisting.
'Straight' oils are mainly mineral/lard and extreme-pressure (E.P.) cutting oils designed to be used neat. They have very good lubricating properties and therefore are essential for slow heavy cutting operations.
Water-base fluids are true solutions of salts and other minerals in water; they have very good cooling properties, and are clean and clear. Those containing sodium nitrite or sodium carbonate are rust-resisting.

The most efficient method of applying cutting fluids is to use a pump, oil tray and reservoir, to give a slow continuous stream over the cutting action. If this is not possible an oil can may be used.

Table 15. Suggested Cutting Fluids

(*Note:* The exact fluid should be determined by a practical trial on the particular work and machine. The fluids are given in order of general popularity.)

Metal	Cutting Fluids			
Aluminium and Alloys	Paraffin	dry	straight	soluble
Brass, Copper, and Bronze	Dry	soluble	straight	paraffin
Cast Iron	Dry	Dry and compressed air		
Steel	Soluble	straight	water-base (mainly grinding)	

11.6 Lubrication

One of the most common applications of lubricants is to bearings.

The oil film should prevent metallic contact between the journal and bearings and depends upon the viscosity of the oil. If the viscosity of the oil is too low the film may be broken, and if too high, frictional resistance to movement is increased. Gears under severe conditions (e.g. hypoid gears) require extreme-pressure (E.P.) lubricants.

Oil is generally considered to be more effective than grease, and is to be preferred if the sealing arrangements are adequate. Methods of applying oil include:

> *Oil bath and splash systems:* slow and medium speeds
> *Circulating systems:* medium speeds
> *Spray or mist:* high speeds

Grease is usually employed where temperatures are not excessive and the sealing arrangements are inadequate for oil. Grease has excellent self-sealing properties and also acts as a dirt excluder. Methods of applying grease include:

> *Grease packing:* not severe conditions, and infrequent replenishment required.
> *Compression cup (or) pressure gun application:* periodic addition of fresh grease.

Mechanical lubricators (or) centralised pressure systems: severe conditions, frequent and regular addition of fresh grease (e.g. metal rolling mills).

11.7 Surface Finishes

The surface finish of metal may be left in a number of conditions before applying the final protection.

Cast iron and other rough surfaces have sharp edges removed by grinding or filing, and are then wire brushed by hand or power. Large workshops may have special equipment such as shot blasting.

The majority of work pieces are given no further finishing after machining or filing. Work which must be accurate to another surface can be scraped, see 8.5, or lapped. *Lapping* requires a lap of softer material than the work, e.g. a grey cast iron lap on hardened steel and a copper or lead lap on soft steel. This ensures that the paste (very fine abrasive powder and oil or grease) is embedded in the lap and not in the work surface. The lap is rubbed over the work under light pressure and in a varied and random motion. For circular work *honing* can be employed: fine abrasive sticks are held in a special holding device either in the bore or externally and moved over the rotating work.

Work which does not require such accuracy can be draw-filed and perhaps emery clothed. An attractive finish on small bright surfaces can be imparted by holding a piece of wooden dowel, say 5 mm diameter in the drill chuck, applying a small amount of abrasive paste and 'spotting' the work all over.

In the past it has been a very popular practice to colour metals by chemical means. Hundreds of formulae are in existence, particularly

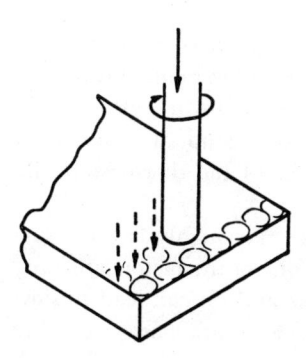

Fig. 344. 'Spotting'

for the copper alloys (e.g. for oxi-finishes on copper and silver, use a dilute solution of about 3 grams of potassium sulphide (liver of sulphur) per litre, at room temperature or slightly warmer). If a quantity of work is to be coloured, proprietary powders and solutions are available. Iron and steel can be coloured by heating and plunging into oil.

11.8 Surface Protection

A primary essential to all work is absolute cleanliness. If the surface of the metal is to be seen, a convenient method is to lacquer. Cold lacquering is practicable, but the temperature must be at least 18°C and the atmosphere dust free. An alternative method is to apply beeswax and then polish with a soft cloth.

Electrodeposition or electroplating is the deposition of one metal upon another by electro-chemical processes. A very low voltage direct current is required, generally between 4 and 10 volts.

The article is first chemically cleaned and scoured, and then immersed in dilute acid (sulphuric or hydrochloric) to remove any oxide film, before being swilled and hung from a central cathode. Nickel and copper plating are possible with simple equipment.

Anodising (anodic oxidation) is the process of thickening the natural oxide film on an aluminium surface. The article to be anodised is made the anode of a bath with a lead cathode lining and containing an electrolyte capable of liberating oxygen, which combines with the parent metal at the anode face. The new aluminium oxide film is therefore integral with the metal surface and not a surface deposit.

The anodic film has a minutely porous cellular structure, which can absorb dyestuffs ranging from pastel shades to vivid primary colours.

Plastic For special purposes such as wire baskets for soap, vegetables, etc., *plastic coating* is now widely used. One method is to heat the article to approximately 200°C and immerse in a proprietary powder; brush off excess and fuse the remainder to an even coat at 160°C. The oven used should be evenly heated and thermostatically controlled.

Paint finishes should be applied over thoroughly cleaned surfaces since the condition of the surface is one of the factors affecting the durability of the paint system. Grease and oil can lead to slow drying of the paint and to poor adhesion. Rust and rust-promoting agents may cause paint failure months after the finish has been applied. De-rusting fluids are based mainly on phosphoric acid with suitable inhibitors and wetting agents. Their main function is to remove traces of rust and give an etched surface to the metal to improve paint adhesion.

Best results are normally obtained by the application of a painting system comprising several coats of paint, each of which has its own specific function. The primer provides the initial adhesion and gives corrosion resistance; the undercoats provide an opaque background of uniform colour for the finishing coats which, in turn, provide gloss, colour and durability.

Paint systems may range from a single coat of finish to a multi-coat system of primer or primer-surfacer, filler and finish. The system to adopt depends on the initial state of the metal, and on the durability and appearance required of the paint coating. For example, on smooth sheet metal 1 or 2 coats of finish will often give adequate performance for most purposes but an additional coat of primer will give a system with increased build and durability. On rougher metal 2 or 3 coats of primer-surfacer, followed by finish, may be necessary to obtain a good appearance, while on metal castings a full system of primer, filler and finish is generally required.

12

Economic Considerations

The thoughtful reader will have noticed as he read parts of this book that there was often a choice between two or more metals for a particular purpose and between technical methods for achieving virtually the same result. The student who pursues this enquiry further may find that his studies lead him to what he might have considered academic subjects separate from his own interests, such as economics, geography and history. Unfortunately educational bodies and text books have given little encouragement to this interesting development of technical subjects at secondary education level. At University and in industry the student will soon find that economic considerations can be just as important as the technical.

In a book of this size it will be impossible to do more than illustrate some of the avenues that can be explored. The selection of one from two metals which could equally fulfil the technical requirements will require the consideration of several factors such as the length of life of the project and the rate of interest, as illustrated below.

Metal (hypothetical)	Durability of metal (years)	Cost of project (£)	Annual repayments (£) at Interest Rates of 0%	5%	20%
x	10	100	10	$12\frac{1}{2}$	20
y	50	200	4	9	24
z	100	300	3	$10\frac{1}{2}$	33

Thus, when the rate of interest is relatively low we should tend to select the more durable metals, despite the fact that the initial cost may be higher.

ECONOMIC CONSIDERATIONS

One simple method of comparing techniques is by a break-even chart. Before this can be constructed the costs involved must be grouped:

Fixed costs: Interest on capital, depreciation and other costs which must be met even if the machine or equipment is not used.

Variable costs: Power, materials, labour and other costs which vary with production.

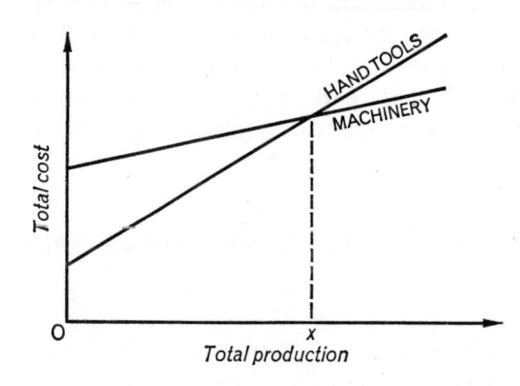

Fig. 345. Break-even chart

In the hypothetical example there are two methods, one by a simple labour intensive method using hand tools and the other using expensive machinery but little labour. It will be seen that up to x units of production, the hand method is most economical.

In workshops it is not uncommon for inventions to be made, which may range from special tools for the particular job in hand, to others which are likely to have market potential. In the latter case the problem is to decide how the inventor can profit from his idea. The simplest method is in factories which have suggestion boxes and pay employees for good ideas whilst the most involved is for the inventor to patent and enter into commercial production and marketing. An interim approach is to apply for a provisional specification and then to come to an agreement with a firm who will manufacture and market the invention.

The first step towards a patent is to write to:

> The Patent Office, 25 Southampton Buildings,
> Chancery Lane, London WC2A 1AY

to ask for the official pamphlet 'Applying for a Patent', and then to decide if it is worth proceeding, with or without the assistance of a patent agent.

The selection of metals and techniques, and the problem of patenting are but a brief introduction to some of the interesting subjects which the student may wish to study in greater depth. These might range from methods of selecting the most profitable product for a specified production unit, to a study of the location of industry.

Those students who wish to undertake practical projects in a very realistic manner should consider the commercial aspects as well as the technical. For example, students could produce alternative designs and quotations for seats in the park or playground equipment for a school. The following may be used as a guide, to help with the quotation.

Example. Fixed and Variable Costs to produce 4 Bench Seats

Fixed Costs

	Total Costs	Unit
Depreciation (e.g. calculate for each major piece of equipment $\dfrac{\text{purchase price} \times \text{hours of use}}{\text{hours in life of equipment}}$)	£1	£0·25
Maintenance	0	0
Salaries	0	0
Administrative and other expenses	2	0·50
Total Fixed Costs	3	0·75

Variable Costs

Labour	0	0
Materials: Metal	30	7·50
Miscellaneous	6	1·50
Other (e.g. electricity)	1	0·25
Total Variable Costs	37	9·25
Grand Total	40	
Average Unit Cost		10·00

A school or college would probably only aim to cover Variable Costs, excluding labour, although it would be an interesting exercise to attempt an estimate of Fixed Costs. The question of the profit margin is more complicated and cannot be adequately discussed here.

Appendix A

Table 1 Tempering Temperatures, p. 24; 2 Workshop tests and methods of identification, p. 27; 3 Pattern-makers' contraction allowances, p. 33; 4 Flame temperatures, p. 42; 5 Soft solders, p. 44; 6 Silver solders, p. 49; 7 Brazing alloys, p. 50; 8 Rivets, p. 53; 9 Tooth size of hand hacksaw blades, p. 121; 10 Chisel angles, p. 123; 11 Threading lubricants, p. 150; 12 Feeds for high-speed steel twist drills, p. 162; 13 Lathe tool angles, p. 186; 14 Cutting speeds, p. 193; 15 Cutting fluids, p. 226.

Table 16. Cutting Speeds and Tool Angles for various materials

Material	Cutting speed Metres per minute	Front clearance	Side clearance	Back or top rake	Side rake
Aluminium — soft alloy	120–240	9	9	30	15
Aluminium — hard alloy	90–180	9	9	30	15
Brass	90–180	7	6	0	5
Bronze — free cutting	90–180	5	5	0	2
Bronze — tough	30– 60	10	12	8	10
Cast Iron	20– 30	5	4	10	9
Copper	20– 45	5	5	20	25
Die-Castings (zinc)	60– 90	8	8	8	10
Magnesium Alloy	180–300	10	10	8	6
Plastics — cast resin	60–180	10	12	30	25
Plastics — laminated	60–180	7	7	25	25
Steel — mild	30– 60	8	6	20	15
Steel — high carbon	10– 25	6	5	10	5
Steel — stainless	20– 45	8	6	8	5
Wood	150–300	15	15	25	25

Courtesy: Boxford Machine Tools Ltd.

APPENDIX A

Table 17. ISO Metric Coarse Thread Form (see Figs 307 and 308)

nom. dia.	pitch	basic major diameter	basic effective diameter	basic minor diameter of external threads	basic minor diameter of internal threads	recommended tapping drill size	clearance drill size
mm	mm	mm	mm	mm	mm	mm	mm
1	0.25	1.000	0.838	0.693	0.729	0.75	1.05
1.1	0.25	1.100	0.938	0.793	0.829	0.85	1.15
1.2	0.25	1.200	1.038	0.893	0.929	0.95	1.25
1.4	0.30	1.400	1.205	1.032	1.075	1.10	1.45
1.6	0.35	1.600	1.373	1.170	1.221	1.25	1.65
1.8	0.35	1.800	1.573	1.370	1.421	1.45	1.85
2	0.40	2.000	1.740	1.509	1.567	1.60	2.05
2.2	0.45	2.200	1.908	1.648	1.713	1.75	2.25
2.5	0.45	2.500	2.208	1.948	2.013	2.05	2.60
3	0.50	3.000	2.675	2.387	2.459	2.50	3.10
3.5	0.60	3.500	3.110	2.764	2.850	2.90	3.60
4	0.70	4.000	3.545	3.141	3.242	3.30	4.10
4.5	0.75	4.500	4.013	3.580	3.688	3.70	4.60
5	0.80	5.000	4.480	4.019	4.134	4.20	5.10
6	1.00	6.000	5.350	4.773	4.917	5.00	6.10
7	1.00	7.000	6.350	5.773	5.917	6.00	7.20
8	1.25	8.000	7.188	6.466	6.647	6.80	8.20
9	1.25	9.000	8.188	7.466	7.647	7.80	9.20
10	1.50	10.000	9.026	8.160	8.376	8.50	10.20
11	1.50	11.000	10.026	9.160	9.376	9.50	11.20
12	1.75	12.000	10.863	9.853	10.106	10.20	12.20
14	2.00	14.000	12.701	11.546	11.835	12.00	14.25
16	2.00	16.000	14.701	13.546	13.835	14.00	16.25
18	2.50	18.000	16.376	14.933	15.294	15.50	18.25
20	2.50	20.000	18.376	16.933	17.294	17.50	20.25
22	2.50	22.000	20.376	18.933	19.294	19.50	22.25
24	3.00	24.000	22.051	20.319	20.752	21.00	24.25
27	3.00	27.000	25.051	23.319	23.752	24.00	27.25
30	3.50	30.000	27.727	25.706	26.211	26.50	30.50
33	3.50	33.000	30.727	28.706	29.211	29.50	33.50
36	4.00	36.000	33.402	31.093	31.670	32.00	36.50
39	4.00	39.000	36.402	34.093	34.670	35.00	39.50
42	4.50	42.000	39.077	36.479	37.129	37.50	42.50
45	4.50	45.000	42.077	39.479	40.129	40.50	45.50
48	5.00	48.000	44.752	41.866	42.587	43.00	48.50
52	5.00	52.000	48.752	45.866	46.587	47.00	53.00
56	5.50	56.000	52.428	49.252	50.046	50.50	57.00

I.S.O. METRIC COARSE THREAD FORM

r = Basic Radius = ·1443 p
hn = Basic Height of Internal Thread & Depth of Thread Engagement = ·54127 p
hs = Basic Height of External Thread = .61344 p
p = Pitch

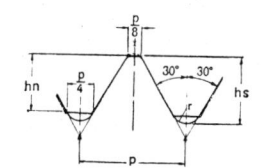

Courtesy:
The Sheffield Twist Drill & Steel Co. Ltd.

ISO Metric Coarse Threads are likely to be the most widely used. Those who require full details are referred to:

British Standard 3643: Specification for ISO Metric Screw Threads
Part 1: 1963   *Thread Data and Standard Thread Series*
Part 2: 1966   *Limits and Tolerances for Coarse Pitch Series Threads*
Part 3: 1967   *Limits and Tolerances for Fine Pitch Threads (Constant Pitch Series)*

Table 18. Standard Diameters for Wire

Diameter, mm (First choice)		
0·020	0·200	2·00
0·025	0·250	2·50
0·032	0·315	3·15
0·040	0·400	4·00
0·050	0·500	5·00
0·063	0·630	6·30
0·080	0·800	8·00
0·100	1·000	10·0
0·125	1·250	12·5
0·160	1·600	16·0

Source: BS 4391: 1969

Table 19. Standard Thicknesses for Sheet and Strip

Thickness, mm (First choice)		
0·020	0·16	1·2
0·025	0·20	1·6
0·030	0·25	2·0
0·040	0·30	2·5
0·050	0·40	3·0
0·060	0·50	4·0
0·080	0·60	5·0
0·100	0·80	6·0
0·120	1·00	8·0
		10·0

Source: BS 4391: 1969

Table 20. Suggested Limits from ISO Recommendations

Tolerances in standard holes (in millimetres) — 2 Classes

	Nominal Diameters	0–3	3–6	6–10	10–18	18–30	30–50	50–80	80–120
H7	High Limit	+0·010	+0·012	+0·015	+0·018	+0·021	+0·025	+0·030	+0·035
	Low Limit	0·0	0·0	0·0	0·0	0·0	0·0	0·0	0·0
H8	High Limit	+0·014	+0·018	+0·022	+0·027	+0·033	+0·039	+0·046	+0·054
	Low Limit	0·0	0·0	0·0	0·0	0·0	0·0	0·0	0·0

Interference (Drive Fit) allowances on shafts for various fits

	Nominal Diameters	0–3	3–6	6–10	10–18	18–30	30–50	50–80	80–120
p6	High Limit	+0·012	+0·020	+0·024	+0·029	+0·035	+0·042	+0·051	+0·059
	Low Limit	+0·006	+0·012	+0·015	+0·018	+0·022	+0·026	+0·032	+0·037
	Tolerance	0·006	0·008	0·009	0·011	0·013	0·016	0·019	0·022

Transition (Push Fit)

		0–3	3–6	6–10	10–18	18–30	30–50	50–80	80–120
k6	High Limit	+0·006	+0·009	+0·010	+0·012	+0·015	+0·018	+0·021	+0·025
	Low Limit	+0·0	+0·001	+0·001	+0·001	+0·002	+0·002	+0·002	+0·003
	Tolerance	0·006	0·008	0·009	0·011	0·013	0·016	0·019	0·022

Clearance (Close Running Fit)

		0–3	3–6	6–10	10–18	18–30	30–50	50–80	80–120
g6	High Limit	−0·002	−0·004	−0·005	−0·006	−0·007	−0·009	−0·010	−0·012
	Low Limit	−0·008	−0·012	−0·014	−0·017	−0·020	−0·025	−0·029	−0·034
	Tolerance	0·006	0·008	0·009	0·011	0·013	0·016	0·019	0·022

Courtesy: Boxford Machine Tools Ltd.

Table 21. ISO Morse Taper Shanks Dimensions in millimetres *Courtesy: T. S. Harrison & Sons Ltd.*

Number of taper	Dia. of plug at small end	Dia. at end of socket	Shank Whole length	Shank Depth	Depth of hole	Standard plug depth	Tongue Thickness	Tongue Length	Keyway Width	Keyway Length	End of socket to keyway	Percentage taper
	D	A	B	S	H	P	t	T	W	L	K	
0	6·4	9·045	59·5	56·5	52	50	3·9	6·5	4·2	15	49	5·2
1	9·4	12·065	65·5	62	56	53·5	5·2	8·5	5·5	19	52	5
2	14·6	17·780	80	75	67	64	6·3	10	6·6	22	62	5
3	19·8	23·825	99	94	84	81	7·9	13	8·2	27	78	5
4	25·9	31·267	124	117·5	107	102·5	11·9	16	12·2	32	98	5·2
5	37·6	44·399	156	149·5	135	129·5	15·9	19	16·2	38	125	5·3
6	53·9	63·348	218	210	188	182	19	27	19·3	47	177	5·2

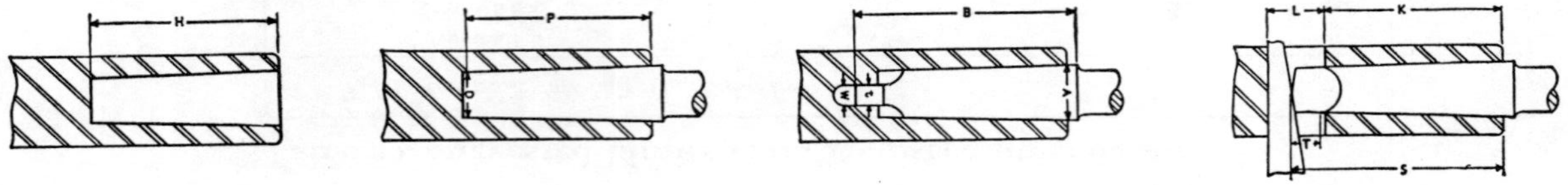

APPENDIX A

Table 22. Natural Tangents (in ½ Degrees)

Degrees		Degrees		Degrees		Degrees	
0	0·0000	23	0·4245	46	1·0355	69	2·6051
	0·0087		0·4348		1·0538		2·6746
1	0·0175	24	0·4452	47	1·0724	70	2·7475
	0·0262		0·4557		1·0913		2·8239
2	0·0349	25	0·4663	48	1·1106	71	2·9042
	0·0437		0·4770		1·1303		2·9887
3	0·0524	26	0·4877	49	1·1504	72	3·0777
	0·0612		0·4986		1·1708		3·1716
4	0·0699	27	0·5095	50	1·1918	73	3·2709
	0·0787		0·5206		1·2131		3·3759
5	0·0875	28	0·5317	51	1·2349	74	3·4874
	0·0963		0·5430		1·2572		3·6059
6	0·1051	29	0·5543	52	1·2799	75	3·7321
	0·1139		0·5658		1·3032		3·8667
7	0·1228	30	0·5774	53	1·3270	76	4·0108
	0·1317		0·5890		1·3514		4·1653
8	0·1405	31	0·6009	54	1·3764	77	4·3315
	0·1495		0·6128		1·4019		4·5107
9	0·1584	32	0·6249	55	1·4281	78	4·7046
	0·1673		0·6371		1·4550		4·9152
10	0·1763	33	0·6494	56	1·4826	79	5·1446
	0·1853		0·6619		1·5108		5·3955
11	0·1944	34	0·6745	57	1·5399	80	5·6713
	0·2035		0·6873		1·5697		5·9758
12	0·2126	35	0·7002	58	1·6003	81	6·3138
	0·2217		0·7133		1·6319		6·6912
13	0·2309	36	0·7265	59	1·6643	82	7·1154
	0·2401		0·7400		1·6977		7·5958
14	0·2493	37	0·7536	60	1·7321	83	8·1443
	0·2586		0·7673		1·7675		8·7769
15	0·2679	38	0·7813	61	1·8040	84	9·5144
	0·2773		0·7954		1·8418		10·39
16	0·2867	39	0·8098	62	1·8807	85	11·43
	0·2962		0·8243		1·9210		12·71
17	0·3057	40	0·8391	63	1·9626	86	14·30
	0·3153		0·8541		2·0057		16·35
18	0·3249	41	0·8693	64	2·0503	87	19·08
	0·3346		0·8847		2·0965		22·90
19	0·3443	42	0·9004	65	2·1445	88	28·64
	0·3541		0·9163		2·1943		38·19
20	0·3640	43	0·9325	66	2·2460	89	57·29
	0·3739		0·9490		2·2998		114·6
21	0·3839	44	0·9657	67	2·3559		
	0·3939		0·9827		2·4142		to infinity
22	0·4040	45	1·000	68	2·4751		
	0·4142		1·0176		2·5386		

Table 23. Useful Miscellaneous Data

Length
- 1 yd = 0·9144 m
- 1 ft = 0·3048 m
- 1 in = 25·4 mm
- 1 'thou' = 25·4 μm

Area
- 1 ft^2 = 0·0929 m^2
- 1 in^2 = 645·16 mm^2

Volume and Capacity
- 1 gal = 4·546 litres
- 1 pt = 0·568 litre
- 1 in^3 = 16·387 cm^3

Mass
- 1 ton = 1016 kg
- 1 cwt = 50·8 kg
- 1 lb = 0·454 kg

To convert °Fahrenheit to °Celsius, subtract 32 and multiply by $\frac{5}{9}$.
To convert °Centigrade to °Fahrenheit, multiply by $\frac{9}{5}$ and add 32.

Circumference of a circle = Diameter × 3·1416
Area of a circle = (Radius)^2 × 3·1416
Volume of a sphere = $\dfrac{(\text{Diameter})^3 \times 3 \cdot 1416}{6}$.

Factor by which the unit is to be multiplied	Prefix	Symbol
1 000 000 = 10^6	mega	M
1 000 = 10^3	kilo	k
0·001 = 10^{-3}	milli	m
0·000 001 = 10^{-6}	micro	μ

Appendix B

Past Question Papers for the Certificate of Secondary Education and the General Certificate of Education

Arranged in approximate chapter groupings and designated
C.S.E.1., C.S.E.2.,...for the Certificate of Secondary Education
O.1., O.2., ...for Ordinary level Metalwork
E.1., E.2., ...for Ordinary level Engineering Workshop
Theory and Practice
A.1., A.2., ...for Advanced level Metalwork

1 Metals

C.S.E.1. Give one reason for:
(a) water taps being made of brass or chromium-plated brass;
(b) surface plates being made of cast iron;
(c) the skin of an aeroplane being made of an aluminium alloy;
(d) some mild steel sheets being coated with zinc;
(e) the wire of an electric cable being made of copper;
(f) a centre punch being made of high-carbon steel.

(WJEC)

C.S.E.2. What is meant by the term 'case hardening'? How is this operation carried out? Give an example of when you would use the process of case hardening.

(EM)

O.1. (a) Describe the properties of (i) copper and (ii) cast iron and state two examples of the use of each.

(b) What is an alloy? Name three alloys commonly found in the workshop and state one use and the composition of each.

(LU)

O.2. Plain carbon steels may be classified as Low Carbon, Medium Carbon, or High Carbon. What do you understand by this? What would you expect to happen to each of these steels if they were heated to red heat and then (a) allowed to cool slowly, (b) cooled quickly in water?

Give, with reasons, an example of the type of work for which you consider each of these classes of steel to be most suitable.

(AEB)

O.3. Tools such as scribers, screwdrivers, drills and chisels have to be subjected to some form of heat treatment before they are suitable for use. Give an account of the treatment you would give a cold chisel, explaining why it is necessary, and making certain that you specify exactly the material from which you would make the cold chisel.

(O&C)

O.4. Explain what is meant by an alloy and state why alloys are used so extensively in all branches of metalworking.

Using a grid like the one below, list four different alloys and give the constituent metals and approximate proportions, the outstanding working properties and the main uses of each.

Alloy	Constituent metals and %s	Main working properties	Uses

(LU)

E.1. Give one instance of a workshop situation in which each of the following materials may be used: high carbon steel, medium carbon steel, half hard copper sheet, aluminium. For each of the situations

APPENDIX B   243

you mention state the properties inherent in the material which make it a suitable choice.

(OLE)

E.2. A plain carbon steel containing 0·6% carbon is supplied in its soft state. How may this be hardened? Write fully on the precautions you would take to ensure successful hardening of the metal in both sheet and bar form. What steps would you take to reduce some of the hardness again in both sheet and bar form?

(OLE)

E.3. (i) The jaws of a small mild steel spanner must be prevented from wearing in use.

Describe the heat treatment used to do this.

(ii) Describe in detail the process of hardening and tempering a scriber, mentioning the metal from which you should make the scriber.

(NU)

A.1. (a) Briefly describe the production of copper noting particularly the raw materials involved and the source of these materials.

(b) List the physical characteristics of copper and explain how these properties are affected when it is alloyed with zinc in varying proportions.

(c) State the uses of some of the copper-zinc alloys in the school workshop.

(LU)

A.2. Below are listed some items which are to be manufactured.

Alongside each item are three suggested metals which could be used. Write down the metals in order of preference (most appropriate first) and give reasons for your choice in each case. (Note: it is sufficient to give one reason why your first choice is preferable to your second and one reason why your second choice is better than your third.)

(a) Decorative metal bowl	70/30 brass, mild steel, copper,
(b) Foil to be used for wrapping food	mild steel, aluminium, copper

(c) Ship's propeller | cast iron, high carbon steel, manganese bronze

(d) A crane hook | wrought iron, mild steel, cast iron

(e) A worm wheel mating with a steel gear wheel | high carbon steel, phosphor bronze, duralumin

(f) A long bar required to be hard at one end | mild steel, copper, 50/50 brass

(NU)

2 Preliminary Considerations

C.S.E.1. What special rules apply for your safety when you use: (a) a lathe, (b) an emery wheel, (c) bench shears or guillotine, (d) a pickle bath?

(S)

C.S.E.2. There are a number of sources of danger in the metalwork room. For each of the following say clearly, in a few words, what the danger might be and also what precaution you would take to prevent an accident when:
(a) drilling a hole in thin sheet metal;
(b) adding cold metal to a crucible of molten metal;
(c) forging a number of pieces of metal which have been allowed to cool naturally from red heat;
(d) measuring the length of a knurl on the lathe;
(e) stacking long lengths of metal.

(SE)

O.1. 'Safety in the School Workshop.' Discuss this with reference to (a) clothing, (b) swarf, (c) hot working of metals, (d) protection of eyes when using machines.

What do you consider to be the value of the emergency stop buttons in the workshop?

(WJEC)

O.2. State two dangers which exist when carrying out each of the following operations and in each case describe the precautions you would take to avoid the possibility of an accident.

APPENDIX B

(a) Joining metal pieces together by brazing at the brazing hearth.
(b) Buffing a small copper dish on a polishing machine.
(c) Pickling copper to remove the scale after annealing.
(d) Turning a 50 mm diameter brass bar in the lathe.

(AEB)*

E.1. (a) What special precautions should be taken when setting up and turning brass?

(b) List six items that one should expect to find in a school workshop's first-aid box.

(AEB)

A.1. Safety in the school workshops is of utmost importance at all times. State, with reasons, the safety precautions you would observe when using the following machines and apparatus: (a) the drilling machine, (b) the centre lathe, (c) the grinding wheel, (d) the brazing hearth.

(WJEC)

3 Foundrywork

C.S.E.1. Make a sketch and notes to explain the use of each of the following used in casting.

(a) Moulding box or flask. (b) A combined wedge and flat rammer. (c) A sprue pin. (d) A crucible.

(EA)

C.S.E.2. 'The pattern maker must have a good knowledge of foundry work if the pattern is to produce the desired result.'

List eight requirements for a really good pattern.

(NW)

O.1. Use your ruler to draw a rectangle 200 mm long × 150 mm wide. This rectangle represents the outline of a sectional elevation of two moulding boxes clamped together and ready for pouring the molten metal.

Within the rectangle draw all the relevant details you would expect to see, labelling the ten most important factors, but excluding the clamping device.

(OLE)

O.2. (a) Explain: (i) how you would assess the suitability of foundry sand for moulding and (ii) what steps you would take to restore it to condition if found unsatisfactory.

(b) Why and when is parting sand (or powder) used?

(c) Sketch and identify three moulding tools and explain how they are used.

(CU)

O.3. Describe in note form how you would cast an aluminium disc 100 mm diameter by 19 mm thick having a 19 mm dia. hole at its centre. Add sketches where these help to clarify your notes.

(OLE)*

E.1. Explain, clearly, what is meant by three of the following as used in foundry work:
(a) cope and drag,
(b) runner, riser and vent,
(c) solid and split patterns,
(d) cores and core prints.

Use sketches to clarify your answers.

(AEB)

A.1. Sketch pictorially a small hand wheel, e.g. that found on the tailstock of a lathe, and also draw a vertical section through it. Describe how you would cast and finish in an aluminium alloy the wheel you have drawn. You may assume that the sand has been previously prepared and is ready for use.

(OLE)

4 Joining Processes

C.S.E.1. What happens to produce a joint when molten solder is in contact with the metal being joined?

(WM)

C.S.E.2. From what materials are soft solders made? What is meant by 'tinning' the soldering bit (iron)?

(S)

O.1. (a) Explain in detail the meaning of the terms: tinning, sweating, oxidation.

APPENDIX B 247

(b) (i) What is the purpose of using a flux when soldering?

(ii) Identify two different soft soldering jobs, one for which an active (acid) flux would be suitable and another for which a passive (resin based) flux must be used.

Give reasons for your choice and explain fully the soldering process for one of the joints you have selected.

(CU)

O.2. There are several methods of ensuring that a nut does not work loose on a bolt. Make sketches of three methods with which you are familiar, and state the reasons which would govern your choice in the use of each you have drawn.

(WJEC)

O.3. By brief notes and clear sketches describe the processes by which the following metals may be joined together.
(a) Thin sheet metal: (i) making use of heat, (ii) without using heat.
(b) Rods, bars and thicker sheet metal.

(O&C)

O.4. Make sketches illustrating jobs in which you would use the process of (a) soft soldering, (b) silver soldering and (c) brazing.

Describe fully the various stages involved in carrying out one of these processes.

(LU)

O.5. Name and sketch two kinds of rivet.

Describe, with sketches, how you would fasten together two pieces of 25 × 6 mm mild steel bar using one rivet of each kind.

(AEB)*

E.1. Why is a flux necessary when soldering? Name the fluxes and solders used for (a) hard soldering, (b) soft soldering.

Describe the process of hard soldering.

(AEB)

E.2. Two pipes, 38 mm in diameter, are to be brazed together to form a 'T' piece. The pipes are of brass having a high melting point and they are shaped ready for joining.

Describe fully the brazing process.

(AEB)*

A.1. Discuss the factors which determine when each of the following methods is used for joining two pieces of metal together: (*a*) welding, (*b*) brazing, (*c*) silver soldering, (*d*) soft soldering.

In each case, explain, in detail, the precautions necessary to ensure a successful joint.

(WJEC)

A.2. Write a short essay on 'Fluxes in the School Workshop'.

(AEB)

A.3. (*a*) Make sketches of five types of rivet with which you are familiar and state a use for each particular type.

(*b*) State the amount of shank required to form the head on each type relative to the diameter of the rivet.

(*c*) Show by means of sketches the method of forming a snap head when closing a rivet joining two pieces of 3 mm plate.

(WJEC)*

5 Sheetmetalwork

C.S.E.1. (*a*) Give three reasons why edge finishes are so important in tinplate work.

(*b*) What should you use to clean and polish tinplate articles?

(*c*) What should be used to mark out construction lines on tinplate and why should it be used?

(*d*) Two pieces of steel sheet are to be joined by a line of rivets. Describe a method that would ensure that the holes for the rivets, in the two sheets, are exactly matched to each other.

(WM)

C.S.E.2. An open top box is to be made in tinplate to hold nails. Illustrate and describe two methods of finishing the top edges of the box to prevent cutting oneself on the sharp edges round the top of the box.

(EM)

O.1. Make sketches of the following tools used in tinplate work: a hatchet stake; a bick iron; a creasing iron; a pair of folding bars; a rawhide mallet. From these tools, choose any three and illustrate one use for each.

(WJEC)

APPENDIX B

O.2. Make sketches of the following tinsmith's tools: snips; a paning hammer; a hand groover. What use is made of each of the above tools?

(OLE)

O.3. Explain, illustrating your answer with sketches, two of the following tinsmithing processes.
(i) Making a grooved seam.
(ii) Throwing up an edge, as in making the bottom of an oilcan.
(iii) Wiring an edge.

(WJEC)

O.4. Sketch two ways of making a flat seam tinplate joint, two ways of making a circular seam joint and two ways of finishing edges on tinned plate work. Carefully explain how you would make one example from each of the above groups.

(OLE)

E.1. What is the fault when
(a) in cutting tinplate a pair of snips produces a 'burr',
(b) a countersunk rivet cannot be closed effectively?
Describe the method of constructing a splayed rectangular baking tray when the corner has a riveted lap joint and the top has a wired edge.

(AEB)

E.2. (a) What are the most common forms of riveted joint?
(b) Why are fluxes used in soldering and brazing?
(c) A sheet metal tray is formed by bending up the four sides from a marked-out base. Which of the above-mentioned processes would you use for the corner joints when a tray is made from:
(i) 2·0 mm steel sheet, (ii) 1·2 mm brass sheet, (iii) 0·8 mm tinned plate?

(AEB)

A.1. Describe how you would produce a smooth and stiffened edge to a cylindrical vessel being made from (a) tinplate, (b) sheet copper:
(i) by adding or applying wire in some form;
(ii) without adding or applying any wire.

(AEB)

6 Silversmithing

C.S.E.1. Explain by notes and/or sketches the meaning of the following terms: (a) planishing, (b) raising, (c) annealing.

(WJEC)

C.S.E.2. Explain in detail how you would make a small copper tray by the use of sinking.

(WM)

O.1. A cylindrical tankard in gilding metal is being made in the school workshop. The long seam in the body has been soldered with hard silver solder.

Describe in detail how a slightly domed bottom could be made and silver soldered on to the body so that the doming rises inside the tankard. Illustrate your answer and name all materials which you would use.

(WJEC)

O.2. Describe, with the aid of sketches, either
(a) the raising of a vase from a single sheet of copper, or
(b) the production of a pierced pattern, including the preparation, sawing and finishing to shape.

(NU)

O.3. (a) why is it frequently necessary to planish work in copper and gilding metal? Explain how you would planish a small circular hollowed bowl.

(b) Describe in detail how you would silver solder a circular base ring on this bowl.

(O&C)

O.4. Make a dimensioned working drawing of a tankard approximately 125 mm high and 75 mm diameter to be made in gilding metal. Give all constructional details.

(SU)*

O.5. By sketches, show how you would bind the soft iron wire around a truncated cone preparatory to silver soldering the butt joint. If the joint is not satisfactory what are possible causes of failure and what precautions should you take to ensure success?

(OLE)

APPENDIX B

O.6. Make a sketch of a small beaten metal sweet dish on three legs, and explain in detail the final processes of cleaning and polishing it.

(OLE)

A.1. Wire in many forms is applied to beaten metalwork. State two reasons for the use of 'wires' in beaten metalwork. Use sketches and notes to show the form of two different 'wires' which you could make and give a relevant example of the use of each. Describe how you would make and apply one of these 'wires' to the example of work you have given.

(AEB)

A.2. Using sketches to illustrate your answer, give the sequence of operations necessary to make one of the following:
(a) a cast brass handle for a tankard;
(b) a built-up stop-hinge for a rectangular box.

(NU)

A.3. Explain the following processes, giving typical situations, preferably from your own experience, where they would be used: snarling, caulking, stitching, chasing.

(CU)

A.4. The lid of a box made from sheet metal may be located by means of a bezel which is fixed inside the box and over which the lid fits.
  Describe in detail how you would make and fix such a bezel for
(a) a circular brass box of internal diameter 75 mm;
(b) a rectangular brass box of internal size 125 mm by 80 mm.

(AEB)*

A.5. Sketch a design for either the salt or the pepper container of a condiment set which could be made principally from gilding metal sheet. The size, form, and construction of the container, including the means of filling it, should be clearly shown. Briefly describe the successive stages in the making of the container.

(LU)

A.6. Make several design outlines of a trophy in the form of a cup which could be made in the craft-room from gilding metal, and,

selecting the one you like best, produce:
 (i) a well-proportioned detailed sketch,
 (ii) a list of the processes involved in its construction.

(WJEC)

7 Forgework

C.S.E.1. (a) What is the correct procedure when cutting with a hardie?

(b) Explain 'hot short' and 'cold short'.

(c) Why do many blacksmiths prefer to use wrought iron rather than mild steel?

(d) Sketch a pair of open-mouthed tongs, clearly illustrating the jaws.

(WM)

C.S.E.2. State what is meant by the term 'upsetting'. Freehand drawings may be made to assist in this answer.

(M)

O.1. Sketch the plan of a smith's anvil and label the working face, the beak, the punching hole, the hardie hole and the soft ledge or table.

Use sketches and brief notes to describe a forging operation which makes use of any one of the parts you have labelled.

Name the material from which each of the following parts is made:
(i) the working face, (ii) the beak.

(NU)

O.2. Sketches for this question must be freehand and pictorial.
(i) Sketch a bottom fuller.
(ii) Sketch the result of fullering on the wider face of a piece of black mild steel 40 mm wide by 18 mm thick.
(iii) A decorative twist 75 mm long is to be made in the middle of a piece of 9 mm square mild steel 450 mm long. Briefly state how you would make this twist and particularly how you would ensure straightness in the rod and evenness of the twist.

(OLE)

O.3. With the aid of sketches describe how you would weld to-

APPENDIX B 253

gether two pieces of 15 mm diameter mild steel end to end, using the blacksmith's weld.

(SU)*

O.4. Show diagrammatically the means of creating the forced air which is supplied to a forge and its passage to the fire. How is the fire lit? What is a dirty fire, and what makes it so? Why is it unwise to forge with a dirty fire?

(OLE)

O.5. Explain step by step the processes involved in forging an eye, of diameter 38 mm, on the end of a piece of 6 mm diameter mild steel rod. Illustrate your answer with suitable sketches.

(WJEC)*

O.6. How could you produce a 12 mm diameter hole in a bar of wrought iron which is, to begin with, 12 mm wide and 5 mm thick?

(AEB)*

O.7. Describe with the aid of sketches how you would make an 'S' scroll such as could be used in a wrought-iron gate. On traditional wrought-iron work the hole for fixing the scroll to the frame was punched. What is the difference between a drilled and punched hole? What advantages has one over the other? How is a square hole forged in a bar?

(OLE)

E.1. Principally by the use of sketches and added brief notes show how:
(a) a blunt round point is drawn down on a 12 mm diameter mild steel rod;
(b) a 60 mm long twist is put in the middle of a 300 mm long 9 mm square bar of mild steel;
(c) a sharp right-angle bend is formed in a piece of 9 mm square mild steel bar;
(d) a ring handle 60 mm inside diameter is formed on the end of a 6 mm diameter mild steel rod.

(OLE)*

E.2. With the aid of sketches (where possible), describe five of the following:

(*a*) drawing down, (*b*) upsetting, (*c*) blacksmith's weld, (*d*) hot and cold bending, (*e*) tinning, (*f*) sweating, (*g*) shrinking.

(AEB)

A.1. The upsetting or jumping up of a length of metal may be achieved in a number of ways. Describe these processes and sketch three examples of work which require upsetting for their making.

'C' scrolls and 'S' scrolls, with or without flared ends, form an important motif in wrought iron work. Sketch these scrolls and describe the making of an 'S' scroll with flared ends.

(OLE)

A.2. (*a*) Describe four distinct processes, e.g. 'drawing down', which are used by the blacksmith in working wrought iron.

(*b*) Make dimensioned sketches of a wrought iron bracket suitable for carrying the name plate of a house as a hanging sign at right-angles to a wall surface.

(LU)

A.3. Describe how the flare and the twist are used in the decorative treatment of wrought iron work.

(OLE)

8 Benchwork

C.S.E.1. For which processes would you correctly use each of the following tools?

(*a*) Odd-leg calipers, (*b*) Centre punch, (*c*) Boring bar.

(M)

C.S.E.2. Make a large, clear sketch of a 0–25 mm micrometer caliper set to 6·72 mm. Name the parts of the micrometer.

(EA)*

O.1. It is frequently necessary when working in metal to have available precision measuring and testing equipment. Name two such pieces of equipment and explain fully how to use one of them. Include a large well-labelled drawing in your answer.

(O&C)

O.2. List the sequence of operations for drilling and tapping a blind

APPENDIX B 255

hole in mild steel, given that the thread is to be M 6 and a full thread is required for a depth of 12 mm.

State four precautions you consider necessary to ensure success.

(NU)

O.3. Sketch a circular die.

Describe how this type of die is fitted into the stock and show how adjustment is made.

State two precautions to be taken to ensure a good result when cutting a thread on a rod.

(NU)

O.4. Sketch, approximately full size, a pair of outside calipers and with annotated sketches describe the method of making the calipers.

(LU)

O.5. Make sketches and describe the uses of any three of the following tools:
(a) odd-leg calipers, (b) centre square, (c) spring dividers, (d) depth gauge, (e) vee block.

(WJEC)

O.6. A hacksaw blade must be tight and taut when in use. Show, with the aid of sketches, how the frame is adjusted to achieve this.

(AEB)

O.7. (a) Why is it necessary for hacksaw blades to have teeth of different pitch?

(b) State three precautions to be observed if good service is to be obtained from a hacksaw.

(NU)

O.8. Name five different kinds of file and state the uses of each. Why are files made with different 'cuts'?

State what is meant by a 'safe-edge' file and give an example of its use.

(AEB)

O.9. (a) Make a large sketch of a handled half-round file, naming the parts.

(b) What is (i) drawfiling, (ii) pinning?
(c) Sketch two forms of vice clamps.
(d) Is a file uniformly tempered throughout? Give reasons for your answer.
(OLE)

E.1. (i) Make a sketch in large detail of the barrel of a 0–25 mm micrometer set to 8·418 mm.
(ii) What provision is made for adjusting this micrometer for wear on the anvil?
(iii) How would you test the micrometer for wear on the anvil?
(NU)

E.2. Two pieces of 5 mm mild steel, prepared to size, are to be lap riveted together. Three 5 mm snap head rivets are to be used and the joint has to have flush riveting on one side. Describe with the aid of sketches how you should mark out, drill and rivet the plates together.
(NU)

E.3. (a) Make a sketch of sufficient of a vernier caliper gauge to show clearly a reading of 61·58 mm. Your drawing should be approximately twice full size and the vernier scale should have 25 divisions.
(b) In each case state one precaution you would take to: (i) ensure an accurate reading, (ii) preserve the accuracy of the instrument.
(NU)*

E.4. Give the name of a tool specifically designed for accurate testing of (a) narrow gaps, (b) horizontal levels, (c) internal diameters, (d) depth of blind holes, (e) spherical roundness, (f) angles, (g) internal and external radii.
Sketch two of the tools you have mentioned and briefly describe their particular features and the method of using them.
(OLE)

E.5. (a) Describe three methods which may be used to determine the centre of the end of a cylindrical bar. One method must make use of a surfacing gauge.
(b) State, with reasons, which method is the most accurate.
(NU)

APPENDIX B 257

E.6. Name three types of cold chisel in common use, and with the aid of sketches explain the difference between their cutting edges.
Give one use for each of the chisels named.
(NU)

E.7. One outer face of a 100 mm × 75 mm × 75 mm cast iron angle plate is to be hand-scraped flat.
(a) Sketch a suitable type of scraper. Name the scraper and show clearly the form of the cutting edges.
(b) How are these cutting edges prepared and maintained?
(c) What method can be used to indicate where metal must be removed by the scraper?
(AEB)*

A.1. (a) With the aid of sketches explain the cutting action of (i) a flat cold chisel; (ii) a pair of tin snips; (iii) bench shears.
(b) Make a sketch of bench shears and show how the maximum leverage is obtained.
(c) What are the advantages and disadvantages is using bench shears to cut: (i) small diameter mild steel rods; (ii) sheet metal?
(d) What safety factors should be observed when fitting bench shears into a school workshop?
(LU)

A.2. Differentiate between the following pairs of tools and explain when you would use each:
(a) reamer: mandrel;
(b) screw-cutting gauge: screw pitch gauge;
(c) boring tool: boring bar;
(d) vernier micrometer caliper: vernier caliper gauge;
(e) wire gauge: feeler gauge.
(AEB)

A.3. By means of a simple line diagram show the construction of a dial test indicator. By using further annotated line diagrams show how you would use it to test:
(a) parallelism on a vertical plane between the centres of a lathe;
(b) the flatness of the table of a horizontal milling machine;
(c) parallelism of the arbor of a milling machine;
(d) the flatness of the table of a pillar drilling machine. (OLE)

A.4. Explain clearly the difference between a precision measuring tool and a comparator. Into which category would you place each of the following:
(a) an internal micrometer;
(b) a dial test indicator;
(c) a plug gauge;
(d) Johansson's blocks.
  Name and sketch one further example of each type of instrument.
(WJEC)

9 Drilling

C.S.E.1. (a) Show by means of a sketch how you would change the speed of a belt-driven machine drill which has no gearbox.

(b) Show by means of a sketch how a taper shank drill is removed from the hollow spindle of the drilling machine.
(WJEC)

C.S.E.2. When using a drilling machine to drill a 12 mm diameter hole 25 mm deep and with its centre 25 mm from the edge of a 75 mm steel cube, you find that the drill overheats.
(a) Describe two ways in which you could prevent the overheating.
(b) How would you ensure that it cut exactly to the right depth?
(c) What preliminary work would you do to the block to help the 12 mm drill to cut more easily?
(d) After drilling, how would you test to find if the hole was the correct distance from the edge of the block?
(L)*

O.1. A flat drill is to be made from 10 mm diameter carbon tool steel. With the use of sketches describe the operations necessary for forging and sharpening the drill ready for use. The tools used should be shown in your sketches.
(SU)

O.2. The making of a piece of sports equipment involves drilling a 12 mm dia. hole centrally through a plate of mild steel which is 150 mm square and 10 mm thick. Assuming that there is no machine vice available which is large enough to hold this, show how the plate could be held securely for drilling on the drilling machine table.

APPENDIX B

State whether you would choose a high or a low spindle speed for this operation, giving two reasons for your choice.

(NU)

O.3. Explain how you would drill an 8 mm diameter hole in a 25 mm diameter bar: (*a*) on the axis, (*b*) on a diameter.

(AEB)

O.4. (*a*) Draw freehand a side elevation of the cutting end of a twist drill, showing a short portion of the body; show also a cross section of the drill. Your drawing should show the drill about 40 mm diameter and clearly state the angles to which it should be ground.

(*b*) In the absence of a 12 mm twist drill describe with the aid of sketches how you could make a simple drill from a suitable piece of tool steel about 10 mm in diameter.

(LU)

E.1. (*a*) What precautions should be taken to ensure that a hole of 12 mm dia. is drilled in the correct position and to the correct size?

(*b*) Explain briefly why tee bolts that are used to clamp work in place on a machine table should be as close as possible to the work piece that is to be held.

(AEB)*

E.2. A blank mild steel flange casting has the boss face and the base of the flange machined parallel. The diameter of the boss is 50 mm and the base ϕ 125 mm. Three holes equispaced and 9·5 mm diameter are to be drilled through the flange on a 90 mm P.C.D. Drilled centrally through the boss is a ϕ 30 mm hole.

Describe in list form exactly how you would mark out and drill these holes. At each stage state the name of the tools and equipment you would use.

(OLE)

A.1. In what ways should drills be modified in relation to the hardness of the material being worked? Show by sketches the chip shape produced on each of three materials and hence discuss the problems of lubrication and cooling in relation to drilling.

(OLE)

A.2. Make a vertical sectional sketch through the head, spindle and chuck of a sensitive drilling machine, showing clearly how the tool functions. Why is it called a *sensitive* drilling machine?

(OLE)

10 Lathework

C.S.E.1. When would the use of a FOUR jaw lathe chuck be preferable to the use of a THREE jaw chuck?

(M)

C.S.E.2. Describe the steps you would take before mounting a 25 mm diameter mild steel bar 300 mm long, between centres in the lathe. Make a sketch of the bar mounted in the lathe and label the parts of the lathe shown.

(WJEC)*

O.1. State three different methods of holding work ready for turning on a centre lathe.

Using sketches and notes give for each method one example of work which shows its correct use. Give reasons for your answers.

(AEB)

O.2. Your are working on a lathe which is chattering and producing poor quality turned work. Consider all the reasons which might give rise to chattering and explain fully how you would attempt to cure the problem.

(O&C)

O.3. Make a freehand sketch of two views of a lathe tool-post holder, showing clearly how the tool is adjusted to cut on centre. Why is it important that the tool be adjusted to its correct height? Describe in detail how you would set up a lathe and prepare a piece of mild steel bar for turning between centres.

(OLE)

O.4. Explain the meaning of five of the following lathework terms: backlash, mandrel, carrier, surfacing, tolerance, back gear, face plate, packing.

(SU)

APPENDIX B   261

E.1. (a) With the aid of suitable sketches describe the mechanism of the 3-jaw self-centring lathe chuck.

(b) Why are these chucks usually provided with two sets of jaws? Sketch one jaw from each set.

(NU)

E.2. Make a freehand sketch of two views of a lathe tool-post holder showing clearly how the tool is adjusted to cut on centre height. Why is it important that the tool be adjusted to its correct height?

Describe in detail how you would set up a lathe and prepare a piece of mild steel bar for turning between centres.

(OLE)

E.3. (a) State four methods of holding work in a centre-lathe.

(b) Discuss the advantages and disadvantages of each of these methods and specify their particular application in general workshop use.

(AEB)

E.4. Sketch and describe a mandrel as used on a lathe. Give an example of its use.

A bar being turned on a lathe is found to be tapered. State two faults which could cause this and briefly explain how to correct each of them.

(NU)

E.5. What is meant by the terms *rake* and *clearance* as applied to cutting edges?

(a) Show, with the aid of sketches, how and why these angles vary for three of the following materials: brass, cast iron, tool steel, mild steel and aluminium.

(b) How does an error in setting a lathe tool to centre height affect these angles?

(AEB)

E.6. (a) Describe two methods of taper turning, stating under what circumstances each would be used.

(b) What are the following? (i) Dial indicator, (ii) dead and live centres, (iii) centre square, (iv) headstock.

(AEB)

A.1. Make freehand sketches of the details of a simple lathe tailstock showing: (a) how it is attached to the bed; (b) how its centre can be fixed in an axial position; (c) how the axis of the barrel can be moved across the bed of the lathe for taper turning.

(NU)

A.2. Discuss five different methods of holding work in a lathe (excluding the three jaw chuck) and state the advantages and limitations of each particular method.

(LU)

A.3. The methods used for turning a taper depend to a large extent upon the degree of taper required. Discuss these methods and state, where applicable,
(a) any disadvantages inherent in the methods, and (b) the formulae needed to set up the work.

(OLE)

A.4. A lathe has recently been used for taper turning and the tailstock has been offset for this purpose.
(a) Explain in detail the procedure for re-setting the tailstock to ensure the correct alignment of centres.
(b) Sketch and name the gauge used in the above operation. Describe briefly the working principles of this instrument.

(LU)

11 Machinework

C.S.E.1. (a) Use notes and sketches to illustrate how two different machining operations can be carried out on a milling machine.

(b) Sketch and describe two methods of holding work whilst milling.

(c) Give the names of two types of milling cutter and explain briefly the use of each.

(L)

C.S.E.2. Various 'finishes' are carried out on metals both to improve appearance and to check erosion. Other than paint or brush enamelling, give a brief description of how to produce two 'finishes' that could be done in the school workshop.

(NW)

APPENDIX B

O.1. Give examples of types of work which may be carried out on a shaping or on a milling machine. Sketch a piece of work that is being cut on either of these machines, showing the parts of the machine that are near to the work.

(SU)

O.2. What lubricants, if any, would you use if you were turning: (i) mild steel, (ii) brass, (iii) copper, (iv) aluminium, (v) cast iron? Describe carefully the effect of efficient lubrication.

(OLE)

E.1. Describe with the use of diagrams how you fix a tool into a shaping machine and how you set the clapper box when machining a perpendicular plane surface.

(OLE)

E.2. (*a*) A casting with a flange 18 mm thick is to be secured to the table of a milling machine using tee-bolts and clamps. Make a sectional diagram through one of the tee-bolts to show the set-up.

(*b*) Sketch the arbor of a horizontal milling machine with a plain cutter in position. Show the spacing collars and the method of supporting the arbor at its outer end.

(NU)

E.3. Sketch and describe each of the following as used on a milling machine: (*a*) parallel block; (*b*) vee block; (*c*) angle plate. Briefly indicate one use of each.

(NU)

E.4. (*a*) Sketch the assembly of a grinding wheel on the spindle of a bench tool grinder. Name the parts and give reasons for their use.

(*b*) Describe briefly one method of dressing a grinding wheel.

(AEB)

E.5. Explain why it is advisable to use cutting oils when machining certain metals. Name two types of cutting oil stating which should be used when machining mild steel. State why it is not necessary to use a cutting oil when machining cast iron.

(AEB)

A.1. Explain the importance of the following features normally adopted in the design of a shaping machine:
(a) the return stroke is faster than the cutting stroke;
(b) the tool box is hinged;
(c) the tool box can be rotated in a plane perpendicular to the movement of the ram;
(d) the vertical slide can rotate;
(e) the length of the stroke is variable.

How would you test that the movement of the vertical slide was vertical when the setting indicated that this should be so?

Use sketches to illustrate your procedure.

(NU)

A.2. A shaft has a keyway $10 + 0\cdot 15$ mm wide, 5 mm deep, and a total length of 75 mm with semi-circular ends.

Explain how you would obtain this keyway using: (a) a milling machine, (b) hand tools only.

How would you measure the width of the keyway to the accuracy required?

(NU)

A.3. Why is aluminium oxide considered to be a suitable grit material for the manufacture of high speed grindstones, and what other materials are used for the purpose?

Explain why several different materials are used as bonding agents and name two such materials.

What factors would you consider when choosing a grinding wheel for the removal of (a) hard metals, (b) soft metals?

(WJEC)

A.4. (a) What causes a grinding wheel to become glazed, and why is it undesirable to use the wheel in this condition?

(b) Sketch and describe a tool used to dress a grinding wheel and explain how it is used.

(c) Discuss briefly the characteristics and uses of each of four abrasives, excluding emery, used in metalwork.

(CU)

A.5. In some machines the cutting tool rotates and in others it moves in a straight line. Similarly in some machines the work rotates and in others it moves in a straight line. Name three machines which, by using different combinations of these work and tool movements, produce a plane surface.

Give, with reasons, examples of work which would be done on each of the machines you have named and which would not normally be done on either of the others.

(AEB)

A.6. Write an essay on 'Metal Finishing'.

(AEB)

Index

Main references are italicised

A
Abrasives, *224*, *225*
Acid lining, 5
Acme thread, 204
Adaptor, 155
Admiralty brass, 15
Age-hardening, 13
Allotropy, 21
Alloy steels, 9
Alumina, 11
Aluminium, *11–13*
Aluminium alloys, 13
Aluminium bronze, 16
Aluminium fluxes, 44
Aluminium oxide, 222, 224
Ammonium chloride, 43
Angle plate, 112, 216, 217
Annealing, 22, 23
Anodic oxidation, 228
Anodising, 228
Anvil, *94–5*
Arbor, 155, 156
Arc Furnace, 7, 8
Art metalwork, 71
Austenite, 21

B
Babbitt, 18
Back gear, 168, 169
Backlash, 211
Basic lining, 5
Basic oxygen process, *6–7*
Bauxite, 11, 224
Beaded edge, 65
Beaten metalwork, 71
Beck iron, 62
Bed, 168
Beeswax, 86, 228
Bench shearing machine, *61*
Bench vice, 114–16
Bending (Sheetmetalwork), *64–5*
Bending bars and jigs (Forgework), 97
Bending jigs (Silversmithing), 88
Bessemer process, 5–6
Bezel, 83
Bevel protractors, 141
Bick iron, 62
Billets, 9
Blacksmiths' forge welding, 51, 52
Blast furnace, *3–5*
Blister copper, 14
Blocking hammer, 74
Blooms, 9, 11
Blue-print, 32
Bolting, *151–2*
Bolts, 54
Borax, 44

INDEX

Borax cones, 50
Boring, *201*
Boring bar, 201
Boring tool, 201
Boron carbide, 222
Bossing mallet, 64, 73, 74
Bottom stakes, 77, 78
Bottoming tap, 148-9
Box spanner, 151
Brass, *15-16*
Brass back saw, 87
Brazing, *50-51*
Breast drill, 153
Britannia metal, 19
Bronze, *16*
Bronze coinage, 16
Bronze welding, 51
Buffing, 91, 92
Built-up work, *82-5*
Burnt borax, 52
Butt rammer, 36

C

Caliper gauge, 139, 143
Calipers, inside, 134
 outside, 134-5
 vernier, 136-41
Cap screws, 53, 54
Cape chisel, 124
Capillary attraction, 49, 50
Carbon steel lathe tools, 182, 183 186
Carrier, 176
Cartridge brass, 15
Case-hardening, *25-7*
Cast alloys, 13-14
Castings, *35-40*
Cast iron, *9-10*
Castle nuts, 55
Catch plate, 176
Caulking, 77
Cementite, 20
Centre drill, 173, 174

Centre finder, 172
Centre punch, 114
Centre reamer, 174
Centres, *172-7*
Chaplets, 35, 39
Chasers, 212, 213
Chasing, *89-90*
Chasing dial, 211
Chatter, 130
Chemical colouring, 227
Chenier, 82
Chill plates, 39
Chisel, 101-2, 123-5
Chuck, 155, 156, 169-73
Circular split die, 150
Cladding, 13
Clamps, 112, 216, 217
Clams, 117
Clapping, 217
Cleaning, *71-2*
Clearance, 186, 187
Clinker, 94
Cogging, 9
Cold chisels, 101
Cold Forging, 104
Collar, 194
Collet hammers, 81
Colouring, 227-8
Combination centre drill, 173, 174
Combination set, 110
Concave milling cutter, 221
Converter, 6, 7
Coolants, 225-6
Cope, 35
Copper, *14-15*
Core box, 34, 35
Core diameter, 202
Core drill, 160, 161
Core prints, 35
Cores, *35-6*
Corner lap joint, 68
Corundum, 224
Cotter pin, 55

INDEX

Counterboring, *163*, *165*
Countersinking, *163*, *165*
Countersunk joint, 69
Crank, 78, 79
Crazing, 25
Creasing, 77
Creasing iron, 63, 67
Cross-cut chisel, 124
Crucible, 38
Cry of tin, 18
Cryolite, 12
Cupola furnace, 10
Cutting (Benchwork), *119–25*
Cutting fluids, *225–6*
Cutting lubricants, 225–6
Cutting speeds, 193–4
Cutting tools (Forgework), *101–3*

D
Dashpot, 121, 122
Datum line, 136, 138
'Dead' centre, 172
Depth gauge, 135, 136
Depth gauge micrometer, 138
De-rusting fluids, 229
Design, *29–31*
Developments, *56*
Dial indicator, 171, 211
Dial test indicator, 144, 145, 171
Diameter, full, major or outside, 202
Diamond abrasive, 222
Diamond chisel, 124, 125
Die, 149–51
Die casting, *39–40*, 55
Die holder, 150, 151
Dividers, 108
Dog, 176
Dolly, 146, 147
Dot punch, 113
'Down-cut' milling, 219
Draft, 34
Drafting, 57

Drag, 35, 103
Drawfiling, 130, 131
Drawing down, *99–100*
Drawplate, 82, 86
Dressing, 66
Drift, 102–3
Drill chuck, 155, 156
Drilling machines, *153–6*
Drilling pillar, 153, 154
Drills, *158–63*
Driving pin, 177
Driving plate, 176
Drop forging, *104*
Dross, 38
Ductility, 2

E
Easy silver solder, 50
Edge-over joint, 69
Edges (Sheetmetalwork), *65–8*
Electric arc and resistance welding, 53
Electric process, 7, 8
Electrodeposition, 228
Electroplating, 228
Embossing, 89
Emery, 224
Enamelling, 91
Endmill, 219, 221
Engineering castings, 10
Engraving, 91
Extinguisher stake, 63
Extrusion, 12

F
Face mill, 222
Face plate, *177*, *178*
Facing, 192
Facing tool, 189
Feeder head, 37
Feedshaft, 168
Feel, 134
Feeler gauge, 142

Ferrite, 20
Ferrous, 2
Ferrule, 128, 129
Fettling, 37
Fiducial line, 136
File card, 130
Filing, *125–32*
Finishing, *91–2*
Finishing tool, 188
Fixed steady, 180, 181
Flaring and scrolls, *103–4*
Flask, 35
Flat chasing, 90
Flat chisel, 123, 124
Flat drill, 158
Flat file, 125, 126
Flatter, 100
Flotation, 14, 17, 19
Fluidity, 13
Flush joint, 69
Fluxes, *42–4*
Folding bars, 64
Forge, 93
Forms, 1
Form tools, 190, 201
Foundry iron, 9
Four-jaw chuck, 170–72
Free-cutting brass, 15
Fretting, 50
Full diameter, 202
Fullering, *100–101*
Funnel stake, 63
Fused alumina, 222, 224
Fusibility, 3

G
Galvanising, 20
Gang milling, 217
Gap gauge, 143
Gauges, 59, 111, 135–46, 208, 209, 213
Gilding metal, 15
Golden section, 30

Grain, 50
Grease, 226–7
Grey cast iron, 10
Grinding, *222–4*
Grips, 116, 117
Grooved joint, 69, 70
Grooving tool, 70
Grub screws, 54
Gunmetal, 16

H
Hacksaw, 119–22
Half-centre, 173
Half-moon stake, 62, 63, 67
Half-round chisel, 125
Half-round file, 126
Hallmark, 46, 71
Hammered metalwork, 71
Hammers (engineers), 114, 115
Hand draw tongs, 86
Hand drill, 153
Hand file, 126
Hand hacksaw, 119–21
Hand-powered drilling machine, 153
Hand reamer, 163, 164
Hand turning tools, 182, 183
Hand vice, 117
Hardening, 23
Hardie, 102
Hardness, 2
Hard solders, *47–50*
Hatchet stake, 62, 63
Heads, 78, 79
Headstock, 166, 168
Hearth, 93
Heat conductivity, 3
Heat treatment, *20–25*
Hermaphrodite calipers, 106, 107
High frequency induction furnace, 8
High-speed steel, 9
High-speed steel lathe tools, 184

INDEX 271

High tensile brasses, 16
Holding devices, *114–19*
Hollowing, *73–4*
Honing, 227
Horse, 78
Hot chisels, 101
Huntington dresser, 223, 224
Hydrochloric acid, 43

I
Independent jaw chuck, *170–72*
Induction furnace, high frequency, 8
Ingots, 8
Inside calipers, 134
Inside micrometer, 138
ISO Metric thread, 203–4

J
Jack, 216
Jennies, 106, 107
Jenny calipers, 106, 107
Jobber's drill, 158
Joints (Sheetmetalwork), 41, *69–70*
Jumping-up, 98, 99
Junior hacksaw, 121–2

K
Killed spirits of salts, 43
Knife file, 127
Knife tool, 189
Knocked-up joint, 69, 70
Knurling tool, 191, 192

L
Lacquer, 228
Ladle, 8
'Laffite' plate, 52
Lap joint, 69
Lapping, 227
Lathe boring table, 201

Lathe carrier, 176
Lathe dog, 176
Lathes, *166–9*
Lathe tools, *182–92*
LD–AC Converter process, 6–7
Lead, *17*
Lead of a screw, 202
Leadscrew, 168
Leather sandbag, 73–4
Ledloy steels, 9
Leg vice, *96–8*
Light alloys, *13–14*
'Live' centre, 172
Lock nuts, 55
Low temperature silver brazing alloys, 47
Lubrication, 226–7

M
Machine reamer, 163, 164
Machine vice, 156, 157
Major diameter, 202
Malleability, 2
Malleable cast iron, 10
Mallets, *64*
Mandrels, 62, 79, *177–80*
Marking out (Benchwork), *105–14*
Marking out (Sheetmetalwork), *58*
Marking-out tables, 111
Martensite, 23
Matte, 14
Matting tool, 90
Measurement, *134–46*
Methods of holding work, *156–8*
Metric threads, 203–4
Metric trapezoidal thread, 205
Metric verniers, 139–41
Micrometer, 135–9
Micrometer collar, 194
Milling, *217–22*
Milling cutter nomenclature, 220
Mill scale, 8
Minor diameter, 202

Modern 'Wrought Ironwork', 11
Mops, 92
Moulding box, 35
Mouse-tail file, 126
Multi-flute core drills, 160, 161
Muntz metal, 15

N
Needle file, 128
Nippers, 123
Nodular cast iron, 10
Non-ferrous, 2
Normalising, 23
Notching, 57
Nozzles, 8
Nut mandrel, 179
Nuts, 55

O
Odd-legs, 106, 107
Off-hand grinding, 222–4
Oil, 226
Open-ended spanner, 151
Open hearth case-hardening, 25, 26
Open hearth process, 5–6
Outside calipers, 134, 135
Outside diameter, 202
Oxy-acetylene welding, 53
Oxygen converter process, 6

P
Pack carburising, 25
Pad handles, 122, 123
Paillons, 50
Paint finishes, 228–9
Paned-down joint, 69
Panels, 50
Paning hammer, 67
Parallel strips, 216, 217
Parallel turning, 193–5
Parting-off tool, 189, 190
Parting powder, 36–7

Patterns, 33–4
Pearlite, 20
Peg rammer, 36
Pencil, 50
Permanent joints, 41
Pewter, 19
Phillip's recess, 54
Phosphor bronze, 16
Pickle, 72
Piercing, *88–9*
Pig iron, *3–5*, 9, 10
Pin gauge, 143
Pins, 130
Pin tongs, 117, 118
Pin vice, 117, 118
Piping, 99
Pitch, 53, 202
Pitch bowl, 89
Plain milling cutter, 220
Planing machine, 215
Planishing, *79–82*, 90
Plastic coating, 228
Pliers, 118, 119
Plug gauge, 143, 144
Plug tap, 149
Plumbago, 38
Plumbers' solder, 47
Point grinding, 159
Poker 94
Pouring, 7, 8
Pouring basin, 37
Power-driven sensitive drilling machine, 154–5
Power hacksaw, 121, 122
Pozidriv, 54
Precision files, 128
Precision rollers and spheres, 145
Precision needle files, 128
Printing metal, 19
Production, 1
Properties, 1, *2–3*
Puddling furnace, 11
Punches (Benchwork), 113–14

INDEX

Punches (Forgework), 102–3
Punches (Sheetmetalwork), 61

Q
Quick helix drills, 160, 161

R
Rack and pinion, 154
Radius gauge, 142, 143
Raising, 74–7
Rake, 94, 186, 187
Ratchet brace, 153, 154
Rat-tail file, 126
Rawhide mallet, 64
Reaming, 163, 164
Reducing, 8
Repoussé, 89, 90
Repoussé hammer, 90
Resin, 43
Rifflers, 128, 129
Ring gauge, 143, 144
Ring screw gauge, 144, 213
Ring spanner, 151
Riser, 37, 38
Riveting, 146–8
Rivets, 53
Rolling and wire drawing, 85–7
Root diameter, 202
Roughing tool, 188
Round bottom stake, 63
Round file, 126
Round-nosed tool, 188, 189
Rule, 105
Runner, 37
Runner sticks, 37

S
Safety, 28–9
Sal ammoniac, 43
Sand slinging, 36
Sates, 102
Scarf, 52
Score marks, 130

Scrapers, 83, 132–3
Scraping, 132–3
Screwcutting, 201–14
Screwcutting gauge, 207, 208
Screwdriver, 152
Screw extractor, 149, 152
Screw gauge, 213
Screw pitch gauge, 207, 209
Screws etc., 53–6
Screw thread gauge, 207, 209
Scriber, 105, 106
Scribing block, 111
Scrolls, 103–4, 169
Second tap, 148, 149
Sections, 9
Self-centring chuck, 169–70
Sensitive drilling machine, 154–5
Set, 147
Set hammer, 100
Sets, 102
Set screws, 54
Setting protractor, 109, 110
Shaping and planing machines, 215–17
Shaping machine, 215–17
Shell moulding, 40
Sheradising, 20
Side and face milling cutter, 221
Side stake, 63
Silicon carbide, 222, 224
Silver brazing alloys, 47–9
Silver sand, 52
Silver soldering procedure, 50
Silver solders, 47–9
Sine bar, 145
Sinking, 72–3
Skim bob, 37
Slabs, 9
Sledge hammer, 95
Slice, 94
Sliding bevel, 109
Sliding (parallel turning), 193–5
Slot punch, 103

Slotted nuts, 55
Slow helix drills, 160, 161
Smith's hearth, *93–4*
Snap, 146, 147, 148
Snarling iron, 89
Snips, *59–60*
Soaking pit, 8
Soft solders, *44–7*
Soldering irons, 46
Soluble oils, 225
Sources, 1
Sources of heat, *41–2*
Spanners, 151
Special mandrels, 179
Spelter, 51
Spherical turning attachment, 191
Spheroidal cast iron, 10
Spindle, 168
Spindle speeds, 193–4
Spirits of salts, 43
Split die, 149, 150, 151
Split pin, 55
Spotfacing cutter, 163, 165
Sprue cup, 37
Sprue pins, 37
Square file, 127
Square thread, 204
Stakes (Sheetmetalwork), *62–3*
Stakes (Silversmithing), *77–9*
Standard lathe mandrel, 178
Star-type dresser, 223, 224
Steadies, *181–2*
Steel, *5–9*
Stirrup, 112
Stitching, 84
Stock, 149
Stopper rods, 8
Straight oils, 225
Strength, 2
Strickle off, 37
Stub mandrels, 179, 180
Studs, 54, 55
Surface finishes, *227–8*

Surface gauge, 111
Surface plate, 110, 111
Surface protection, *227–8*
Surfacing, *192–3*
Swage block, 95
Swaging, *101*
Sweated, 47

T
Tack, 46
Tailstock, 166, 167, 175, 197–9
Tallow, 43
Tam-o'-Shanter stone, 91, 225
Tang, 128, 129
Tap bolt, 54, 55
Taper flat file, 125, 126
Taper tap, 148, 149
Taper turning, *195–201*
Taper turning attachment, 199, 200
Taps, 148, 149
Tap wrench, 148, 149
'T' bolt, 217
Teeming, 8
Tempering, 23–4
Template, 76, 143
Temporary joints, 41
Tension file, 128, 129
Threading, *148–51*
Threading tool gauge, 207, 209
Threads, *203–14*
Three-square file, 127
Thumb screws, 54
Tin, *17–18*
Tinmen's anvil, 62
Tinmen's groove punch, 69, 70
Tinmen's hollow punches, 61
Tinmen's mallet, 64, 65
Tinplate, 18
'T' nut, 217
Tongs, 95, 96
Toolmakers' clamps, 118
Toolpost grinder, 173, 174

INDEX

Toolposts, 185
Tool steel, 9
Toughness, 2
Tracer, 90
Trammels, 108, 109
Travelling steady, 181–2
Tray hammer, 72
Treblet, 79
Tripoli, 92
Try square, 109
Tubular box spanner, 151
Tue iron, 93
Tumbler gear, 168
Tungsten carbide tipped tools, 184
Tup, 104
Tuyere, 93
Twist drills, 158–63
Twisted bars, 97

U
Universal bevel, 109
'Up-cut' milling, 218, 219
Upsetting, *98–9*
Uses, 1

V
'V' grooves, 82, 83
Vee blocks, 112
Vent holes, 37
Vernier caliper gauge, 139–41
Vertical milling, 222
Vices, 114–18, 156–8

Viscosity, 226

W
Warding file, 127
Water-base fluids, 225
Water bosh, 93
Water of Ayr stone, 91, 225
Welding, *51–3*
White cast iron, 10
White metal, *18–19*
Wing compasses, 108
Wing nuts, 56
Wire and sheet gauges, *59*
Wire drawing, 85–7
Wired edge, 66
Wiring, 84
Wires, application of, *87–8*
Witness mark, 172
Working, 1
Working drawings, *31–2*
Workshop tests and methods of identification, *27*
Wrench, 151
Wrought alloys, 13
Wrought forms, 13
Wrought iron, *11*

Y
Yellow metal, 15

Z
Zinc, *19–20*
Zinc chloride, 43